CRY
FROM THE
DEEP

CRY
FROM THE
DEEP

THE SUBMARINE DISASTER
THAT RIVETED THE WORLD AND
PUT THE NEW RUSSIA TO THE
ULTIMATE TEST

RAMSEY FLYNN

HarperCollins*Publishers*

HarperCollins books may be purchased for educational, business, or sales promotional use. For information, please write: Special Markets Department, Harper-Collins Publishers Inc., 10 East 53rd Street, New York, NY 10022.

FIRST EDITION

Designed by Joseph Rutt

Printed on acid-free paper

Library of Congress Cataloging-in-Publication Data

Flynn, Ramsey.
  Cry from the deep: the submarine disaster that riveted the world and put the new Russia to the ultimate test. — 1st ed.
    p. cm.
  ISBN 0-06-621171-9
  1. Kursk (Submarine) 2. Submarine disasters — Russia (Federation). 3. Submarine disasters — Barents Sea. 4. Russia (Federation). Voenno-Morskoæ Flot — Submarine forces. I. Title.

VK1282.R8F589   2004
910'.9163'24 — dc22

                                                                2004047526

04 05 06 07 08 WB/RRD 10 9 8 7 6 5 4 3 2 1

To Mary Jane and Bill Flynn,
who have always been there and always will be.

And to Betty,
who has sustained me when little else could.

CONTENTS

PREFACE

When I first proposed this story to a magazine editor in mid-August 2000, the event was only a day old and the world was riveted by the televised images of a rescue in progress. There were reports of trapped sailors knocking from inside a sunken submarine in a shallow area of the Barents Sea, and experts agreed they could be brought out alive. Though the Russians had mysteriously rebuffed foreign-rescue offers, some of those foreigners leaped into action anyway. I was optimistic.

I'd envisioned something like the feel-good story of the long-shot *Apollo 13* rescue, only better: saving the *Kursk* submariners would go down in history as an international bonding experience. Lingering East-West tensions would fade as former enemies joined in a common purpose, pooling the best resources and bravest rescuers to bring those boys out alive. In my eighteen-year career, I'd chronicled more than my share of tragedy. This would be different.

Instead I watched with growing dismay as the Russian government threw a befuddling series of obstacles into the paths of foreign rescuers, and the reports of the submariners' tapping disappeared.

The difficulty in unraveling this new riddle of why Russia had seemingly sabotaged a rescue of its own men now loomed like an enormous Rubik's Cube. My stock-in-trade was to untangle complicated stories until I could present the truth. It's difficult enough with happy outcomes, but now I'd be asking impolite questions of notoriously tight-lipped officials—in a country I'd never been to, in a language I'd never spoken, in a mysterious and complex world of undersea espionage and warfare that I'd always found deeply baffling.

One of my first phone calls was to the Russian embassy in Washington, D.C., where I'd hoped to start getting the proper clearances to work in this former "evil empire." "What makes you think I can help you with this?" asked Yuri Zubarev, the embassy's press attaché.

Well, what, indeed? As an unaffiliated, independent journalist, I was looking at a yearlong process just to get "accredited" to report from within Russia. And accreditation was only the first in a series of escalating hurdles. I opted for a business visa—which would afford me no access whatsoever to "official" press facilities and events—and finally set foot on Russian soil in late October, some seventy-five days after the wreck. But the country was still in a state of shock, with official allegations that an American spy sub rammed the *Kursk* just reaching a shrill crescendo.

At the end of my first week I was wandering around the streets of St. Petersburg in a cold rain, gamely employing my twelve-word vocabulary in a vain attempt to find the apartment of a helpful American expat with translator connections. After an hour or so in the steady downpour, I reluctantly called him on my cell phone. But standing at a five-way intersection where all the signs were written in an alien alphabet, I still could not match his careful instructions; he had to head out into the rain himself to come rescue me. It seemed everything about this project was going to be very hard work.

The ensuing years demanded that every success be hard-won: five reporting trips to Russia; many hundreds of interviews; countless ransackings through online Russian media archives; carefully arranged discussions with on-scene military officials; generous technical advisers and dedicated translators every step of the way—for three and a half years. And this was only for the Russian side of the story.

This narrative account is more than 90 percent factual. The remainder is "informed scenario," mostly involving events experienced by the men whose lives were lost. In an effort to craft these sequences responsibly, I have tried to reconstruct them with the help of forensic findings, recovered tapes of onboard dialogues, notes found on submariners' bodies, ships' logs, Russian naval protocol, family interviews, the firsthand testimony of key participants, and intensive professional guidance.

Most of the three-hundred-plus subjects I've interviewed for this book agreed to stay on the record. Though their contributions are not attributed within the narrative, I have compiled a liberal accounting in a separate appendix at the book's end.

Some general explanations on sources: While I have sifted many thousands of documents about this tragedy—including countless news reports and narrative treatments and other original documents that have never been publicized—I have tried wherever possible to get close to the subjects themselves for firsthand interviews. Perhaps the most consistently maddening aspect of this story was that the truth always appeared to be a moving target, one in which even those closely involved routinely resorted to speculation about what had happened around them. The "facts" persistently refused to sit still. For this reason, I repeatedly interviewed as many subjects for key scenes as possible, occasionally subjecting some poor souls to multiple rounds of questioning.

Reconstructed dialogues among living persons come from my own interviews with the subjects involved, or occasionally from published interviews conducted by other journalists. Very infrequently—and only in exchanges of low consequence—I have resorted to descriptions from intimates who either witnessed the exchanges or received the accounts from participants at a later date.

In some cases that describe a living subject's interior thoughts, many of the rules mentioned above apply. But in some instances, my reconstruction is also based on statements later expressed in interviews that, in my judgment, seemed credibly applied within the moment of dramatic events that form the narrative.

Also in rare cases, I have used firsthand material from subjects who could not allow their names to be published. This includes all dialogues onboard the *Kursk* and between the *Kursk* and the *Peter the Great*, once the sub entered the open sea on its way to the exercise. Those records come from a source close to the Russian investigation.

All weather descriptions come from the records of reporting stations responsible for the times and places described.

Most accounts of actions among key Western actors in the drama are based on my interviews with the subjects themselves, many of whom spoke publicly about the *Kursk* event for the first time. This includes former U.S. Deputy Secretary of State Strobe Talbott, who used his own verbatim notes from the first meeting between Presidents Clinton and Putin several weeks after the tragedy to give me an accurate account of that meeting.

For the book's formidable technical challenges, I relied most heavily on Lars Hanson, a retired American naval commander and engineer whom I'd stumbled upon while aiding National Geographic Television's own *Kursk* account in the spring of 2002. I'd worked with a number of other technical advisers with limited success, but Lars's moxie was of an entirely different order; he rolled up his sleeves and feverishly worked through the *Kursk* tragedy's many mysteries, drawing on a stunning range of high-level skill sets. There were many times when I simply felt like Lars's legman, supplying him with key bits of information as he educated me in the world of American and Russian submarines. He certainly could have written this book by himself if he'd wanted to.

But for all of his tireless guidance, it must be said that I sometimes chose advice with which Lars disagreed, knowing full well that I did so at my peril. Which is to say I accept full responsibility for any errors in this document.

This project's most highly skilled American translator is a U.S. Navy warrant officer who contacted me in early 2002 and initially offered me his "fact-checking" services gratis. I suspect that Robert "Rip" Burns soon came to worry over what he'd gotten himself into, as I shamelessly lured him into ever more time-consuming translation projects of Russian documents that kept finding their way into my possession. The man has never told me no, though he's certainly had a right to. Rip routinely provided precious gems of information never published in the West, and over time his work constituted meaningful original reporting.

On the Russian side, my confused wanderings on the rainy streets of St. Petersburg that day in November 2000 bore remarkable fruit. My ex-pat friend's wife connected me with a formidably talented translator/fixer. Anna Korovina, who had been a high-school exchange student for a year in Illinois, quickly displayed a keen natural interest in this effort. She understood my desire to talk to *everybody involved*, and consistently risked her regular job to make time for my endless reporting needs. Anna had been born and raised in Murmansk (the Arctic hub of Russia's submarine world), she lived and worked in naval-centric St. Petersburg, and she had friends in Moscow. Suddenly, I had couches to sleep on in all the primary locations. Anna quickly tuned into my need to defeat the Russian habit of hoarding precious contact information, as she automatically remembered to ask for the phone numbers and e-mail addresses of key targets at the end of each interview. She also fended off the persistent scoldings of the many Cold War military dinosaurs we encountered, who tried to convince her that she was aiding and abetting the enemy. Anna's impassioned defenses often converted some of these same critics into our best sources, whom she continued to pursue in the long periods between my visits. With my scripted interviews in hand, Anna quizzed many of these subjects on her own. In one remarkable case, she successfully tracked down obscure contact information for families of each key member of the *Kursk*'s torpedo team, winning us interviews that helped humanize these little-known men who'd been saddled with an impossibly dangerous task. For that and many similar such exclusives, I came to trust Anna as *Cry from the Deep*'s Special Correspondent.

For an overall technical review, I relied on the careful and wise reading of U.S. Rear Admiral (Ret.) Thomas Evans, whose knowledge of and love for the world of submarines is quite nearly boundless. Early in our correspondence, "Admiral Tom" took personal time to give my two young boys and their friends a one-on-one tour of the Cold War Submarines Museum at the Smithsonian's Institute of American History, where he serves part-time as a docent. He was a patient and avuncular delight that day, and remained so throughout his skillful work on this book.

Some important outside contributors should also be highlighted up front. While I had remarkable access to all of the living characters in the first chapters, Olga Kolesnikova, wife of the submariner who wrote the poignant note that gives this book its title, refused to cooperate with my interview requests. (In a brief personal exchange, she expressed offense that I'd spent too much time interviewing others about her husband, instead of coming to her first for the real story.) I have portrayed Olga through the use of voluminous video material and the testimony of others, but owe a special debt to prominent Russian journalist and friend Nikolay Cherkashin. It is his book, *Into the Abyss: The Loss of the Kursk: Timeline, Theories, Fates*, that provides some of the key "missing moments" in Olga's relationship with her husband.

I have also relied on some of the original reporting of another prominent Russian *Kursk* author, Vladimir Shigin. His time line of events surrounding the *Kursk's* demise held up very well over time, and he was able to interview a number of key subjects exclusively. His fine book on the tragedy, *Empty Mooring*, will stand for years as among the most definitive.

And I must doff my cap to British TV journalist Robert Moore, who was based in Moscow at the time of the disaster and captured it from the ground up. His book, *A Time to Die*, provided an unparalleled depiction of British and Norwegian rescuers attempting to help the Russians. Moore negotiated exclusive access to one of the Western rescue vessels as it raced to the scene, and reported on moments that could not be adequately replicated by someone who wasn't there. In certain sequences that depict exchanges between Russian officials and the head of the on-site Norwegian diving operation, Moore's terrific material is my only source.

Though I hope *Cry from the Deep* will find its place among the defining accounts of this pivotal moment in international relations, I am nevertheless convinced there are truths about the *Kursk* case that have eluded me. My publisher sympathizes with this lingering concern, and has agreed to support a Web site (http://www.cryfromthedeep.com) where updated facts of this case will be posted as they emerge.

CRY
FROM THE
DEEP

1

WIVES' DAY
VIDYAYEVO NAVAL GARRISON, PIER EIGHT
SUNDAY AFTERNOON, JULY 9, 2000

The wives hush when they first spot the giant black hulk. It's more squat than in the photographs they've seen, yet somehow more imposing. It looks like a capsized ocean liner draped in a shroud. The three couples murmur as they file out of the shuttle bus past the armed guards and hear the popping of bay water slapping the submarine's hull. The dark colossus dwarfs them as they draw closer, and the collars of the wives' coats flap in the diesel-scented breeze. Dmitry Kolesnikov, or "Dima," guides his wife Olga up the steel gangway to the sub's broad deck. He wants to make sure she feels comfortable meeting his beloved metal mistress. He wants his new bride to love her, too.

Olga is mystified. Why does her husband love this thing? Why do he and his friends speak of it with a reverence that makes the wives jealous? Why have they all staked their futures on $100-a-month salaries in a remote little fjord in the Arctic Circle? For *this*?

Standing in front of the *Kursk*'s imposing conning tower, Olga shields her eyes from a sky brightly veiled with high sweeps of ice-crystal clouds. At fifty-two degrees, the weather feels oddly autumnal, even though it's a Sunday afternoon in July. "Olechka!" says Dima, using her pet name while boyishly tugging her aside to proudly describe the *Kursk*'s topside fittings, quickly losing her in the inevitable jargon. She regards the vessel's great red crest emblazoned at the front of the central tower. The crest—a golden double-headed eagle that evokes Russia's wariness about foreign invaders from all directions—is already bleached from its few storied voyages.

The couples have been bonding into a submariners' "family," a very useful thing in Vidyayevo, the spartan garrison town on the Kola Peninsula where they all must live. Vidyayevo's cinder-block apartment buildings are rudimentary, riddled with peeling paint, power outages, heating problems, leaky plumbing, and water shortages. It is the kind of place where people wake up on dark winter mornings to find their teapots filled with ice. Life in Vidyayevo is all about making do. When the few shops close in the evenings, a spontaneous marketplace emerges in the treeless spaces between the apartment buildings, with a few entrepreneurial men selling sodas, beer, and cigarettes out of their jacket pockets, supplementing the handful of small kiosks that keep later hours.

So these loose-knit "families" share cars and sometimes apartments and often foodstuffs and tools and videos. For many of the town's nine thousand people, such communal habits make Vidyayevo a socially intimate place. The younger wives pride themselves on their collective culinary ventures, especially when making a group stew—one contributing, say, beets or ham; another cabbage, or perhaps the prized mushrooms that appear after the late-summer rains, like manna springing from beneath the dwarf conifers and wild berry bushes that hug the rocky hillsides in a Darwinian struggle for Arctic sunlight.

Such routines have forged a stubborn indomitability in Russia's submarine community here, which clings proudly to a few terrifying prowlers of the deep that help assure their motherland's increasingly tenuous claim to world power. The *Kursk* is a potent leftover from the vast Soviet empire that stood toe-to-toe against an imperialist West for seventy years, and senior state officials believe the giant submarine still has an important future in helping to preserve Russia's place in the international pecking order. The six-year-old *Kursk* is among a shrinking handful of supersubs that can silently traverse the ocean depths and unleash a nuclear strike against an enemy navy's carrier battle group any time the Kremlin gives the orders. The young men posted to the *Kursk* guarantee that such orders will be carried out.

"This hull will be my blanket while I am away," says Dima as he leads Olga through an interior passageway on one of the *Kursk*'s upper decks. "It will keep me warm and safe while I dream of you." The two take turns with the video camera they've brought along to record the day's visit. With the other two couples wandering off to their husbands' assigned compartments, Dima shows Olga the mysterious workings of his cloistered world. Olga is already getting accustomed to the strange scents—a subtle blend of solvents and mechanical lubricants—as Dima beckons her forward. She pans the camera across a cul-de-sac of control panels.

"Ty zdyes komanduyesh?" Olga asks. You are in charge here? It is a claustrophobic space, painted a wan yellow-green, crammed with pipes, wires, switches, meters, and gauges. Dima carefully ducks his head around a low-hanging piece of overhead equipment as he describes the console from which he oversees the eight-man turbine crew that runs the *Kursk*'s forward turbine compartment. He explains broadly how the console tracks the performance of his section of the propulsion system, including the giant turbines that dominate the decks below him. Sensing her bewilderment, Dima suddenly becomes animated, showing Olga how he can recline on a rise in the floor and nap with his legs braced against the wall. Olga gasps at the contorted arrangement, but Dima boasts about his clever adaptation. "And if there is an emergency," he begins, then abruptly leaps from the floor and, darting his head left and right, hissing as if he's spitting bullets for punctuation—*"fut! fut! fut!"*—shows Olga how he can snap into action with the shrill call of a "battle alarm."

Moments later, Dima takes the camera and zooms in on Olga dancing toward him, Broadway-style, clicking her fingers as she performs a series of half pirouettes. "Take me with you to the sea," she pleads playfully.

"I can't," Dima says. "It's a bad omen to have a woman on the sub."

"I promise to smile at everybody," she says, dancing closer, her smartly bobbed, hennaed hair perfectly framing the girlish pout that blooms across her lips.

"Well," Dima teases, "if you're going to smile at everybody, there can be no talk about having you on the sub."

Olga's luminous face fills the camera frame. "I promise I will smile only at your superiors so you can get promoted," she persists. "And you will become an admiral."

"*Da?*" asks Dima. *Yes?*

"*Da,*" answers Olga.

"*Nyet!*"

Sometimes Dima finds it hard to believe this dancing goddess is his wife. He always considered himself an awkward galoot of a man, spirited and romantic but cursed with a soft outer layer of baby fat, his red hair and pale complexion conspiring to keep him in the "good friends" category with the young women in his life. His shyness around them had kept him returning to the same fiery-tempered high school girlfriend his parents disapproved of, but who was always there when Dima came home on leave, stealing away with him even amid her second failing marriage.

Inna had always wanted to marry Dima, and would do it even now, but he refused to quit the submarine service and become a commercial seafarer, despite Inna's insistence that doing so would give them a comfortable life.

Dmitry Romanovich Kolesnikov had foundered about briefly after high school in his hometown of St. Petersburg, where he'd distinguished himself as a party boy nicknamed "Koleso," the Russian word for "wheel." An academic achiever with a love of poetry and the classic Russian writers, he cultivated an endearing habit of coining comic patronymic Russian middle names for his party mates, with whom he belted out the Soviet-subversive songs of his favorite Russian rock group, DDT. He was especially close to his high school friend and drinking mate Maksim Guskov, whose reputation as an incorrigible "bad boy" made him even more unpopular with the Kolesnikov parents than Inna was. But Dima treasured these relationships, and in those final post–high school months of 1990 he felt whipsawed between the social comforts of St. Petersburg and the austere career path blazed by his father, who retired from the service as a highly respected captain first rank. Eventually Dima retreated to his room at his parents' apartment, and after days of stewing finally came to a decision: he'd join the navy. Overweight, he quickly embraced a strict diet of yogurt and cucumbers that lasted for weeks, losing enough of the two-hundred-plus pounds from his six-three frame to make the cut.

After five years in the naval academy, Kolesnikov and his two closest classmates won assignments to the motherland's finest sub, the *Kursk*. The trio found themselves virtually penned up in Vidyayevo—one of the remote Arctic locations where the farthest reach of the Gulf Stream keeps the fjords ice-free—a place so lacking in diversions that alcohol fueled the off-duty hours of nearly every unmarried officer. Armed mostly with bottles of Mr. Officer–brand vodka, Dima fell hard, and too many of his days disappeared into a fog. He would get into fistfights while carousing with naval college classmate Rashid Aryapov, but their more diplomatic classmate, Sergey Lubushkin, would usually manage to steer them clear of bigger trouble.

Lubushkin eventually homed in on an attractive young woman in a nearby town, and one night he persuaded her to join him and his friends at a café there. When the flattered young woman ordered something from the menu, the three men suddenly made excuses about needing to wash their hands and departed for the bathroom. Once there, they pooled their money, ensuring that they could collectively afford Sergey's date.

For Dima Kolesnikov, the personal loan of a few rubles turned into a wise investment. Sergey and his Olga soon married, and the newlywed Olga Lubushkina often found herself cooking for Dima as a houseguest—and occasionally for Rashid as well. The good-natured young wife sometimes joked that her marriage to Sergey was a three-for-one deal.

Dima often stopped by the Lubushkins' cozy apartment after evenings of drinking with Rashid, lounging in a favorite chair and talking for hours. Olga Lubushkina usually enjoyed Dima's company, especially since he often contributed to meals. But there were times when he would settle in for too many hours, just to indulge the comfort of home and family and conversation. Sometimes Sergey had to tell Dima when it was time to leave. "Today is not a visiting day," he would candidly tell Dima. "I am tired of you." Sometimes Dima would playfully protest, saying he was always welcome because he had a "special arrangement with your wife." But as Dima Kolesnikov would reluctantly slip out the door, Olga Lubushkina would worry, knowing that Dima probably subsisted on bits of fruit and cigarettes and alcohol back at his apartment, a dimly lit lair with nothing for decoration except his clothes, which hung on nails punched through peeling brown wallpaper into the concrete.

Dima's parents worried, too, especially about how their son's drinking might jeopardize his naval career. Dima's mother even asked Olga Lubushkina to look after her son and to tell her how Dima was doing.

The concern was well founded. By the summer of 1999, *Kursk* captain Gennady Lyachin had heard enough about Kolesnikov's drinking escapades, and he finally issued a stern ultimatum to the otherwise promising captain-lieutenant: If Kolesnikov couldn't control his drinking, Lyachin said, "I think it will be time for you to leave the sub." The *Kursk* had just been tapped for a particularly critical long-distance mission, Lyachin told him. But one more drunken stunt, one more report of a fistfight, and Kolesnikov would be left behind in Vidyayevo.

A rattled Kolesnikov retreated on leave to St. Petersburg, and slipped back into his old familiar ways. He looked up his dark-haired Inna. He downed more Mr. Officer with his wayward friend Maksim. He told Maksim that the drinking up north was the dominant form of recreation, though fleet conditions were hellish. He talked of how he loved the *Kursk*, but resented how the brutal post-Soviet military cuts forced him to jury-rig repairs. At one point he turned to Maksim and smiled over the way his naval comrades applauded his resourcefulness. "Up north," he said, "my comrades call me 'Golden.'"

"Well, no matter what they say about you up there," Maksim joked, "you'll always be 'Rust' to me."

Despite his continued drinking, Dima's parents sensed he was ready to make a change. They persuaded him that he needed to get "decoded" from alcohol. Dima's mother had plans for him if he could clean up his act: with her doctorate in chemistry, Irina Kolesnikova worked at a nearby grade school, and she'd spotted a pretty young biology teacher there, also named Olga, who was recently divorced. After a newly sobered Dima returned to Vidyayevo to join the *Kursk*'s long-distance mission, his mother sought out the soft-spoken teacher, Olga Borisova, and proposed an introduction. Olga had mixed feelings about the idea of attaching her future to a career navy man, but eventually she agreed to meet him.

Several months later, Dima returned home late on New Year's Eve to mark the coming millennium and, at his mother's insistence, dressed quickly and attended a celebration at his high school. When his mother introduced him to Olga, the awkward Dima was utterly tongue-tied. What could such a beautiful woman possibly see in him?

Olga Borisova quickly appraised the tall man before her. Now a more robust 225 pounds, Dima had outgrown his jacket and pants. She thought he looked a bit like an oversized puppy. Olga smiled. They walked off and attempted conversation, but Kolesnikov seemed so awkward that Olga wondered if the harsh conditions of the North—too much male company, too few creature comforts—had robbed him of any social skills he might have had.

But Olga agreed to see him again despite her first impressions, until Kolesnikov's impaired manner of courtship bottomed out while they were riding the metro in St. Petersburg. At one point the subway train stopped abruptly, sending the passengers collapsing into one another. Trying to protect Olga, the towering Kolesnikov grabbed the back of her jacket collar, dangling her in front of the other passengers like a kitten.

They agreed to stop seeing each other, but Olga soon found herself missing this "clumsy but strong, kind guy."

Dima called and said he hoped he could see her. Then he called again. When he returned to St. Petersburg, he confessed that her teacherly manner had made him feel ill at ease, and that this impediment to their relationship "must be immediately fixed." They began meeting every evening after Olga's classes, often heading to cafés, strolling the picturesque riverbanks, and ordering champagne, even though Dima's hard-won sobriety prevented him from sharing it with her. Before long, Dima took Olga to the Chernaya Rechka, the riverside where beloved Russian poet Alexander Pushkin suffered a mortal wound in a duel with his wife's alleged French paramour. Dima proposed. Olga accepted.

"Let's go see my family and tell them all!" Dima shouted.

"No," said Olga, typically cautious. "I'm not sure they will be very happy. Let's have you go first and get them prepared for the news."

His phone call later was oddly reserved. "Come over," he told her. "We must talk seriously."

"Maybe I shouldn't?"

"*Come!*"

Olga stood anxiously outside the Kolesnikov apartment after ringing the bell. The door swung open to flowers and bear hugs from brother Sasha, mother Irina, and father Roman, who pronounced: "We didn't have a daughter. Now we have one!" The April 28 wedding was for family only.

The newlywed Olga Kolesnikova allowed herself modest hopes before making her first pilgrimage to Vidyayevo just two months later, in summer 2000. Dima warned her that this place felt like one of the ends of the earth. But when Olga and Dima came to his apartment door, Dima hesitated.

"What's wrong?" asked Olga.

"I'm afraid you'll faint," said Dima. "There are holes in the floor, ragged wallpaper, a sagging sofa. It's not like in St. Petersburg."

"You know," said Olga, standing her ground, "I already like this broken floor and this ragged wallpaper and this sagging sofa, because these are our walls."

Kolesnikov swung open the door.

Olga Kolesnikova beheld the "creepy walls" of their first home together, and couldn't help thinking: *This barren little bachelor's space is the home of a captain-lieutenant?*

Dima flopped into a big stuffed chair and tried to humor her, joking sheepishly about his wall "art." Olga tried to feign nonchalance, but would later tell her mother, "I thought I'd married the poorest officer in the whole Russian Navy."

But now—on this Sunday afternoon aboard the *Kursk*, surrounded by the impressive technology of her new husband's amazing submarine—

Olga gushes an oath of spousal loyalty. "You have a very difficult job," she says with disarming sincerity, "and I will love you very strongly and very tender!" She stares at him wide-eyed. Then she seals the promise by blowing a kiss into the camera.

Dima Kolesnikov considered the introduction between his lovely new wife and his great steel mistress a success, but he and his Olechka agreed she should return to St. Petersburg before his next big mission, planned as a high-stakes weapons-firing exercise in the Barents Sea to the north. An unadorned former bachelor's apartment was no place for a young wife to await her seafaring husband. Besides, perhaps Olechka and her mother could find some things in St. Petersburg to make the apartment feel more like home.

With the matter settled, Dima persuaded a friend, a fellow *Kursk* crewman, to drive them to the train station in Murmansk, ninety minutes away. When Ivan Nessen arrived to pick them up, he was struck by the contrast of this earnestly smiling couple standing at the threshold of such a drab little apartment. Ivan thought it testified to the powerful love they must share.

At the train station, Dima Kolesnikov couldn't keep it together. Olechka tried to soothe her "Mitya" as he clung to her and sobbed like a baby.

2

LOADING UP
BOLSHAYA LOPATKA DOCK, ZAPADNAYA LITSA BAY
THURSDAY, AUGUST 10, 2000, 1700 HOURS

The leviathan *Kursk* floats quietly alongside a loading pier at a ramshackle Arctic naval site in the Zapadnaya Litsa fjord, taking on armaments for one of the most important military tests in post-Soviet history—a three-day fleet-wide battle exercise. The submarine represents a billion dollars of this cash-strapped country's finest technology—a 14,700-ton predator cloaked in a three-inch-thick layer of black rubber that helps dampen internal noise and shields her from detection by opposing submarines—or from the signals of an enemy's acoustic homing torpedoes. It is as long as two jumbo jets, five stories high, and sixty feet wide. There are ten airtight compartments. Twin nuclear reactors. Twin propellers. A closed-circuit video system. A small swimming pool. A sauna. Onboard mascots, including Vasily the cat. It's all wrapped in an enormous double hull, with a twelve-foot void between the inner and outer hulls amidships that helps ensure the enemy can't sink her even with a direct hit. The hull gap also houses the forward-tilting launch tubes of twenty-four giant cruise missiles designed to wreck aircraft carriers—or entire cities, when fitted with nuclear warheads. She can also carry up to twenty-eight torpedoes, one newly modified version of which is now being loaded. As a select few officers and torpedo-factory representatives watch, a decrepit crane gingerly lowers the sleek, twenty-two-foot-long weapon through the torpedo-loading hatch into the *Kursk*'s torpedo room.

Deep inside, the rest of the *Kursk*'s 118 men casually linger near their stations. Toward the stern, an excited Captain-Lieutenant Dmitry Kolesnikov rules over a low-level hum of turbogenerators. While Kolesnikov commands the seventh compartment's turbine systems, best friend Rashid Aryapov, in charge of the *Kursk*'s main engines and propulsion train, commands the adjacent sixth from various locations. The command structure makes Rashid senior to Dima, a detail that has never chilled their friendship.

Although from different worlds—Dima hails from the Christian North, Rashid from the South's Muslim Uzbekistan—ten years of common experience have made them almost inseparable. The thickset Dima sometimes calls his wiry, dark-featured friend "Sayyid," after a popular film character from the Russian classic *White Sun of the Desert*. The two make an odd pair. Though nearly a foot taller than Sayyid and more book smart, "Zolotoy"—Dima's "Golden" nickname among *Kursk* mates—often defers to his more philosophical southern friend, which has sometimes kept them out of trouble. By happenstance, a sobered-up Dima was exchanging marriage vows with his new Olga on the same day a love-struck Rashid was proposing to a shy young Muslim girl named Khalima in Rashid's native Uzbekistan.

Now Dima and Rashid keep photos of their new brides taped to the ceilings of their bunk spaces aboard the *Kursk*. The third member of their academy trio, Captain-Lieutenant Sergey Lubushkin, has taken up his post as commander of a remote control communications group two compartments forward of the heavily shielded reactor compartment. The tall and easygoing Lubushkin recently shed his reputation as an overly patient officer by cursing over the *Kursk*'s intercom when a junior officer failed to respond promptly to his orders. It was quite a break from the usual "Would you please," with which "Lubu" prefaced every request. The sudden display of temper brought peals of laughter throughout the sub, and a hearty round of congratulations.

Much seems right with the world of the three happily married friends—especially if they can guide the *Kursk* through the next three days of critical battle trials and get home soon to their young wives. But here in their after compartments, the men are starting to wonder why the torpedoes are taking so long. They've heard there's something out of order with the torpedoes, which is making the *Kursk* late for the exercise. Their commander must be deeply displeased.

From President Vladimir Putin on down, most of Russia's military establishment awaits these exercises in a state of high anticipation. The armada now setting out into the Barents represents a key test of an emerging do-more-with-less defense philosophy of Russia's little-known new leader. With his nation deeply impoverished, Putin wants his military men to focus on quality, not volume. The Soviet collapse has left the vast bulk of the once-mighty Northern Fleet rusting at its piers. Wary of military challenges to his shaky authority, former president Boris Yeltsin brutally slashed defense spending to a paltry 5 percent of its 1990 level under the Soviet Union, and the navy has felt some of the worst of it. Russia's fleet of nuclear submarines has rapidly dwindled—from 114 in 1990 to sixty-seven in 1996 to thirty-four today, not all of which are seaworthy enough to leave their piers. Most of the decommissioned nuclear subs have been mothballed while still afloat, making tempting targets for metal scavengers so brazen that even the deteriorating nuclear reactors don't scare them.

Russia's official sub-dismantling program is so small, sloppy, and moribund that environmental experts describe the Northern Fleet's 130 abandoned nuclear subs as "floating Chernobyls." This is an exaggeration, but the decaying nuclear subs are a deadly menace just the same. So many of these forgotten undersea warships infest the bays and inlets of the Kola Peninsula that radio stations in Murmansk, the city at its center, sometimes provide radiation reports along with the weather updates. But even as environmentalists vex over the peninsula's spiraling potential for nuclear disaster, the Kola's residents have so far been "lucky" to suffer only small accidents—a smattering of limited radioactive leaks from subs and unsecured disposal sites.

The decommissioned subs at least supply spare parts to some of the few active subs, but the fleet's rescue vessels have not benefited from such spoils. Safety has become a casualty of the economic collapse; the best rescue vessels have been scrapped or sold or rented to paying customers. Russia's two best wreck-assessment submersibles—the *Mir-1* and *Mir-2*—are currently more than three thousand miles away in the North Atlantic, collecting their share of the $35,000-per-trip fees charged to take high-end Western adventurers more than two miles deep for a look at the sunken *Titanic* wreckage south of Greenland. The Northern Fleet's remaining rescue assets rely on a poorly maintained mother ship to support a few submarine rescue submersibles, the crews of which are ill equipped and undertrained. On the rare occasions when the rescue crews actually do train, they usually run drills in shallow water within sight of their docks.

Even the Northern Fleet "deep-sea" divers so valuable to rescue efforts are qualified only for depths down to two hundred feet, well shy of the depths where most Russian subs ply the Barents. The true deep-sea divers—the highly trained "saturation" specialists conditioned for the more technically challenging deep-water work—have also suffered critical cutbacks: they've all but disappeared during the 1990s, either to retirement or to better-paying jobs in the commercial oil industry. Only a handful still train in St. Petersburg with the Black Sea Fleet. But they also lack equipment: if there's a problem deeper than two hundred feet, the Russian Navy's divers no longer have the proper surface support gear to be of much help.

Submarines, while among the most lethal ships in the navy, are also its most vulnerable. But Northern Fleet officials take comfort in knowing the *Kursk* has its own clever rescue system wedged into the conning tower, or "sail," an escape pod capable of whisking 115 sailors safely to the surface. Fleet officials have even planned a mock disaster-and-rescue to follow this week's exercises, just to put the rescue team through its paces.

The summer's war games have been well advertised in military circles since May, and various NATO vessels began drawing up new deployment schedules in anticipation of the big show. As the critical dates draw near, six NATO vessels begin staking out their positions in and around the Barents—not that the Cold War's end has won them an invitation.

It's been more than ten years since the Berlin Wall came down, but Russia and the NATO countries still behave much like enemies at the operational level, spying on one another's military activities in preparation for a conflict whose underpinnings seem no longer to exist. The Barents exercise is choreographed to assume an invasion by Western forces: virtually all of the militarily significant countries to the west are NATO countries. The Russians are putting to sea a thirty-six-ship armada with the *Kursk* as its premier underwater heavyweight.

As the Barents event gears up, Russia is in a bad mood. The weekend's military display will mark a new post–Cold War escalation of tensions between Russia and the West. Russia felt humiliated after being brushed aside seventeen months earlier, when NATO countries boldly disregarded Russian objections to the U.S.-led bombing of former Soviet protectorate Yugoslavia in March 1999.

Some Russians saw the Balkan conflict as a purely internal civil struggle undeserving of outside interference. Many viewed the action more personally, as though NATO were bombing Russian soil itself, seemingly dismissing this battered but still proud former superpower as a viable threat. So was this the new world order, some Russian pundits wondered, with the arrogant Cold War victor throwing its weight around?

"NATO is an agent of war, not peace," fumed defense ministry general Leonid Ivashov in early April 1999. "It's a criminal organization that does not have the right to exist."

It was against this backdrop that former KGB colonel Vladimir Putin's phenomenal rise began to peak. For months he'd been appealing to Russia's crushed national ego as a pro-military prime minister with a strong interest in restoring the once-great Russian military machine, especially its navy, which he warned should not be treated "like a poor relative." With then-president Boris Yeltsin unraveling on the world stage from a toxic mix of alcohol, corruptive cronyism, and cardiac troubles, Putin closely managed Russia's response to NATO's actions in the Balkans. As prime minister, Putin signed off on a plan to send an attack submarine to the Balkans for a symbolic display of Russian displeasure. It would be Russia's first foray to the Mediterranean in ten years, and the main job went to the motherland's most deadly silent stalker, the *Kursk*.

Captain Gennady Lyachin and his *Kursk* crew answered the Kremlin's call with relish, setting out from Vidyayevo on August 3, 1999, for a seventy-six-day patrol, secretly sailing around Norway and England and through the Strait of Gibraltar into the dark blue Mediterranean. Some of Lyachin's officers fondly recall the moment when their beloved commander first used his periscope to view the Mediterranean conditions; he asked if some of the crew wanted a look. As they eagerly crowded the periscope stand, Lyachin asked them to stand back. Then he focused the scope's light into the palm of his hand and cupped the warm image, bringing sighs of delight from the sun-starved crew.

The *Kursk* soon homed in on the primary target of her harassment mission, a prized aircraft carrier operating with the American Sixth Fleet, the USS *Theodore Roosevelt*. The sub—fully loaded with her arsenal of "Shipwreck" missiles—settled into the *Roosevelt's* noisy wake in the Adriatic Sea near the Yugoslavian coast. Lyachin and his crew initially did their best to elude NATO detection, shutting down unnecessary mechanical devices, talking in low voices, and removing hard-soled shoes in favor of soft-soled "boat slippers."

Roosevelt's officers knew something was up, but kept losing track of the *Kursk's* position, eventually diverting nine P-3 Orion submarine tracker patrol aircraft from tank-spotting flights over Kosovo to get a fix on the unwanted predator.

This was precisely what Russia wanted, and Captain Lyachin exploited the moment to his crew's benefit. He ordered that a signal from the *Kursk's* upward-looking camera be beamed throughout the sub's closed-circuit video system. Astonished crew from bow to stern gasped at the visual sensation of fish swimming above them, and above that, an up-close-and-personal view of the hull of a giant American warship. And above that, Lyachin and others would later tell them, were NATO's submarine search planes slicing the sky.

By this point, Lyachin and his crew were happy that NATO had discovered them and become so alarmed. By the time the *Kursk* finally broke away, NATO had definitely gotten the message: Moscow may be down, but she's not out. Russian opposition could not be dismissed without consequences. Even in a post-Soviet world, there would still be limits to the military affairs of Western cowboys.

Her saber-rattling task thus accomplished, the *Kursk* began a second mission to the northern Atlantic, just to probe the wary U.S. patrols off the northeastern United States, much like in the old days of the Cold War.

The deployment's only serious blemish was a fire in one of the turbine compartments that caused heavy smoke, rendering some sailors unconscious and stirring panic among the other compartment crewmen. Lyachin and his damage-control assistant ably ordered the crew to settle down and fight the fire, while evacuating several unconscious men to the *Kursk*'s sickbay. Though the crew was shaken, their abilities to solve the crisis without serious harm bolstered confidence in themselves, and in Lyachin's skill amid potential catastrophe.

When Lyachin and his men debarked onto a Northern Fleet pier that October 19, the proud commander briskly saluted his superiors and barely concealed a smile in announcing his mission's success. Then he and his men settled into a pier-side celebration, complete with a roast suckling pig and brass band.

Lyachin won even greater satisfaction after learning of the late-October congressional testimony of U.S. Sixth Fleet vice admiral Daniel J. Murphy Jr. The chagrined U.S. commander described the *Kursk*'s harassment of his fleet as "inconvenient." He testified that the formidable Russian attack sub possessed "the very best technology," and presented "the highest difficulty in tracking and locating." He complained that the Russian sub forced his NATO patrol aircraft to divide their time between "looking for a tank one day and then looking for a submarine on the following day."

After learning more details of the *Kursk*'s impact in the Mediterranean, Lyachin shared with a Russian newspaper how his vessel's stalking prowess had cost NATO $23 million in diverted assets just to keep an eye on him. "We did not give the adversary's forces any rest," he proclaimed. He was quickly summoned to Moscow to debrief a pleased Prime Minister Putin.

Buoyed by the *Kursk*'s Mediterranean adventure—and still rankled by

NATO's unrelenting pursuit of Yugoslavia's Serbian leader Slobodan Milosevic—Putin announced plans for a series of ambitious naval upgrades. He proposed to reestablish a higher and more permanent Russian naval profile in the Mediterranean, this time to include the dazzling presence of Russia's only remaining aircraft carrier, the *Admiral Kuznetsov*. He wanted the bigger deployment to return to the Med before the end of 2000.

To a Russian Navy still feeling the pain from ten years of deep neglect, this felt like a new lease on life. To a Russian people yearning for a taste of their nation's former clout, it felt like national resurgence.

When an exhausted Boris Yeltsin suddenly named the little-known Putin his acting successor on December 31, 1999, senior navy officials instantly began courting their favored presidential candidate by launching two intercontinental ballistic missiles. To further celebrate Putin's spring electoral victory, Northern Fleet officials then invited the new president for a visit to the Kola Peninsula, feting him with an overnight stay onboard a nuclear submarine. Putin, the son of a submariner and the product of the navy-centric St. Petersburg, engaged in the baptismal rites of an honorary sailor—drinking a cup of seawater and planting a kiss on a greasy sledgehammer—then bunked in a space near the vessel's torpedo compartment. He donned a navy cap and greatcoat to watch a sub-launched ballistic missile leap into the cobalt Arctic sky and hurtle across the thinly populated Arctic Russia toward Kamchatka. Putin then stood on a snow-dusted Northern Fleet pier and began to detail his ten-year plan for the Russian Navy: First, he announced the great Barents exercise for the coming summer. Then he said that it would be only a dress rehearsal for a much bigger display—a bold fall deployment to the Mediterranean.

To all parties, it looked as though the dying Russian Navy was back in business.

The pledged buildup scored a direct hit with the ailing Russian psyche. One journalist greeted the news with patriotic fervor in the April 18 edition of *Rossiiskaya Gazeta*: "Yes, we know how to make war. Yes, we no longer want to hear Tomahawk missiles on the heads of the Serbs, the Iraqis, and the Arabs."

"This time," proclaimed an ebullient Vice Admiral Nikolay Mikheev three days later, "our presence will be even higher than it was in Soviet times."

On May 11, Russia's Military News Agency formally announced the exercise plan, the eager NATO vessels to lock in their schedules. The United States would send five spy vessels; Norway would send one. The opportunity was too good for Western intelligence gatherers to pass up.

3

ENDLESS SPYING GAME

BARENTS SEA

THURSDAY, AUGUST 10, 2000 (NOT FIXED IN TIME BEYOND DAY)

The entire 542,000-square-mile Barents Basin is more wired for sound than usual, and everybody in the Northern Fleet knows it.

NATO's tried-and-true system of underwater hydrophones flanks the Barents to the west, designed to alert the alliance to any Russian naval activity that ventures beyond the Northern Fleet's traditional exercise range. Norwegian P-3 sub trackers occasionally ply the skies, from where they can drop sonobuoys to detect submarines. Orbiting satellites have been programmed to catch glimpses of surface activities from space, with some able to bounce real-time data gathered from U.S. vessels below. They can beam fleeting images of Russia's naval activities back to analysts in Norfolk, Virginia, and Fort Meade, Maryland, four thousand miles away.

Radar sites boldly dot the Norwegian shores facing east and north. The Norwegians have also contributed the stalwart *Marjatta*, a surface surveillance vessel that has become a familiar Barents fixture to Northern Fleet veterans. A similar American surface vessel, the USNS *Loyal*, will trail one of its mile-long twin sonar array cables from a safe 180 miles northwest of the designated exercise site, gathering underwater sound. The *Loyal*'s electronic surveillance system can also collect voice and other electronic transmissions from surface stations and satellites.

Three U.S. spy subs prowl the area's waters. The tiny *NR-1* research sub lingers to the west in the Norwegian Sea—primarily assigned to a separate, classified mission. But members of the *NR-1*'s twelve-man crew could also use their sub's exterior mechanical arms to gather any weapons materials left behind by the Russian war games. The NR-1 can be aided in such a mission by its surface support ship, the *Caroline Chouest*. And the *Chouest* can retrieve the NR-1 on short notice, speeding to any site where it might be summoned.

But the real NATO heavyweights are two modernized Los Angeles–class attack subs that have already staked out hiding places in this traditional Cold War submarine playground. The USS *Toledo* will cover the big picture; the USS *Memphis* will home in on *Kursk*.

The *Memphis* crew is particularly geared up. The *Memphis* is the American navy's premier testing platform for the latest in underwater technology, and its crew has been eager to try out some new acoustic equipment that extends its listening capability far beyond that of any known opponent. The new system is a radical departure, employing the most powerful computer processors offered by the commercial sector. The *Memphis* has recently been custom-fitted to allow quick switches to the latest top-secret gadgetry, including signal-processing software and classified sound-collection devices. The listening arrangement is aided by twin mile-long towed sonar array cables—at $3 million a pop—a system hailed as breakthrough technology and still improving.

The *Memphis*'s listening equipment was installed in the spring, and now the crew is ready to try it against the best thing the Russians have to offer. The *Memphis* even has a seasoned commander who has been on board for two years now, a former senior submarine school instructor whose motivational zeal has greatly boosted flagging morale from the previous command regime. Barents deployments are the grail of the American submariners' world, since only the most proficient crews are selected.

The average depth of the Barents Sea is 750 feet, just 250 feet deeper than the *Kursk* is long, leaving little room for adventurous moves. During the more openly contentious Cold War years, the Barents—the world's most active hornets' nest for East-West submarine spy games— was the site of at least six collisions between Soviet and NATO subs. Post-collapse, there have been two more accidents.

The men of the *Memphis* are confident their long-range listening capabilities will help them get the job done from a greater distance.

On the eve of the August exercise, Vladimir Putin's Kremlin finds itself on the defensive, seemingly buffeted by alarming trends on every domestic front. Russia's population is shrinking dramatically, and life expectancy is dropping; the average Russian man will be lucky to see his fifty-ninth birthday. The nation is ranked third in the world for violent death. Its gross domestic product equals that of Peru. A handful of widely loathed "oligarchs"—former Yeltsin business cronies who greedily exploited his reckless giveaway of state assets as part of a Western-inspired "economic shock therapy"—are rapidly spiriting billions out of the country. Many have also bought up major media operations, which they are increasingly turning against the apparently authoritarian new president with a KGB past.

One of Russia's most-sought-after exports is human beings: childless Westerners comb the desperate orphanages for babies; lonely men shop for mail-order brides; scam artists dupe some women into sexual slavery; unemployed scientists leap for better prospects abroad. And the people who stay behind are caught up in a distressingly chaotic economy plagued by organized crime, complete with gangland killings and rampant bribe taking. Many thousands of young children wander the streets homeless, begging at metro stations for subsistence and sniffing glue for escape.

The painful post-communist transition has prompted bouts of nostalgia among older Russians for the relative ease and order of Soviet times, with little heed paid to the harsh reality that the bankrupt Soviet system itself helped bring about the mess that Putin now faces.

Some of the challenge gets personal for the tenderfoot president: as prime minister just the year before, Putin led the battle cry to renew the war against Chechen separatists. The ensuing siege there has become a national nightmare, providing a relentlessly steady body count that has driven mothers' rights groups to seize their sons from the battle zones. By early August 2000, the Kremlin is actively trying to convince skeptical Russians that a series of deadly bombings in Moscow—one just a week before the Barents games—were the work of Chechen terrorists, while some of the swaggeringly independent media are suggesting that the Kremlin staged the attacks in a dark ploy to prop up support for the divisive war.

Given the mysterious new leader's lifelong career in a widely despised KGB, the idea of killing innocent Russians for political gain doesn't seem so far-fetched. When the benignly enigmatic Vladimir Putin was first introduced to the Russian people as Yeltsin's choice for the battered nation's new leader, one Western journalist made headlines by asking the very question so fundamental to any would-be democracy: "Who is Putin?"

Despite a well-crafted political campaign aimed at the March 2000 elections, including portrayals of Putin as a dynamic man of action—flying in the back of a fighter jet over Chechnya, displaying his judo skills in a visit with students, sharing personal anecdotes for his campaign biography—the mystery still lingers six months into his presidency: Who is Russia's new leader, and where does he plan to take the country? Will he return to Soviet-style secrecy and deception? How does he feel about free speech? Private ownership? What are the priorities between people's lives and the needs of the state? Which way to the new Russia?

A steady stream of high-ranking pilgrims have been penciled into Putin's Kremlin schedule on the eve of the Barents exercise. There is a two-hour rapprochement with ex-president Mikhail Gorbachev on Thursday, an inaugural visit with Yasser Arafat on Friday morning, and a tense session Friday evening, in which Putin must settle a long-running public squabble between his top two military men. The new president's final decision on that dispute could carry enormous consequences for Russia's future: Should he prop up Russia's faltering global clout by steering his tiny defense budget toward nuclear forces, which would favor the navy's nuclear-equipped missile boats? Or does the Chechnya problem herald a growing need for more conventional weapons on the home front?

The pro-nuclear Russian defense minister, Marshal Igor Sergeyev—already looking older than his sixty-two years and a popular target of ouster rumors—is counting on the Northern Fleet to make his case this weekend, regardless of Putin's Friday-night rulings.

For Putin, the flotilla now heading into the Barents could mark a breakout point—a great way to celebrate the new president's one hundredth day in office, which he will observe with his family on the sandy beaches of the Black Sea on Monday, August 14.

When the new president eventually slips into the Mediterranean climate of the Black Sea on Saturday, August 12, he will still feel connected to his far-flung operations, including his naval exercise three thousand miles to the north. Several top military men in his normal traveling entourage will pass him updates from the Barents. Minding the store from Moscow will be Defense Minister Sergeyev, the nation's most senior career military man, and the one with an immediate professional stake in the weekend's outcome.

In the Barents itself, directly overseeing the exercise, will be Northern Fleet commander Vyacheslav Popov, a quintessential Soviet-era admiral. In his fifties, his red walrus mustache turning gray from the salty Arctic spray, Popov has lately demonstrated his agility in adapting to rapidly changing East-West dynamics by forging a friendship with his nearest NATO counterpart in Norway. Yet Popov couldn't be more imbued with a patriotic fealty to the Kremlin. As he looks out over the bridge of the nuclear cruiser *Peter the Great*, Popov knows how much stock his new leader—and, by extension, his tormented nation—places in the gathering flotilla.

4

DANGEROUSLY LATE
BOLSHAYA LOPATKA DOCK, ZAPADNAYA LITSA BAY
THURSDAY, AUGUST 10, 2130 HOURS

"Chyort poberi!"—Damn it to hell!—mutters a weapons officer at the dock in Zapadnaya Litsa Bay, where the *Kursk*'s torpedo-loading process is suffering the direct effects of the navy's long-neglected weapons cranes. Hours past the *Kursk*'s intended departure time, a newly modified electric torpedo is taking too long to load.

The holdup only adds to a much bigger worry for Captain Lyachin and his crew. For the past week, a huge and notoriously temperamental liquid-fueled torpedo, loaded on August 3, has kept the torpedo men on edge. Because of a series of unforeseen changes among the torpedo crew in recent weeks, most of them are unfamiliar with the weapon's highly specialized systems, but they know that its improper handling can bring catastrophic consequences.

This particular torpedo, technically called "Type 65–76," is so large and unwieldy that sailors casually refer to it as the *"tolstushka,"* or "Fat Girl." It's the world's biggest torpedo, weighing in at nearly 4.5 tons, more than three midsized cars. It stretches thirty-six feet, the length of an average school bus. Its girth, eighty inches, is that of a circus fat lady, hence its nickname. Salty weapons handlers also like to joke that its massive phallic dimensions prove that it was "designed by a very lonely woman."

The Fat Girl's destructive capability may strike fear in the hearts of Russia's enemies, but its volatile propulsion chemistry also frightens many Russian sailors.

The Fat Girl was borne of a very Faustian bargain. In their headlong race for military parity with the West, Russian weapons designers progressively embraced a propulsion system for the Fat Girl that their Western counterparts had long ago rejected as too unstable. While many liquid-fueled torpedoes used compressed air as a fuel oxidizer, the Fat Girl employs high-test hydrogen peroxide, or HTP.

The benefits of HTP are threefold: It makes torpedoes run faster and much longer—two highly coveted advantages in any sub-to-ship duel on the high seas. HTP is also a vastly cheaper oxidizer than those favored by Western navies, which helped compensate for their capitalist enemies' richer defense budgets. Each Fat Girl could be manufactured and fueled at a cost to the Soviet state of 300,000 rubles, less than $11,000 at year-2000 exchange rates. This compares with the approximate $1 million cost per unit of many Western torpedoes.

But HTP also brings real danger. The oxidizer is composed of 85 percent pure hydrogen peroxide, as opposed to the 5 percent solutions found in some household products. This makes HTP capable of slowly corroding through certain materials, destroying rubberized gaskets and valves connected with its own container, and then seeping through microcracks in the welded seams of a torpedo's casing. Once exposed to outside elements, HTP can come in contact with even more volatile materials that can trigger a dangerous chemical breakdown. And known catalysts include way too many materials commonly found in torpedo rooms: rust, oil, grease, hydraulics, clothing, dirt, and even certain metals, some of which are found in the alloys of torpedo components and their launching tubes. Contamination causes HTP to break apart violently into oxygen and water, expanding in volume by 4,500 times and generating very high temperatures. Such a burst can ignite the weapon's fuel, which is forty-two gallons of kerosene.

Smaller HTP forerunners had anchored Soviet torpedo arsenals since the 1950s, but in 1976, designers unveiled the goliath Fat Girl and soon amassed a stockpile of five hundred. American arms negotiators over the years targeted the Fat Girl arsenal in nuclear arms talks, complaining particularly about one disturbing aspect: While the conventional version of the giant weapon used a precise antiship, wake-homing guidance system, the nuclear version designed for attack on enemy shore installations had no guidance system at all. This made the nuclear version strictly a "point-and-shoot" weapon, which could easily stray.

In exchange for U.S. concessions, Russia agreed to reduce the five hundred Fat Girl torpedoes in its arsenal, knowing perfectly well that their powerful SS-N-19 "Granit" missiles (NATO code-named "Shipwreck") were a better alternative: the Shipwrecks weren't limited to water; they could travel 280 miles in minutes by air and hit their targets with pinpoint accuracy. And unlike the Fat Girl, they could be programmed to strike land-locked American cities beyond the coastal zones.

In the last years of the Soviet Union, weapons men emptied hundreds of Fat Girls of their fuel and electronic components, often slicing up the metal casings for use in children's playgrounds.

By the summer of 2000, the Russians still have one hundred *tols-tushkas* in the arsenal, and think the resurgent chill with the Americans makes it prudent to ensure its navy still knows how to use them. But as with the rest of Russia's dramatically collapsing post-Soviet navy, the Fat Girls are aging poorly—along with the knowledge of how to use them. In a rare instance, the Northern Fleet's *Smolensk* submarine successfully fired one Fat Girl in the spring of 2000. None of the *Kursk*'s torpedo men had participated, but crewmen from the *Smolensk* have tried to share their knowledge in the days leading up to the forthcoming exercise.

Even when stored in their warehouses, the Fat Girls keep their handlers nervous. Achieving the torpedoes' intended service life of twenty years requires a maintenance overhaul at ten years. But some of the Fat Girls don't even make it that far before they start failing in their storage racks. When weapons experts periodically inspect the Fat Girls, they sometimes spot alarming signs of leakage. During the course of supplying the practice torpedoes for the Barents exercise, at least four of the leaking giant weapons have been disabled and discarded.

If early leaks are not detected in time, HTP weapons begin to heat up, developing a palpable "fever" as the oxidizer begins to decompose. If left unventilated, the torpedo's internal temperature can soar to one thousand degrees Fahrenheit. Weapons handlers describe such a torpedo as "enraged," especially if the process graduates to the stage where an acrid white vapor begins seeping from the torpedo casing. In the depot, an enraged torpedo requires dangerous emergency disposal procedures. In a torpedo room, such a weapon begs for speedy ejection into the sea.

To monitor HTP weapons, submarines are equipped with "bubble sensors"—clear glass tubes coiled above the weapon to show bubble generation levels as an indicator of the HTP's decomposition rate. When the number of bubbles reaches a certain threshold, the gauge automatically triggers a spray of seawater to cool the torpedo down. Such an event also sets off a shrill alarm, signaling torpedo men that they have no more than six hours to eject the torpedo or risk explosion.

Though Western navies once tried to harness HTP's more attractive powers, a series of mishaps forced its broad rejection by the 1970s. In 1955, an HTP-fueled torpedo exploded in the forward section of the British sub HMS *Sidon*, killing thirteen men and sinking the sub at its pier. The United Kingdom consequently scrapped its entire HTP-torpedo arsenal. U.S. submarine designers, hoping to power an entire submarine using HTP, devised a miniature prototype called the X-1. In 1957, the X-1 also blew up pier-side, ending that idea as well.

Although these reports were widely reported by the time the Fat Girls were designed, Soviet weapons designers have long distinguished themselves among their international peers for their higher tolerance for risk. If they could adequately manage the HTP's dangers, Soviet weapons designers seemed to think, the advantage over their Western enemies made the extra risks worthwhile.

But the Soviet embrace of unstable gas-steam weapons like the HTP torpedoes exacted a cruel price, even if the growing death knell associated with their ill-timed detonations was muffled almost completely beneath the veil of Soviet-era secrecy.

One of the first reports of such a gas-steam torpedo destroying a Soviet sub occurred at the Northern Fleet's Polyarny sub base on the Kola

Peninsula on January 11, 1962. It was just nine days prior to the B-37 sub-marine's planned deployment to escort nuclear missiles to the Caribbean, and B-37 commander Captain First Rank Anatoly Begeba returned from vacation early that morning for a planned ceremonial flag raising. One of his weapons men approached him. "Commander," the man said, "the fleet is loading garbage on our sub!" Though not an HTP weapon, the gas-steam torpedo involved shared a similarly volatile oxidizer system. The alarmed torpedo man told Begeba that the fleet, apparently hop-ing to rid the arsenals of aging stocks, had sent unstable liquid-fueled weapons that were four years overdue for maintenance. Worse, Begeba also had orders to see that these torpedoes were pressurized in their racks at twice their normal "stored" level while still moored at the pier. This would put them on a hair trigger before setting out on the high-stakes mis-sion; if the Americans learned of the Soviet plan in Cuba, this deploy-ment could get hot. Still, Begeba thought the order unnecessarily foolhardy, and refused to comply until his commander formally put it in writing. The commander did, leaving Begeba no choice.

By 0810 that morning, the torpedoes were pressurized at the ordered level, with Commander Begeba topside and aft, inspecting his vessel's exterior. Begeba didn't hear the blast ten minutes later, but remembers seeing a bright flash toward the bow and then finding himself in the icy water. The sub sank rapidly, taking seventy-eight young lives with it. A criminal indictment for Commander Begeba quickly followed. Begeba's formally documented protest of the torpedo-pressure order eventually won his exoneration.

The B-37's unstable torpedo oxidizer issue emerged at trial, but failed to halt the Soviet adoption of the even more unstable fuel oxidizer pre-sented in the HTP weapons. In short order, HTP blasts rocked a sub in the Black Sea Fleet in 1966, a Pacific Fleet sub in 1970, and then two more Northern Fleet subs in 1972 and 1977. Yet the HTP torpedoes kept coming, with little public evidence that Soviet weapons designers were especially concerned about the pattern.

•   •   •

For the men of the *Kursk*, the Fat Girl's history is distressing enough, but the rumors that the weapon aboard their sub could become a leaker started shortly after its August 3 loading. The *Kursk*'s *tolstushka* had arrived that day with a flood of paperwork irregularities—many chain-of-custody signatures were simply missing—with little or no indication at all that the torpedo had received its proper midlife overhaul. But sloppy paperwork was all too common in the post-Soviet navy, and its officers learned to compensate as best they could. After thoroughly inspecting the giant torpedo, the *Kursk*'s young new weapons officer had accepted it for loading.

As if the weapon's paperwork irregularities weren't alarming enough, that August 3 loading had also gone poorly. The *Kursk*'s ungainly Fat Girl endured rough handling at this same Bolshaya Lopatka dock when it nearly crashed to the pier. Weapons officers and others looked on anxiously as the long-neglected crane's heavy slings and rusty chains began to lose their grip on the giant torpedo, forcing the crane's operator to lower it roughly back to the pier. Weapons inspectors carefully studied the torpedo's streaked green casing for fuel leaks or other anomalies, but didn't find any. They could find no material reason to reject it. As an added precaution, one of the senior torpedo base officers double-checked the weapon's onboard installation himself, personally ensuring that it was safely secured and its special monitoring system properly attached. Still, the *Kursk*'s wary torpedo men began watching it closely.

Captain Lyachin is normally a patient sort, but the declining Arctic light finds him pacing the pier like a restless cat, occasionally running the fingers of one hand up and down his cheek and pulling on his chin in his signature display of worry. The sky is dominated by a thick layer of thunderstorms that have yet to act up, though a light mist makes Lyachin unhappy about leaving his topside torpedo doors open much longer. At a moist fifty degrees, the sky could really open up at any moment.

The *Kursk*'s loading problems have now placed her well behind schedule, and Lyachin will have to explain the delay while getting clearances to enter the designated range for the first of his three planned weapons demonstrations—test-firing his powerful cruise missiles. Lyachin has been at this dock since noon. It's now approaching 2200 hours, and the *Kursk* is supposed to be in position by 0400. While he's still tied to the dock, other vessels in the fleet are already engaged in the exercise.

› Tonight's last-minute torpedo loading involves a different weapon than the Fat Girl, and it galls Lyachin that this is his third attempt to pick it up. This newly modified practice torpedo is a common and smaller weapon, known as the USET-80, whose electric propulsion system at least makes it generally safe to handle. On the most recent of his six previous weapons-loading visits since spring to this dock in Zapadnaya Litsa—a ninety-minute journey from the parallel fjord that shelters Vidyayevo to the east—Lyachin was told the weapon simply wasn't ready. And now that it *is* ready, the cranes and their operators, as usual, are not up to the job.

The poorly maintained loading cranes have become a thorn in the side of the entire Russian Navy. Vessel commanders and weapons officers have complained bitterly about their frequent malfunctions, but the constant budget shortfalls have progressively forced their shutdown. The cranes were produced in Odessa, Ukraine, now an independent republic no longer united with Russia under the Soviet Union's banner. Russia hasn't funded its loading cranes from that factory since 1987, and the cranes' last maintenance contracts expired in 1998. Even if the Russian government had the funds, they're reluctant to remain dependent on a non-Russian producer for such a crucial element of their defense system. Meanwhile, no native Russian company has stepped in to fill the void.

In February 1999, senior naval officers, arguing that a foreign-produced torpedo-loading system is better than none at all, finally persuaded navy commander in chief Admiral Vladimir Kuroyedov to formally request new funding directly through Russia's Interior Ministry. Kuroyedov did his part, declaring to the Moscow authorities that fleet vessels could not unload their combat weapons after returning to shore because the decrepit cranes posed a serious safety hazard. The regular off-loadings are critical to inspection and maintenance of the weapons, he argued.

The crane failures were mounting ominously, Kuroyedov reported:

of the fourteen cranes used for lifting hundred-ton loads, only three worked; of the sixty-three designed to lift forty tons, only seventeen worked. And these were shared between the entire Russian Navy's four fleets, which made the Northern Fleet's share of functioning cranes smaller still.

Moscow responded by earmarking $17.4 million for new cranes and renewed maintenance contracts. In March 2000, Russia's Security Council even asked Deputy Prime Minister Ilya Klebanov to oversee the budgeting issues relating to the cranes, to ensure that the money allotted for their upgrade made it into the right hands. But despite this, powerful forces in the Russian Defense Ministry used the funds to help build another submarine. Soon thereafter, in June 2000, a deficient crane used by the Pacific Fleet caused a loading accident releasing toxic fuel from a submarine-launched ballistic missile. One crewman was killed, and another eleven were injured.

The decaying cranes have also reduced the fleet's safety margin in a less visible way. Fleet rules revised in the Gorbachev era barred submarines from carrying combat-ready torpedoes into an exercise where only dummy warheads may be fired. Though many fleet commanders have questioned the value of such "rules" with regard to designated "constant readiness" vessels like the *Kursk,* one thing is not in dispute: Most of the weapons now loaded on the *Kursk* carry live warheads, and the vessel has no hope of unloading them with the compromised crane system at the pier. And with the docks in Zapadnaya Litsa now straining to shoulder most of the Northern Fleet's weapons-loading needs—since so many other nearby sub bases have lost their crane capabilities altogether—the problem extends fleetwide. Other fleet sub commanders will share the *Kursk*'s additional weapons risks for the exercise. Most of them are carrying combat weapons, and several are also carrying the untrustworthy Fat Girl torpedoes.

Captain Lyachin's uneasy pacing has accelerated at the loading dock as he feels the pressure weighing on him from every front. When the crane operator returns from a poorly timed dinner break, the operator barely has time to finish the final loading of the USET-80.

Prematurely aged after twenty-three years of service—a tenure that entitles him to a monthly salary of about $250 in a country where the median income is $350—Lyachin has watched the Russian Navy's decline with growing dismay, though he's still proud of what he and his crew have been able to accomplish. But if his *Kursk* is the finest sub in the fleet, he often wonders, Why can't he get better weapons support? *Here we go again*, thinks Lyachin, trying to steel himself for this high-stakes all-fleet exercise—with a handful of senior officers from division headquarters along for the ride to observe his every move.

Lyachin intends to retire after this exercise, and he even hopes to cast his boat slippers over the side on the return trip, a traditional gesture signifying that his submarining days are behind him. He'd like to end his active duty career—and his years in the north with his beloved Irina's—on a successful note.

As Lyachin makes a final appraisal of his men engaged in the torpedo loading, he takes a special comfort in the presence of one man—Captain Third Rank Murat Baigarin. Baigarin was supposed to be transferring back to St. Petersburg by now, and Lyachin had to call in some favors to change the seasoned weapons officer's plans.

Baigarin is a former member of the *Kursk* crew, much beloved and trusted by her senior men. He'd left the crew in March to become a division headquarters officer before receiving orders to transfer to the naval college in St. Petersburg. Lyachin hated to coerce Baigarin into abruptly abandoning his plans, but he felt he had no other choice. Baigarin is the only one among them who knows the Fat Girl. And quite uncharacteristically, Lyachin had personally hunted for Baigarin in the days just before the exercise.

His torpedo crew's lack of experience with the Fat Girl came from an unlikely chain of personnel problems. First, the torpedo officer specifically trained for the Fat Girl exercise had to be removed for insubordination. Then the lead torpedo man designated and trained to handle the weapon was suddenly hospitalized after getting injured in a fight. Another torpedo man trained for the Fat Girl as an alternate had been allowed by Lyachin to extend his summer leave—before Lyachin saw the crew crisis coming. Then the flag officer from division headquarters assigned to oversee the Fat Girl's shooting practice had taken ill. Though the warrant officer who commanded the torpedo compartment was both seasoned and competent, the Fat Girl was new to him. The sudden loss of experience just days before setting out constituted an emergency.

When Murat Baigarin and his wife, Svetlana, and their kids returned to their garrison apartment on August 6 after a preparatory visit to St. Petersburg, they planned to finish packing quickly for the big move south. But within hours, the Baigarins bumped into *Kursk* warrant officer Ivan Nessen, who was clearly agitated. Nessen told them about the Fat Girl worries, and that the sub's torpedo compartment commander was babysitting the unfamiliar weapon. Then Nessen, a confidante of Captain Lyachin, took Murat aside and told him Lyachin was anxious to talk with him. Might Murat provide one last favor for the old crew before departing for St. Petersburg?

Sympathetic but reluctant, Murat hoped Lyachin would find another qualified headquarters officer for the exercise, but as he and Svetlana tried to settle into their apartment late on the evening of Monday, August 7, other *Kursk* crewmen stopped by to encourage Murat to help, including the torpedo compartment commander.

Murat, a dark-haired, thickset man of thirty-seven, then spoke with Svetlana. "They've taken a headache on board," Murat sighed. "They need me." As soon as the exercise was over, he promised, he would return and help her and their two young boys finish packing.

The unusual level of concern surrounding the Fat Girl set off a quiet ripple of rumors around Vidyayevo. One rising young officer, navigator Senior Lieutenant Sergey Tylik, told his mother just hours before departing that the sub had "death on board." Of course, this could mean anything, Nadezhda Tylik told herself, deciding that he simply meant that the *Kursk* was carrying its usual deadly arsenal. She comforted herself with the *Kursk's* celebrated indestructibility. In any case, her ambitious Sergey didn't elaborate before kissing his wife and new baby girl and setting out.

By the time the *Kursk* arrived at her loading dock in Bolshaya Lopatka, Lyachin and his reconstituted weapons team had tried to reassure themselves that they now had adequate experience aboard to tame the notoriously moody Fat Girl. They also noted that it would be gone within thirty-six hours.

As the long day approaches 2200, sunset, Lyachin finally, impatiently, signals to the watch officer that it's time to go. "*Davai poyekhali*," he says.

The *Kursk*'s torpedo room is now fully loaded with the equivalent of twenty tons of TNT.

5
GETTING UNDER WAY
BOLSHAYA LOPATKA DOCK, ZAPADNAYA LITSA FJORD
AUGUST 10, 2000, 2200 HOURS

The *Kursk's* topside crewmen clear away gear and secure the loading hatches. The watch officer orders the engines warmed, propelling commanders in compartments seven and eight into action. In the seventh, Captain-Lieutenant Dmitry Kolesnikov listens as his throttle man "puffs" the engines. The throttle man opens the throttles, then quickly shuts them again. The action brings a thump and rumble from the depths of the ship. As the engine hums and warms over the next fifteen minutes, Kolesnikov breathes in the familiar, welcome scents of moist heat and hot oil that fill his compartment.

"Stand by to get under way!" shouts the deck watch officer, signaling nearby tugboats to take up their positions. Within minutes, the nearby tugs nose up to the *Kursk* and throw lines across her deck. As the mooring crew casts off dock lines fore and aft, the tugs slowly pull the massive submarine sideways away from the pier. It is 2230. "All ahead one-third!" the watch officer shouts.

The *Kursk's* reactors have been providing power to all ten compartments during her stay at the dock, so Captain-Lieutenant Rashid Aryapov shifts his attention as his engineers apply power to get the giant propellers turning. Outside in the bay, the great bronze blades bite into the water and propel the giant vessel gracefully forward. The process is eerily silent, with the ship's motion displayed by only a small ripple at her bow. The tug operators deftly reposition around the sub's vulnerable exterior elements—the rudders and stern planes and propellers—gently pointing her northward toward the Barents.

Peering at the dark, fog-shrouded navigating lights out in the fjord, Captain Lyachin barks: "Turns for six knots!" In the seventh compartment, Kolesnikov confirms the rising rpms on his console as the *Kursk* smoothly accelerates. Back in the eighth compartment, his shipmate, Captain-Lieutenant Sergey Sadilenko, confirms that his portion of the engine system has also reached the ordered speed.

After the topside crew secures the *Kursk*'s outer deck and heads below, the tug operators retrieve their lines and slowly fall away in advance of the fjord's narrowing banks. The ship slows. "Proceeding through narrow passage!" the watch officer shouts. As they enter the open water, Lyachin barks out a course: "Steer zero-two-zero degrees! All ahead standard!" The *Kursk* passes the low light marking a reef near the bay's mouth and heads east, parallel to the Kola shores through a half-mile-wide channel. Soon she begins to gently roll and heave in the deeper Motovsky Strait, where Lyachin orders the bridge cleared and rigged for dive, and then slides down the eighteen-foot ladder into the central command post, or CCP, on the uppermost deck of compartment two. This commander's pierside worries are at last beginning to fade.

Lyachin confers with navigator Senior Lieutenant Sergey Tylik about when the *Kursk* will have sufficient depth for safe diving, which will allow the ship to double its speed. Then he orders compartment commanders to prepare. One by one, they confirm that they're ready for dive. The bridge's heavy clamshell fairings have been shut, leaving the tower smooth. The *Kursk* is now streamlined, with nothing to impede the flow of water along her flanks.

"Submerge the ship!" Lyachin orders from inside the CCP. The diving alarm rings, and the men surrounding him in the command post come to life as the vessel seeks her most natural element. The *Kursk*'s exterior diving planes swing out into position. The main ballast tank vents open, and air roars forth. In minutes, there is nothing but a few ripples of disturbed water where her 14,700 tons had been.

After confirming the submerged conditions as normal, Lyachin orders an acceleration to twenty-eight knots. Some time later, he orders the boat to slow and turn northward, toward her operating area.

With his boat now safely under way, Lyachin thinks the time is right to announce a fire drill for the second compartment, his own crowded central command post. Though last fall's Mediterranean mission fire broke out aft of the reactor compartment, Lyachin thinks it's more instructive to test his men with a scenario that knocks out the Kursk's senior command.

Captain Lyachin swivels in his high-backed command chair and presses the intercom microphone to his lips. His voice crackles over the speaker system: "This is a drill. General quarters! There is a fire in compartment two! Control will not answer. Control of the submarine has shifted to assistant to the commander of the aft control point. The primary survival plan: Rescue personnel from the compartment and prevent the fire from reaching adjoining compartments."

In moments the bleating alarm sounds, catapulting the Kursk's men into a frenzy of emergency response actions—leaping for fire hoses, seizing emergency suits and masks, moving in to assist with the evacuation of comrades in trouble.

Lyachin watches as the drill progresses, and winces at some of the problems that unfold. Best for his men to figure things out now, he believes, so they'll be more prepared should a real disaster ever force them to find out what they're made of.

By declaring the fire in his own compartment and stipulating that his intercom is inoperable, Lyachin has also effectively excused himself from participation in the drill, allowing him to focus on the Kursk's progress. Glancing at the navigator's plot, Lyachin notes that she appears to be moving slower than ordered. He punches the intercom button for compartment seven.

"I said 'speed fifteen knots,'" Lyachin says. "But the speed now is fourteen knots."

Kolesnikov answers promptly. "Comrade Captain, speed is fifteen knots."

"But the navigator says fourteen," says Lyachin.

Kolesnikov reviews his gauges. "The log reads fifteen," he asserts, then realizes the reason for the discrepancy. "The navigator is taking into account the current," he says, meaning that the *Kursk* is working upstream.

Not good enough, Lyachin thinks. As the clock keeps pressing, Lyachin worries about the prospect of having to request yet another variance in his already-delayed arrival time. He consults with Tylik. "So, Navigator, how much longer on this course?"

"Until we reach the exercise area," says Tylik.

The *Kursk* slows and comes to periscope depth to communicate with the exercise coordinators. Within minutes, the *Kursk*'s radio room takes a report from an officer who urges the sub to make up for lost time. After jotting down the order, the *Kursk*'s radio operator keys his internal intercom. "Bridge, this is Radio."

"Bridge aye, Radio," answers Lyachin.

"Order from Nakhimov: Proceed on course three four zero at maximum speed. Report when we are on that course."

Lyachin confers with navigator Tylik, reviews the charts himself, then orders the new course as the *Kursk* slips beneath the waves again and accelerates to twenty-eight knots in her headlong drive toward her operating area.

In the small farming village of Boksitogorsk, on Friday morning, August 11, it's a breezy sixty-three degrees as Olga Kolesnikova helps her mother gather the fruit crop under a leaden sky. Inside by midday, they extract both juice and gelatin from the apples, which they plan to mail north to Dima to tide him over until Olga's return. She mailed him a letter for his twenty-seventh birthday, and hopes it arrived before his departure on the *Kursk*. Olga truly loves Dima, and longs to start a family. They've even talked of retiring to this simple farming village when his years in the North are done.

Dima's parents, Irina and Roman, are taking a bus from their home in St. Petersburg to the family's getaway cottage in nearby Estonia. Their worries have eased now that Dima is back on track and married to such a lovely woman. The assignment to Vidyayevo of their second son,

Alexander—also for submarine service—only adds to their cheer. It comforts them to know that the boys can look after each other, and that together they are cementing the family's submarining tradition.

It also helps that Dima has recently begun keeping his parents better informed of his activities, allaying his mother's worries about the dangers of his work. In May, he even wrote her about how to handle the possibility of any future mishap. "If you don't hear from me," he wrote, "don't worry. Just watch the news on TV. They'll tell you what's going on."

Rashid Aryapov's departure for the exercise was easier on his new bride, Khalima, than either of them expected. Though shy and still new to Vidyayevo, Khalima found the garrison town's surroundings surprisingly pleasing. The summer-green hills and rocky outcroppings seemed exotic to her, making for the perfect meeting of "earth and heaven."

She feels calm and comfortable in Vidyayevo, even with Rashid away. She spends time Friday afternoon sprucing up their modest apartment, dwelling on a magnificent new event in their lives. Shortly before Rashid left for the *Kursk*, Khalima told him she was carrying their first child. Rashid was happy, of course, but also worried about taking on the new addition so early in their marriage, especially given the meager salary of a captain-lieutenant, and the difficulties of the coming winter in a town where heating and plumbing could not be counted on. But Khalima is much too happy for worry.

Olga Lubushkina, meanwhile, has returned from her day job in Vidyayevo's passport office, and can hardly keep from smiling as she settles into the apartment she keeps with Sergey. She and her "Seryozha" are still so much in love that she tallies the days of their young marriage when he's not at sea: so far it's 106 days together, 193 days apart. As usual, when he's at sea, Sergey the "walking history reference librarian" has given her a reading "assignment" from one of his history books, telling her gamely to expect a quiz when he returns. He has even drilled her on basic home electrical repairs so she can be more self-reliant when he's on long missions. They still leave love notes for each other in odd locations around the apartment, and she particularly enjoys the elaborate illustrations Seryozha adds to the notes he leaves for her, like the fancy rendering of the

Kursk broaching the surface of the sea. Recently she tried to one-up him by baking a cake shaped like the sub.

Olga is pleased at how her husband and his friends are all settling down. She no longer has to worry about Dima and Rashid going out and getting into fistfights, or Dima spending nights aboard the *Kursk* because his apartment was recently burglarized or lost its electricity. And Dima not drinking anymore — isn't *that* something! His sobriety hasn't changed him a bit; he's still the trio's social leader. He still smokes his "Belamor-canal" cigarettes — a far more affordable vice at 10 rubles a pack (less than 30 cents) than the Mr. Officer vodka still favored by Rashid and Sergey. She almost laughs out loud when she thinks about the men's old routine: As soon as the alcohol started to flow, Rashid's bright white teeth would shine like a beacon, Seryozha would start smiling and winking, and Dima would hand out the goofy patronymic nicknames.

In another apartment nearby, Irina Lyachina is making plans for her son's twenty-first birthday. Though Gleb's birthday is actually on Sunday, August 13, Irina assured her *Kursk* commander husband, whom she calls "Genna," that they would wait until his sub's return on Monday to celebrate. It will make sense for the birthday boy, too — he's busy with duties as a young cadet in the Northern Fleet.

Irina and her daughter, Dasha, have just returned from visiting relatives down south in Genna's ancestral Volgograd region, and the place could use some freshening up. Irina had to say good-bye to Genna on August 5, before she left for the weeklong visit in Volgograd. She thinks now of how she spotted him as she neared their apartment that afternoon, seeing him pacing in front of the window, oddly anxious. She thought it strange that he was home at all, since it was the middle of the day. When she walked in, he told her he'd been waiting for hours to say good-bye.

Typical Genna, Irina thinks. Loyal, earnest, a straight arrow, a steady family man. Sometimes she felt like the luckiest wife in the world. It was her custom always to tell him before parting that he should steer clear of all bars and other women, but this last time she had left it unsaid. After more than twenty years together, such things just didn't need saying anymore. Of course they'd endured some rough patches over the years—including Genna's own drinking problem, now long resolved—along with the customary absences that plague navy families during extended missions.

But Genna's great Mediterranean mission had been a career comeback, of sorts; after the drastic fleet shrinkage during the 1990s, he'd been left ashore without a sub to command. The Mediterranean deployment buoyed their marriage along with Genna's career. She can't wait for his return this time, and the resumption of their plan to retreat to St. Petersburg. She'll be able to teach there. And Genna's been wondering aloud about whether he can pick up some advanced training at the naval college to enhance his status in the reserves. Yes, it's all coming together now.

6

USS *MEMPHIS* PROWLS

SOUTHERN BARENTS SEA
FRIDAY, AUGUST 11, 2000

Aboard the USS *Memphis* some sixty miles north of the Kola Peninsula, Commander Mark Breor slowly rotates the periscope, scanning the surface of the sea, searching for Russian vessels that might be coming over the horizon. He notes a light southwesterly breeze, modest wave heights, and the multiple cloud decks that reduce the sun's glare. Visibility couldn't be any better; he can see clear to the edge of a sharp horizon in every direction.

This is one of the *Memphis's* rare visual appraisals, since seeing without being seen is the name of the submariner's game—and an exposed periscope in the vast emptiness of a calm summer sea destroys the sub's protective mantle of invisibility. Tall and muscled, Captain Breor has imbued the 135-man *Memphis* crew with an infectious enthusiasm. Though some find Breor's John Wayne manner and hard-driving style intimidating, even those cowed by him would choose Breor as their commander in a real-world conflict.

The men gladly snap to with Breor's trademark greeting over the sub's intercom—"Attention, prowlers!"—and have all but forgotten the low morale left by their last commander, a "screamer" whose manner left many planning to leave the navy altogether. That commander was widely perceived as a strictly careerist officer who used the assignment as a stepping-stone; Breor is more warmly recognized as the "skipper" of the highly decorated *Memphis*—always in top form, a beacon of competence.

The men throughout are now "on station" and they try to keep their activity down to a dull murmur—noise can travel outside the hull. Unnecessary systems are turned off. The movies usually shown in the dining area are on hold.

The periscope sweep is meant for tracking big game, but sometimes also happens because submarine commanders find it hard to resist "peeking." With no way of seeing one another in the dark ocean depths, submariners must use "passive" sonar listening to detect another submarine's presence. In addition, the *Memphis* deploys its sensitive sonar array from the stern, maintaining a minimum speed of three knots to keep it from dangling into her propellers, or catching on obstacles on the seabed. The best hunters maintain perfect invisibility during such activity, and hope their prey makes a mistake by carelessly emitting a sound. Sound travels nearly five times faster through water than air, at over three thousand miles per hour. Skilled sonar operators must train well to distinguish between merchant vessels, military surface vessels, other submarines, sea life—"biologics," in submariner's parlance—and even rain. Many sonar trainees tracking events at sea are taken aback when they first hear a certain cacophony of loud popping sounds, only to learn they've picked up a school of "snapping shrimp" passing great distances away.

Though skilled sonar men can divine the approximate directions to underwater objects around them, they have no way of knowing the actual range without "going active" with their sonar and "pinging" on the target. They are also blind in the "baffles"—the acoustically shielded exterior structures designed to protect hydrophones from the sub's own machinery noise—mostly confined to a small area aft of the conning tower. And because they operate in a three-dimensional environment, gauging the depth of nearby vessels is always an educated guess.

Great submariners have been rewarded for closely shadowing enemy subs to gather their sound signatures and design details without being detected. But mistakes are sometimes made, and collisions between opposing subs are a constant hazard. Such close shadowing not only risks lives but also has threatened to turn Cold War games into larger clashes.

The *Memphis*'s new listening equipment can change all that. It can now detect a Russian sub from an unprecedented distance, dramatically reducing the risk of collision.

As the *Kursk* slices through the icy Arctic waters toward her first exercise area in the wee hours of Friday, some of the crew go off shift, stopping into the fourth compartment's midlevel mess hall for crackers and hot borscht or a more substantial meal, or retreating to their bunks to occupy themselves with books or laptop computers or portable stereos. The most popular musical artist among *Kursk* sailors is "Lubeh," something of a folk-rock balladeer with a special feeling for the lives of Russian Navy men separated from their loved ones. One of the group's tunes, "There Beyond the Mists," is a favorite of Lyachin's, and widely embraced by the crew.

> *Blue sea, nothing but sea beyond the stern;*
> *Blue sea, and in the distance the way home;*
> *There beyond the eternal, drunken mists;*
> *There beyond the mists is our native shore. . . .*

With some of the *Kursk* crewmen on midwatch, others turn to their racks to sleep, blissfully shielded from the Arctic summer's early sunrise at 0310.

Shortly before 0900, Captain Lyachin orders his team to bring the *Kursk* to a depth of sixty-three feet, periscope depth, as they approach the designated missile-firing area. Lyachin is expecting to take radio orders from Vice Admiral Oleg Burtsev aboard the *Peter the Great*, the Northern Fleet's only operational nuclear cruiser and command post for the exercise. Captain Lyachin initiates the contact, using his exercise code name, "Vintik" — Russian for "little screw."

"*Peter the Great*," Captain Lyachin says into his radio microphone, "This is Vintik, CO speaking. Over."

"Gennady Petrovich!" says Vice Admiral Burtsev, commander of the First Submarine Flotilla. "Once again, greetings. This is the commander."

"I hope things are well with you, Comrade Commander," Lyachin says. "I am ready to receive orders."

Burtsev confirms the noon starting time for the *Kursk*'s missile-firing window. "First, 'T'-time is 1200. Second, actions are to be carried out in accordance with the command table. Meet the control ship, and jointly identify yourselves on the surface. Establish communications after submerging. Use exercise signals in accordance with the table. Do you understand? Over."

Lyachin finishes jotting down the instructions and then keys his mike. "Understood, Comrade Commander."

"Make sure you maintain constant underwater communications after submerging," says Burtsev. With multiple vessels to coordinate for the missile tests, it's crucial that all submarines in the area monitor their underwater telephone channels or floating radio buoys in case of changed plans. After a pause, Burtsev keys his mike. "I have relayed all orders. I will be standing by."

"Aye-aye, Comrade Commander. Understood," says Lyachin, who checks his watch to note that it's approaching 1000 hours, his next scheduled time to make contact. He transmits: "Have I received from you the final instructions?" Lyachin asks. "Or will we receive more instructions at 1000? Over."

"That is all," says Burtsev. "I will provide no further instructions."

With the *Kursk* now steady on its new course, Lyachin switches to the intercom and orders his planesmen to descend.

Over the coming minutes the *Kursk* settles to a keel depth of 165 feet, and the missile team carefully enters the target coordinates into its computers to guide the two designated Shipwreck missiles precisely to a derelict target vessel more than two hundred miles away. At 1240 Moscow time, the *Kursk* fires its first missile. Thirty-three feet long and weighing more than seven tons, the projectile erupts from one of the twenty-four side-mounted tubes tucked between the sub's inner and outer hulls. The ejection's force causes the sub to roll toward the launch side, giving sailors from bow to stern a sensation similar to what one gets from standing at the rear of a diving board while another man leaps from its front, except that it's in slow motion. Once free of the sea surface, the rocket's engine ignites, propelling the Shipwreck toward its hapless target at two and a half times the speed of sound.

If the missile had been fully armed with a nuclear warhead and the ship engaged in a real-world conflict, it could have shattered an entire air-craft carrier. The *Kursk's* other missiles could be targeted to home in on the carrier's attendant escorts. The Russian sub could then depart from the encounter, proceed to the eastern seaboard of the United States, and, firing nuclear-tipped versions of the same missile, attempt to systematically shut down at least half a dozen land-based military installations. Of course, the *Kursk's* men like to think that such an event would never oc-cur without genuine provocation, but it's nice to know that NATO spies are watching right now. NATO needs a reminder that provoking Russia is still a very bad idea.

While thrilled with the successful launch of the one missile, the *Kursk's* missile systems officers inform Lyachin that the second missile failed to eject properly. One member of the hydroacoustics team reports he detected a distinctly abnormal splashing sound. Such a failure is not altogether uncommon in Russia's navy, but Lyachin nevertheless reports the malfunction to his superiors in a cryptic message through his under-water telephone system.

Returning to periscope depth at 1400 for radio contact with the *Peter the Great*, Lyachin transmits. "Comrade Commander," he reports, "this is commander of Vintik."

"Gennady Petrovich! I received your message," says an ebullient Vice Admiral Burtsev, referring to Lyachin's underwater transmission. "I have no complaints related to your crew's actions. Thanks for your work."

"I serve the fatherland!" Lyachin barks into his radio microphone.

"You should add 'and the flotilla commander!'" jokes Burtsev before signing off.

"And the First Flotilla!" Lyachin returns.

The *Kursk* moves away and maneuvers to a lower depth.

Despite the successful launch, Lyachin still can't hide some disappointment over his crew's chaotic preparation before getting under way. He's now seeing the results, and they are not good enough. He's been forced to take personnel from one of the *Kursk's* sister subs to complete his crew, and coordination problems among the mixed teams are unfolding in front of the headquarters observers on board, some of them Lyachin's own neighbors in Vidyayevo. Right now his men must get things shipshape before facing the sub's next event—a simulated missile attack on the *Peter the Great* planned for early Saturday morning, August 12, followed by the midday launching of torpedoes. The *Kursk* must do better.

With some of the chaos of getting under way having abated—and with most of the off-shift crew now awake at midday on the eleventh—Lyachin feels it's the right time to address the entire boat about the deficiencies. He keys his intercom.

"Attention, crew," his voice crackles. "This is the commander. There have been many personnel failures while readying the submarine for sea, specifically in the material readiness of the boat. Two warning bells have already gone off. Therefore, all personnel are to remain at their posts and carefully inspect their spaces. Report the slightest sign of leaks to Control. Report any signs of smoke immediately. All emergency measures should be set to 'ready.'"

Lyachin's longtime officers—including Kolesnikov and Aryapov and Lubushkin—take the captain's frustrations personally. When referring to him, they use an old Russian word for father, *Batya*. Many of them like to tell the story of how he once took some of them to a bar and offered to treat them. Instead of the beers they expected, he bought them ice cream. When they appeared disappointed, he offered to eat all the ice cream himself. Not all were aware that he'd long sworn off the Great Russian Curse of alcohol addiction.

•   •   •

Nearly 1,000 miles to the south, President Putin lingers at the Kremlin for his last full work day before joining his wife and two teenage daughters on the Black Sea the next day. In his afternoon meeting with Yasser Arafat, Putin urges the Palestinian leader to proceed cautiously with his expressed plan for unilaterally declaring independence from the state of Israel. The exchange is important to Putin. Even with the apparent decline of his nation's superpower status, he still wants Russia to have a seat at the negotiating table.

Putin also feels his meeting earlier in the week with former Soviet President Mikhail Gorbachev went well. The exchange was a two-hour watershed, one that set Putin apart from his political progenitor, Boris Yeltsin. As an architect of Gorbachev's humiliating ouster, Yeltsin had angrily barred Gorbachev from any formal relationship with the Russian government for most of the past decade. But Putin sympathizes with some of Gorbachev's reforms, and views the rapprochement as an important step forward in building bridges between Russia's Soviet past and its uncertain future.

For his part, Gorbachev still championed the spirit of his reforms as head of Moscow's Glasnost Foundation, and shared with Putin his chagrin over the new president's clampdown on Russia's fledgling independent media. More urgently, Gorbachev also urged Putin not to silence the most powerful critic of his government, the privately owned national television network, NTV. Gorbachev knows all too well how Putin must feel about the aggressively impolite network, especially as it leads the increasingly shrill carping over the upstart president's controversial war in Chechnya. Adding insult to injury, NTV is owned by the oligarch Vladimir Gusinsky, a former Yeltsin crony now targeted as a criminal by Putin's government. Putin hates Gusinsky's ability to fight back through his ownership of Russia's most influential broadcasting operation, but Putin nevertheless assured Gorbachev that NTV's journalists could survive a state takeover plan as long as the operation "obeys the law."

By Friday afternoon, Putin takes his seat at the head of a Kremlin conference table to preside over his squabbling military men, one of whom has publicly described another as "criminally insane." Regardless of the disputed priorities, Putin says, Russia's shattered economy means its leaders must do more with less. They must achieve quality without quantity. They must find a way to reduce numbers in ways that better allocate the diminished funds, which should enhance the conditions for individual soldiers and sailors. On this point, Putin reiterates his concern that it's unwise for the defense ministry to keep relying on the "enthusiasm" of its young men regarding military commitments. The sailors throughout Russia's naval fleets can no longer remain shore bound from lack of funds, he says. "If sailors almost never put to sea," he asks, "is everything all right in terms of the structure of the armed forces?"

As Putin speaks in Moscow, one submariner now aboard the *Kursk* makes a comment in his shift log. "We have noted a pressure increase in the oxidizer reservoir over twelve hours," writes Senior Lieutenant Alexey Ivanov-Pavlov, the *Kursk*'s new torpedo control officer. "The pressure increased to $1 \, \text{kg/cm}^2$." He marks the date and time in his log at August 11, 1550.

This pressure increase inside the Fat Girl is within the normal range. It causes no particular alarm.

7
SHOOTING PRACTICE
SOUTHERN BARENTS SEA
SATURDAY, AUGUST 12

Arctic dawn bursts rapidly over the sharp horizon at 0316 on a key day for the Northern Fleet's submarines. Vice Admiral Yuri Boyarkin stands on the bridge of the *Peter the Great* and looks into a dark blue sky. The Barents waves rise just a few feet, stirred by a light southerly wind. Six submarines are scheduled to perform weapons drills today, finishing with torpedo firing. Fleet commander Admiral Vyacheslav Popov ratified the final torpedo plans last night from aboard this same nuclear cruiser, and the details have been transmitted to the submarine commanders. But first Boyarkin must watch the *Kursk* perform a simulated firing of its entire cruise missile arsenal at the *Peter the Great* and its battle group.

At 0608, Captain Lyachin radios Admiral Boyarkin aboard the *Peter the Great* to report that he has arrived in the test area for the planned simulation. Admiral Boyarkin, a stocky man who serves as the fleet's deputy commander for combat training, tells Lyachin, "The ships are opening up, and we will give you an opportunity to change the plan. You should descend immediately and head to the waiting area. How copy? Over."

Lyachin confirms his new course. "I am proceeding according to the mission. Over."

"You understood me," says Boyarkin. "Report when you have completed the exercise."

At 0620 Captain Lyachin orders an emergency descent and settles at a new depth. Within ten minutes, the *Kursk's* sonar team has detected a target, classifying it generically as a "surface warship," which it tracks for most of the next hour while the missile crew prepares a launch. The weapons men run through a series of commands and system protocols to demonstrate their proficiency at a mass launch aimed at the destruction of an enemy battle group. By 0835, the simulated attack is complete.

At 0851, Lyachin comes to periscope depth and radios the *Peter the Great*. After confirming that Admiral Boyarkin is at the receiver, Lyachin transmits: "Comrade Commander, I have completed the combat exercise. Nothing unusual to report."

"I approve," Boyarkin responds heartily. "Everything's correct. But you also have a report to issue regarding leaving the area. That is all."

"Aye-aye," says Lyachin. "We are standing by."

Minutes later, Lyachin reports via shortwave to command headquarters in Severomorsk that the *Kursk* has arrived in the planned location for its torpedo exercise. The Severomorsk officer relays word back to the *Peter the Great*.

As he acknowledges the *Kursk's* transition, Admiral Boyarkin is vaguely apprehensive for Lyachin and his crew. Boyarkin has run the fleet's Combat Training Directorate for years now, and has complained on the record, frequently and pointedly, about how the Russian Navy's meager resources grossly crippled training throughout the 1990s. His fleet's antisubmarine hunter-killer group had too little fuel even to participate in the Barents exercise in the fall of 1998. Chronic fuel shortages also forced sweeping cutbacks in personnel training, virtually rusting the sailors themselves. And then there was the rising tide of failing equipment. In the 1998 exercise, the entire Northern Fleet had to forfeit participation in an all-navy antiaircraft competition because the launchers for drone target planes no longer worked at all.

Boyarkin shakes his head. He inspected the *Kursk* prior to her departure, and he knows all too well the scramble it took to get her under way. Everybody complained about the cranes. But from Boyarkin's perspective, the ballyhooed crane issue didn't seem so bad. At least they managed to load the exercise weapons. He also disagrees with the idea that the crane shortage leaves too many combat warheads aboard the submarines headed into exercises. He views this supposed "prohibition" as a holdover from the Gorbachev years, before all the money dried up. Boyarkin thinks that in Russia's post-Soviet navy, the real test is making do with the left-over scraps. Everyone in the Northern Fleet feels a bit trapped. What would the state have them do, stay ashore and let it all go to hell?

From the bridge aboard the *Peter the Great*, Boyarkin watches the horizon as, miles beyond his range of sight, the *Kursk* slowly slips beneath the dark surface of the Barents. As the temperature heads toward sixty degrees, buildups have started to appear in the lower cloud decks and the wind is shifting to southwesterly at about eight knots. Though meteorologists at a nearby land station report the visibility is a brilliant twenty-five miles, Boyarkin senses a change in the weather. Next up, torpedoes.

At about the same time back in Vidyayevo, Senior Warrant Officer Ivan Nessen is just waking from a disturbing dream. Nessen was excused from the deployment just before the *Kursk* departed, because Captain Lyachin had received word that his crew's payroll was ready for pickup. Paydays are rare in the navy these days, and after conferring with his senior officers, Lyachin decided it would be a great gesture if Nessen could greet the returning crew with much-awaited funds to reward them and their families.

Nessen now rolls toward his wife and confides that he saw himself standing in an open tomb, next to an open coffin, and saw a woman very familiar to him standing in the pit, "looking sad." He's not sure what to make of it, but he feels rattled.

8

FAILING TO TAME THE FAT GIRL

SOUTHERN BARENTS SEA
SATURDAY, AUGUST 12, 1000 HOURS

BLAST ONE

In the *Kursk*'s forward compartment, the key members of the torpedo team are awaiting orders to begin preparing for today's exercise. The original plan called for shooting two smaller USET-80 torpedoes with experimental new batteries, but all agree that the worrisome Fat Girl must go first. The *Kursk*'s torpedo men say the giant weapon's HTP bubble-sensor monitor shows some activity, and that its oxidizer tank is slightly warmer. This especially worries both Baigarin and Lyachin. They can't wait to make the Fat Girl go away.

The man who has long supervised operations in the *Kursk*'s forward torpedo room is Senior Warrant Officer Abdulkadir Ildarov, a swarthy, even-tempered forty-year-old with a big dark mustache that dominates his face. His wife and two teenage daughters live nearly two thousand miles to the south in Dagestan. He last saw them on July 26, two weeks before setting out for the Barents. He and his wife were surprised to learn during the winter that she'd become pregnant, and Abdulkadir promised he'd be home before the birth in September.

Ildarov's two young torpedo men are recent graduates of basic torpedo-handling classes. The newly promoted squad leader is Seaman Ivan Nefedkov, who will have the honors of preparing today's launch of the Fat Girl from the port 650-mm torpedo tube—a responsibility normally handled by the absent warrant officer laid up in Vidyayevo with the fighting injuries. Nefedkov is a twenty-year-old wrestler who wrote home to his mother in May after he'd been selected for the *Kursk:* "We endlessly clean her," he reported, "with soap foam above our knees."

The *Kursk's* new second torpedo man is Seaman Maksim Borzhov. "Mama, you should be proud of me," read his latest letter home. "I have been taken on such a submarine!" He detailed his excitement about working under the inspiring Captain Lyachin, noting that the commander habitually addressed each crewman by his first name. He shared his delight over being teamed with torpedo-school classmate Nefedkov, who bunks next to him. He wrote that the *Kursk's* officers treated the young enlisted men as "little brothers."

Another key presence in the torpedo room today is forty-two-year-old Mamed Gadzhiyev, a civilian senior engineer from a torpedo factory in Kaspiisk, Dagestan. He is the primary designer of the experimental batteries that have been fitted onto the USET-80 torpedoes. Though the Fat Girl is not his company's weapon and HTP torpedoes are not Gadzhiev's specialty, the team welcomes the engineer's general torpedo expertise.

Gadzhiev told his wife in early summer that he was "going on a mission up north" for two months. He and his close military partner, navy liaison officer Senior Lieutenant Arnold Borisov, left Kaspiisk in late July. When he's out of town, Gadzhiev normally leaves messages at the Dagdizel factory plant for his family, because they have no home phone.

On the *Kursk,* both Gadzhiev and Borisov eagerly await the chance to test their refitted USET-80 weapons. Developing these new batteries has become a pet obsession for Gadzhiev as he tries to respond to Dagdizel's challenge to extend the USET's striking range. The USETs are all-electric torpedoes, and their successful upgrade could reduce dependence on the unstable liquid-fueled weapons. Still, the Dagdizel representatives share the concerns of Baigarin and Lyachin regarding the ill-reputed Fat Girl; they agree it should be first in the shooting order.

Immediately aft of the *Kursk's* torpedo room, twenty-two-year-old Senior Lieutenant Alexey Ivanov-Pavlov will execute the hands-on coordination of the torpedo firings from the central command post, or CCP, which is now a beehive humming with some two dozen men. As the sub's new head of torpedo control, Ivanov-Pavlov is considered something of a prodigy. This rising young star recently crowed about his assignment to the *Kursk* in a rare call home to his parents. Even though he's new to the Fat Girl torpedo, Ivanov-Pavlov had felt under pressure to inspect, accept, and sign for its delivery to the *Kursk* a week before setting out. He feels more at ease now that Captain Baigarin is on board.

Baigarin himself does not feel at ease. Though he is impressed with Ivanov-Pavlov's general weapons smarts, Baigarin wishes he'd been present to help the young officer inspect the *Kursk's* torpedoes before they were loaded. As it was, the *Kursk* had to borrow a weapons systems officer from the *Smolensk*, the sister sub that had the rare experience of successfully firing a Fat Girl the previous spring.

At 1005, the *Kursk's* sonar room detects two echoes. Lyachin orders the sub to slow from eleven knots to six as sonar gathers more data, soon classifying one of the echoes as a group of fishing trawlers, and the other as a very large nuclear cruiser. The cruiser is their target, which is the *Peter the Great*. For the purpose of the exercise, the nuclear cruiser and two of her battle group's other surface vessels are posing as invading Western ships—each keeping two nautical miles apart from the other—passing from northwest to southeast along the designated range.

With the sonar report delivered to the CCP, the room's emotional temperature ratchets up. Captain Lyachin leaves his command chair to survey the sonar screens. He'd like to speed up his approach to the target, just to rid himself of the Fat Girl. But the shooting plan dictates that the other subs must first launch their unarmed torpedoes before the *Kursk* can take her turn. He's still nearly ninety minutes away from the moment when the *Peter the Great* will come within his optimal striking range. If his warming Fat Girl becomes enraged now, Lyachin will have to jettison the torpedo prematurely.

Lyachin orders his helmsman to come to a northwesterly course of 320 degrees, maintaining six knots just below the surface. He then orders Baigarin and the torpedo team to begin preparing the Fat Girl for her big moment.

•   •   •

On the bridge of the *Peter the Great* shortly before 1100, senior fleet officers cluster to monitor the torpedo exercises. Admiral Popov hovers closely over the planning table, his perfectly crisp black uniform accompanied by a black jacket and peak cap, chain-smoking his Chesterfield cigarettes from a thin black holder while musing over the vessels' positions. He is closely flanked by Vice Admirals Burtsev and Boyarkin.

The fair weather has held. The wind is light and variable. Admiral Burtsev thinks the weather is "rosy," the Barents surface calm and perfectly illumined by the sun.

By 1100, most of the subs tasked for torpedo shooting—including the *Borisoglebsk*, the *Daniil Moskovsky*, the *Karelia*, the *Obninsk*, and the *Leopard*—have successfully fired their unarmed weapons, properly targeting their projectiles to pass beneath the *Peter the Great*'s keel and beyond, where they expel their own ballast water and float to the surface until torpedo retrievers can recover them.

This is really magnificent, thinks Admiral Boyarkin, delighting in the growing number of successful shots: twelve torpedoes, including four of the temperamental Fat Girls.

Vice Admiral Burtsev moves from one side of the nuclear cruiser to another, also taking great satisfaction in the firings—especially given his stake in the outcome of this last phase of what is also a fleet-wide prize-shooting contest. Burtsev heads up the fleet's First Submarine Flotilla, and his subs are racking up points against their long-running fleet rivals. After confirming the successful firing by his *Daniil Moskovsky*, Burtsev allows himself a boast. "We've won one more prize," he declares. Popov responds with a knowing chuckle.

Aboard the *Kursk* at 1112, now over thirty miles away, Captain Lyachin begins maneuvering to intercept the *Peter the Great*. Throughout the sub, sailors follow their normal routines, ensuring that all systems are in order. Meanwhile, the *Kursk*'s first lunch shift begins, as sailors not involved in the torpedo exercise trickle into the fourth compartment's upper deck, the sub's mess facility. The torpedo firing is not yet at hand, so the crew is in a relaxed "Battle Readiness Two."

In the CCP, Captain Lyachin orders torpedo systems controller Ivanov-Pavlov and division weapons chief Baigarin to transfer the thirty-six-foot-long Fat Girl—still too warm—from its storage rack and into tube four, port side, inboard, lower bank. Minutes later, successful loading is confirmed.

Good, thinks Captain Lyachin, and orders his diving officer to bring the *Kursk* to periscope depth, then broaches her sail above the Barents surface and raises the radar mast, hoping to get a fix on her quarry. The *Kursk* is beginning her approach.

In the forward torpedo room, Ildarov and Nefedkov examine the heavy bronze-alloy breech door for the fourth tube. They confirm that it's securely latched and shut. But with the specialized oxidizer-monitoring system now disconnected and the weapon fully enclosed within its firing tube, Ildarov and Nefedkov agonize over the disconcerting warming they'd felt around the Fat Girl's casing just moments ago. What if the HTP leaks now? How will they know? If the weapon blows prematurely, can they be confident the blast will eject harmlessly forward, into the sea?

Ildarov is called back to the control compartment to share his concerns with Baigarin, leaving factory representative Gadzhiev and torpedo man Nefedkov to attend to details in the torpedo room. Suddenly, Gadzhiev and Nefedkov snap their heads around at the sound of a muffled hiss from within the tube. The sound is mild at first, then builds to a furious scream.

With the watertight door on the *Kursk's* upper-level deck left open to relieve pressure buildup during launches, men in the CCP immediately aft of the torpedo room can hear the commotion even before Gadzhiev or Nefedkov can reach the intercom.

The electric sensation of an emergency courses through the *Kursk's* forward end. Many have been waiting for the tremor that accompanies a torpedo launch, but this is too early and it doesn't sound right. Confused shouts erupt on the second compartment's upper decks. An enormous roar issues from the first compartment. Then a thunderclap. Gadzhiev and Nefedkov barely get to react before a corona of fire engulfs them. The torpedo tube's eight-hundred-pound breech door blows off the tube's aft end and rockets through the torpedo room, pounding the rear bulkhead. Fractured elements of the Fat Girl follow, bursting through weapons fuel tanks and warheads stored on the nearby racks. Much of tube four's after end is shattered, adding to the shrapnel spray. The Fat Girl's kerosene and HTP ignite into a raging fire.

With an explosive force equal to 220 pounds of TNT, the blast reshapes the compartment's interior landscape in ways its designers never imagined. The powerful shock wave instantly kills those in the torpedo room, and also kills or stuns most of the men in the second compartment's CCP through the open door. Captain Lyachin and several other senior officers are gone. The few remaining control-post survivors are too stunned to act, nearly all deafened as they try to raise themselves up amid the bloodied bodies of comrades all around them. Their forward control systems are now unattended, leaving the *Kursk*'s masts in their raised positions. Smoke races through the sub's ventilation system, instantly injecting every compartment with the alarming scent of very big trouble. Dazed sailors throughout the remaining sections scramble to shut watertight doors and otherwise seal their compartments, then jump for their emergency suits and masks, the same moves they'd practiced in Captain Lyachin's fire drill less than twenty-four hours earlier. As in that drill, Control does not answer.

With no corrective inputs from its CCP controllers, the *Kursk* begins slowly to nose into a dive.

Some survivors struggle to collect their wits, then begin feeling their way through the forward end's thick smoke, hoping to find the ladder in the command post that might get them to the escape module wedged into the tower. Those who reach it find the module entry hatch stuck, and begin hammering at it with any metal object they can find.

Many others attempt damage control, struggling with fire suppression equipment and rapidly forming ragtag teams, shouting and gesturing wildly to compensate for the widespread hearing loss. They jam the passageways and ladders between decks, slowing at the narrow water-tight doors, no longer able to escape feeling the *Kursk*'s growing downward tilt.

Senior Warrant Officer Igor Erasov, the cipher clerk responsible for safeguarding the *Kursk*'s top-secret communications codes, races up the slanting deck for the code box locked in a fourth compartment safe. His training has conditioned him to do whatever it takes to protect the encryption tables and their mechanisms from falling into enemy hands; NATO divers have developed a tradition of combing through Russian vessel wreckage in search of just such precious information. Erasov snakes through the tangle of frightened sailors to retrieve the coding equipment, and seconds later joins the chaotic jam-up below the escape module, fumbling with his oxygen mask with one hand and clutching the code machine to his chest with the other.

In the first compartment, the tube four blast has also damaged the smaller torpedo tube above it, opening a path to the sea. The torpedo room's fire creates a momentary pressure bulge that briefly holds the Barents at bay, allowing the kerosene-and-HTP-driven blaze to rage hotter. Then frigid ocean water begins spraying in at an unremarkable pressure of fourteen pounds per square inch—at periscope depth, only one-third the force of a garden hose. As the *Kursk* descends, the pressure behind that spray will increase dramatically, speeding the flood rate.

Such a flood might normally cool a liquid-fuel weapons fire, but the shrapnel blast has punctured the fuel tanks and exposed the warheads of other weapons in the *Kursk*'s torpedo room. The penetrations in the warheads ignite small hot spots that slowly expand with the rising heat, with the hot spots themselves rapidly approaching six thousand degrees. Other fragments have ruptured the compartment's hydraulic lines, unleashing an incendiary aerosol into the hot furnace. Some of the *Kursk*'s regular weapons load includes torpedo-tube-launched rockets with solid fuel motors that dramatically accelerate the firestorm.

Even as seawater dilutes the HTP and kerosene, the volatile confluence of other combustibles defies the growing body of cold water that swirls down into the compartment's lower decks, drowning a young submariner there, seaman missile mechanic Dmitry Kotkov. Water close to the fire itself instantly converts to steam. The fire expands into a hellish maelstrom.

Unexploded warheads of the *Kursk*'s combat torpedoes are designed to withstand a fuel-fired temperature of 1,600 degrees Fahrenheit at a distance of four feet from the flame for about two minutes. This broadly applied standard is aimed at giving a weapons crew adequate time to douse the flames. The ambient temperature in the torpedo compartment is rapidly approaching five thousand degrees.

The aft compartments blur with action. Dima and Rashid know only that the torpedo shot has gone catastrophically wrong and that Lyachin can't communicate. Rashid works the intercom to coordinate with Dima and also with crewmen just forward of the reactor compartment, where Sergey Lubushkin is located. It's just after 1129 Moscow time.

"Whoa!" shouts a sonar operator aboard the USS *Memphis*, now tracking the *Kursk* from twenty-five miles northwest. "What the hell is this?"

Captain Breor and several other senior *Memphis* officers quickly gather around the dimly lit sonar station to watch the green screens, a few with headsets pressed to their ears. Captain Breor had been expecting a torpedo shot, but this is much too soon. And what he's hearing now is not a normal torpedo shot. He listens intently to the sound of accelerating propellers amid a rumble of metal-on-metal and possible ballast tanks being blown. Then apparent flooding noises. *Dear God.*

One hundred and eighty miles further northwest, a towed sonar array of the USNS *Loyal* also picks up the mysterious sounds. The data is relayed in real time back to analysts in the United States. Norwegian P-3 Orion aircraft gather the data from their strategically dropped sonobuoys. The USS *Toledo* picks it up from the exercise perimeter. Even the NATO's secret hydrophones west of the Barents detect the blast, and well-placed seismometers and human-operated land-based posts add to the flood of data. Few of the NATO observers know what to make of the wild spikes on their charts and in their headsets.

An elaborate seismology site anchored into the granite bedrock of a remote Norwegian hillside 279 miles to the west automatically informs a finely calibrated seismograph of the event farther south near Oslo. It emerges as a prominent tracing on the seismograph paper, unobserved on this late Saturday morning. It shows what looks like a temblor, 2.2 on the Richter scale.

In a small farming village outside St. Petersburg just before midday, it's sublimely warm with a hazy overcast. Olga Kolesnikova knows this is a big day in Dima's exercise, and her thoughts are with him as she excitedly opens a letter from her beloved husband of four months. He writes of how she would be on his mind if the *Kursk* ever ran into the kind of big trouble that could end his life. "I will drown in your eyes," he writes, "like a real submariner, without any sound." He says he hopes fate might grace him with enough time to whisper just a few words out loud to her: "I love you."

In Estonia, Dima's parents relax at a health spa near the getaway cottage, taking a rare break in the brief but sweet northern summer.

In Vidyayevo, Khalima Aryapova believes she is suffering her first bout of morning sickness, then hours later notices her heart is beginning to race. In another apartment, Olga Lubushkina is washing her refrigerator when a particularly annoying song comes on her radio, satirically celebrating how all submariners die together in a wreck, regardless of rank. She never thought it was funny, but with her Seryozha away at sea this time, it makes her cry.

Irina Lyachina feels like she's getting back into her normal routine. The town is quiet today, allowing her to reflect on her family's transitions. She is one of the people who will always have a fondness for Vidyayevo, with the way its people pull together during tough times, which have been many. She will be sorry to say good-bye, but is looking forward to a new life. Genna's arrival for Gleb's birthday on Monday will be a chance for the whole family to be together again. His return from sea always felt like a celebration all by itself.

When the kids were small, little Gleb would mimic his father's protectiveness, trying not to let mama Irina or sister Dasha leave the home without him as an escort. And Dasha mastered the role of daddy's girl, exploiting Genna's desire to spoil her, sometimes pleading with him to "take the wallet from Mama" so he could buy her some little-girl things.

Off-duty *Kursk* warrant officer Ivan Nessen is up and about, repairing the roof above his apartment. Just after he removes the cracked and dried tar from the roof's exterior, a summer rain shower moves in, forcing him to scramble to keep water out of his living room.

In Moscow, the front page of the English-language *Russia Journal* carries a report about President Putin's recent visit with officers of the Baltic Fleet, in which he extolled his nation's planned triumphant return to the Mediterranean in the fall.

Putin himself is still stuck in the Kremlin conducting some last-minute weekend business before his afternoon flight south, meeting with the Duma chairman to talk through priorities for the fall, formally congratulating his country on the official eighty-eighth birthday of the Russian Federation, and prepping for one last meeting for the early afternoon.

9
KILLER BLOW
SOUTHERN BARENTS SEA
SATURDAY, AUGUST 12, 1130 HOURS

BLAST TWO

As the submarine slowly falls toward the shallow seabed, terrified sailors in the aft sections slide against their compartments' bulkheads. Some fall on top of one another during the uncontrolled descent, many bloodied by the edges of clipboards and levers and struts and consoles and furniture and interdeck ladders. Outside the wounded vessel, ragged slices of the great *Kursk* scatter across the dark seabed—a railing, strips of thick black rubber, stray chunks of hull—all kicking up clouds of liquid dust as they settle silently into the silt.

Then a sudden lurch, as the *Kursk* makes contact with the bottom—seventy-six seconds after the blast and at an angle of twenty-six degrees—slamming the sailors against one another like toys. But still the vessel plows forward through the heavy silt that covers the granite seabed, finally surrendering after ninety feet.

Shocked survivors toward the aft take small comfort in the sub's return to a level angle, hoping the worst is over. But survivors near the *Kursk*'s forward end are acutely attuned to the torpedo room fire and flooding. Some cling to a hope that the icy Barents water will cool the two dozen remaining warheads before any can detonate. It doesn't. Precisely two minutes and fifteen seconds after the initial blast, another explosion rocks the Barents, this one twenty times stronger than the first. The blow spikes to a 3.5 Richter equivalent on the seismograph in Norway—its most violent tracing ever—and shows up on other seismographs up to 3,100 miles away. Scientists will later gauge the explosion's force as comparable to four thousand pounds of TNT. Some will also revise its Richter scale reading to 4.2.

The nearby *Memphis* shudders violently, and even men without headphones hear the extraordinary blast. Captain Breor and others in the sonar room brace against their equipment and look at one another wide-eyed as the *Kursk* emits a sickening series of heavy rumbles.

Thirty-two miles to the northwest, the Russian missile sub *Karelia* is also rocked by the blast wave, as its crewmen grab on to parts of their workspaces until it passes. Thirty-seven-year-old Captain Andrey Korablev worries he might have hit another sub. He instantly orders damage reports from all compartments. In moments he compares notes with an admiral riding on board as an observer, and the two soon convince each other it is simply the unusual effect of an underwater weapons detonation, unworthy of disrupting the exercise to make an urgent report.

Another Russian sub—the super-quiet Akula-class *Leopard*—is even closer to the *Kursk*. The *Leopard* is acting as an escort to the *Karelia*, scouting her perimeter in search of enemy subs. The escort practice is secret, and few participants in the Barents exercise are aware of the *Leopard*'s participation. The *Leopard* is fifteen miles from the *Kursk* at the moment of the blast. But unlike the Russian *Karelia* and the American *Memphis*, the *Leopard* faces away from the blast wave, meaning the wave washes smoothly over her hull lengthwise, creating no remarkable sensation. The *Leopard*'s captain does not record the blast at all.

On the surface, the *Peter the Great* registers the shudder from a distance of twenty-nine miles, even felt by some officers on the bridge. The sound of the giant surface cruiser's sonar system is broadcast over the bridge's loudspeakers, which emit a loud acoustic rumble. At the same moment, *Peter the Great* sonarman Senior Lieutenant Andrey Lavriniuk notes a dramatic flash on his screen. All of the data—the sonar report, the audible blast wave, the prominently detected hydrodynamic blow to the cruiser's own hull—are duly reported to the Northern Fleet admirals gathered on the bridge. The data also goes to the command vessel's combat information center and to fire control. Lavriniuk documents the blast's bearing, but is not equipped to get a fix on its range. The cruiser's younger officers, alerted to the blast mystery, await orders, only to be greeted with a perplexing silence.

Popov and Boyarkin and the others acknowledge the reports, but show no alarm. For his part, Boyarkin considers it just another small bit of data amid a stream of other coordination challenges. *Such reports happen sometimes in exercises,* he thinks. *Loud detonations should be expected in weapons exercises. It could be a benign misfire.*

Aboard the *Kursk*, the strained first bulkhead has broken loose from its welded perimeter—violently collapsing as it pistons into the second bulkhead—impossibly compressing entire decks and ladders and consoles and heavy equipment into a chaotic mass mixed with the bodies of young men. The heavyweight periscope shaft barely stands its ground, surreally twisting and withering as the superheated maelstrom sweeps past, following a blast wave that dishes the second bulkhead aft, bursting most of its center and crumpling more decks in the third compartment, raining chaos on the mess quarters, sleeping spaces, and medical clinic of the fourth compartment. It then bursts through the third bulkhead, and finally punches a cavity into the fourth.

The enormous pressure buildup has forced a massive bulge in the *Kursk*'s forward pressure hull, which blows out the starboard dome of the torpedo room, taking out an even larger chunk of the rubber-sheathed outer hull. The cold Barents now storms through the sub all the way to the fourth bulkhead—heavily reinforced at fifty millimeters thick—and stops just forward of Sergey Lubushkin's fifth compartment.

The heavy bronze-alloy torpedo breech door is swept up by the inrushing water and converted into yet another among hundreds of aftbound projectiles.

Senior Warrant Officer Erasov dies standing upright, still clutching the *Kursk*'s secret codes box in a third compartment passageway thick with many of his comrades.

Other third and fourth compartment sailors—more than forty young men—die jammed together into the upper passageways, where they'd lined up in the hope of salvation through the top-mounted escape pod. Their air masks and emergency escape suits are shredded by the cartwheeling debris.

The men who work at instruments in the shielded decks just forward of the reactors are stunned at the sight of their forward bulkhead bulging ominously in toward them, threatening a much broader regional nuclear tragedy. The bulkhead holds, but the few men who work behind it are trapped.

At the *Kursk*'s forward end, hydraulic pipes and dangling hull parts lay chaotically splayed open. Large torpedo parts protrude from a deck ceiling in the third compartment. The heavy steel door of a classified paperwork closet is filleted and twisted until it resembles a propeller.

The *Kursk* lists slightly to port and mildly down at the bow in 380 feet of seawater. She points west-northwest, 288 degrees. The water temperature is thirty-eight degrees Fahrenheit.

Captain Breor and others on the *Memphis* keep listening, but the *Kursk* is silent. Breor is not completely sure what all the data mean, and he's reluctant to make any risky moves to find out. If there's been an enormous accident, then most of the Northern Fleet should be swarming the nearby waters very soon. Best to pull away as quickly as possible to avoid detection.

The other NATO observers are just beginning to pull all the data together. Some already think it's obvious that there's been a major accident. But in accord with the tradition of treating Russia like an enemy until it demonstrates otherwise, none dare to initiate contact with the Northern Fleet to ask if it needs assistance—or, indeed, if the fleet even knows that its mighty *Kursk* is in big trouble.

Aboard the *Peter the Great*, the younger officers remain mystified by the bridge's lack of reaction to the blast reports. Some on the bridge scan the seas with binoculars. Fleet Commander Popov tells his senior officers to keep an eye out. The *Peter the Great* keeps to its course, sailing straight into the *Kursk*'s designated torpedo range, awaiting the exercise shot.

Four thousand miles across the Atlantic, electronic analysts who work the overnight shift at the National Security Agency at Fort Meade, Maryland, have detected a spike in the data coming in from the Barents Sea region shortly after 0330: reports of acoustic anomalies and other abnormal events are streaming in from the USNS *Loyal* and its associated eavesdropping assets. The seismic data looks remarkable. The analysts quickly begin puzzling through what appears to be a major snag in Russia's naval exercise.

The community of analysts chatter back and forth across the Atlantic, circulating data among key NATO assets, most prominently those of the United States and Great Britain. Soon they will rule out the more far-flung possibilities, concluding that the most likely scenario is a downed Russian submarine. Reports are prepared. Select intelligence agents in the field are ordered to keep a close watch.

No NATO rescue assets are contacted.

10
STRUGGLING FOR SURVIVAL
SOUTHERN BARENTS SEA
SATURDAY, AUGUST 12, 1140

BLAST PLUS TEN MINUTES

Operating almost instinctively, *Kursk* sailors in the aft compartments try to move about, to make sense of their wrecked surroundings. Some shout the names of comrades, trying to verify their conditions. The emergency lights are dim. The sound of inrushing water sparks new fear. Without waiting for orders, each able-bodied man begins securing valves and flappers and anything else that helps reduce the flooding. The piercing spray of icy seawater penetrates their clothing, chilling them to the bone. Senior officers fumble for their emergency phone sets. Despite their shock, they are conditioned not to leave their posts—or let their men leave their posts—until ordered to do so by higher authority, but none of the higher authorities are answering on the regular intercom. One by one, the commanders of compartments six, seven, eight, and nine open their emergency intercom packages and try to talk to one another.

Even with the emergency phones, no one in the forward compartments answers. Rashid Aryapov quickly emerges as the senior man in the aft, and he tallies the aft compartments' damage reports. It's clear they will not be able to hold the flooding off forever; water is rising fast from the bilges. All soon agree they must pool their resources in a bid for survival, and decide to gather in the ninth compartment. It's a modest space of two decks, jammed with equipment, normally occupied by just three men. The top deck is a warren of tight corridors that weave around machinery, utility spaces, and storage rooms, with several bunks near the aft. Below the two decks lies a hold that shelters the aft propeller shafts, along with some bilge space.

But if the survivors must seal themselves into a single compartment, the officers agree the ninth is their only option: it is the only aft compartment with an escape hatch. At the compartment's forward end, a ten-foot trunk with hatches top and bottom connects the interior space to the open sea. If the fleet can dispatch its rescue vessels, the submersible pilots will certainly seek out this escape hatch, sealing their vessels to the docking ring above the upper hatch to extract the survivors.

And if the rescuers don't arrive in time? The submariners' training calls for a desperate measure: the trapped men can try sealing themselves, one at a time, into the trunk with emergency escape suits, then locking themselves out of the compartment by sealing the lower hatch and opening the upper one to make a "buoyant ascent." Rapidly rising from such a depth poses the risk of a life-threatening case of the bends for any who can make it to the surface. The frigid sea temperatures would also soon penetrate their suits and become fatal—usually within just a few hours—severely shrinking the timeline when rescuers would have to pluck them from the water. But the trapped submariners may have no other choice.

The aft survivors are still shot through with soaring adrenaline, but the simple act of collectively crafting a rough survival plan restores a crude sense of order.

"Zolotoy!" says Rashid before shutting off his emergency phone, using Dima's nickname even amid the strain. "We haven't heard from Lubu," he says. They both agree Sergey must still be in the fifth compartment, where he was at the time of the explosion. Rashid says he's already tried to open the watertight door at the sixth compartment's forward bulkhead, finding it hopelessly jammed. There is a long silence.

"I must secure the reactors," says Rashid at last, telling Dima to supervise the aftward retreat.

While Rashid takes an assistant and briskly moves toward the sixth compartment's aft bulkhead to verify that his reactors have automatically shut down during the *Kursk's* uncontrolled descent, he wants to further assure their stability. He uses his flashlight to find his reactor control manuals and carefully configures the system to prevent a looming temperature spike. This simple act, Rashid knows, will further protect the regional waters from a nuclear leak.

Further aft, Dima orders the remaining stunned sailors to gather up all emergency supplies—oxygen masks, oxygen regeneration cartridges, emergency escape suits, and food rations—and to start moving into the ninth compartment.

On his way, Dima tests the aft emergency buoy's internal release lever tucked into the overhead, hoping for any sign that the buoy successfully deployed to the surface. If it did, then the buoy's presence should be able to alert rescuers to the fallen *Kursk's* location. Its internal telephone might also provide rescuers with the means to communicate with men in the submarine.

To Dima's great disappointment, the lever moves back and forth but gives no indication of whether or not the buoy has deployed. Two other buoys are located forward, but Dima knows well not to count on any of them. It is a poorly kept secret that—to keep the messenger buoys from ejecting accidentally or from rattling in their seats and revealing the sub's location—submariners often weld them to the hull.

Dima knows that, if no emergency buoy has deployed, the chances of a timely rescue are dramatically slimmer. *They won't know where we are,* thinks Kolesnikov. His mind races. *No external communications device . . . how to signal?*

Shaken, Dima presses on and gathers his remaining emergency supplies. Then, amid the fading battery-supported light, he joins fellow survivors in the last compartment's upper deck. The tangle of corridors is now filled with scared young men, not all of them within Dima's field of view. Many shiver in wet clothing. Others slump with exhaustion. Dima sits on a stair step just inside the watertight door, which is also just below the escape trunk. He finds a notebook and pen, and begins to take roll.

Within minutes, Rashid and his assistant return from their work on the reactor. He maneuvers through the dim light, ordering the men to stay as still as possible, which will reduce their oxygen consumption. The sailors have left him the lower bunk space, and Rashid tries to settle in. A few men are already opening the oxygen regeneration cartridges — the chemical plates designed to remove the compartment's ongoing buildup of deadly carbon dioxide while replacing it with fresh oxygen.

Beneath the escape trunk, Dima jots in his notebook, beginning with the military time: "13:15. All personnel from compartments six, seven and eight moved to the ninth," he writes. "There are 23 of us here. We have made this decision because of the accident. None of us can get out. . . ."

BLAST PLUS TWO HOURS

It could have been a dud, thinks Admiral Popov from aboard the *Peter the Great,* trying to reassure himself. He goes through possibilities: The blast reports could have simply been the sound of the *Kursk* maneuvering her weapons through the torpedo room — sometimes a noisy process heard by neighboring vessels miles away. And if Captain Lyachin wanted to communicate with the *Peter the Great* about a failure to fire, his *Kursk* might have a simple communications problem.

Or maybe Lyachin thinks he has fired successfully, tried to report the torpedo's location, and is now simply hiding in the shooting's aftermath, practicing evasion. *But no torpedoes have been spotted at all.*

Or maybe the *Kursk* failed to detect the *Peter the Great* and her battle group. Lyachin could even have the *Kursk* facing in the wrong direction, trying to detect the target in an empty sector of the sea. It's happened before, like the time in 1998 when the commander of the *Pskov* nuclear attack submarine missed the target battle group's passage entirely, not realizing his error until hours later.

But could a commander as smart as Captain Lyachin make such a scandalous blunder? Popov wonders.

Popov keeps his worries to himself as the *Kursk's* exercise firing window begins to close. He gives an interview to a government television crew onboard the *Peter the Great.* He declares the Northern Fleet's exercises nearly finished, and pronounces them an unqualified success. The taped interview will be broadcast tomorrow, on Sunday.

Popov's fellow admirals detect a trace of concern, but the Northern Fleet commander keeps going through the motions as if all is okay. The interview wraps up just as an onboard helicopter prepares to take him to another exercise vessel, and he asks the remaining commanders on the *Peter the Great* to keep him updated. Popov turns and boards the helicopter as the weather begins to deteriorate. Once aloft, the pilot tells Popov the visibility and cloud ceiling are likely to fall below safe flying levels within a few hours, but conditions should hold for their visit to the nearby aircraft carrier *Admiral Kuznetsov.*

For Vice Admirals Burtsev and Boyarkin, still on the *Peter the Great*, the yawning silence from the *Kursk* has become acute. It's been hours now; they should have heard *something*, and the circumstance creates a quandary: Fleet rules dictate that a command vessel may not leave the range with a failed shooting and a missing submarine. Even one hour past the window should trigger a fleet-wide alarm, including the dispatch of search planes. But such an action could also appear unduly alarmist, in itself an unprofessional show of weakness to superiors. Which way to go? They want orders from Popov.

Popov maintains radio contact with the *Peter the Great*, and soon all of them share the growing apprehension. No one has spotted a torpedo's wake. The torpedo retriever crews are idling, empty-handed. No one has picked up the automated "pinger" signal from a torpedo that has finished its run and floated to the surface. As a wave of thunderstorms moves in from the Northwest, the cloud ceiling descends to 1,400 feet and the temperature drops to fifty-two degrees under a sixteen-knot blow. Rain falls.

Amid the deepening worries, Popov suddenly feels out of position. He wants to return to the *Peter the Great*, but the storm precludes landing a helicopter safely on the heaving deck. He finds it difficult to adequately maintain command from the *Kuznetsov*, whose crew, he feels, is unprepared to function as a headquarters operation. Popov believes his best course is to take the helicopter back to the land-based Northern Fleet headquarters office in Severomorsk, from where other exercise coordinators can help him keep an eye on things.

Ten minutes prior to the *Peter the Great's* departure from the *Kursk's* designated firing range, the ship's log keeper makes a grim entry regarding the missing submarine: "At 1350 we start to operate on the worst variant."

Should the Northern Fleet leadership suddenly choose to act on its worry of a worst-case scenario for the *Kursk*, a series of quick moves might be made. First, the *Peter the Great* could turn around and search along the bearing of their sonar man's recorded blast signal. The fleet could also summon search aircraft right away.

Next, if they could honestly acknowledge their rescue assets are crippled, fleet command could instantly contact NATO headquarters for formal rescue assistance. After all, Russia and NATO should be able to assist each other, since they are no longer at war.

The Northern Fleet could do this more readily, of course, if Russia had not already rejected a series of NATO overtures to participate in regional sub rescue exercises. Throughout the late 1990s, NATO officials had hoped to gain enough Russian trust to craft a regionwide quick-reaction plan for just such cases. But the Russians, according to NATO, objected to the idea of operating on equal footing with countries as small as Denmark.

But there are other approaches. If Popov and his men really want to save lives, they could broadcast a region-wide SOS on one of their open communications channels, signaling to attentive spies in the area their concern over an unfolding catastrophe where time is of the essence, and where the traditional East-West spy game might consider a time-out for a joint search operation.

It would be a bold move, but could work. Possibly the finest submarine rescue operation in the world is based in the United Kingdom. If the British were alerted right now, they could have their own rescue submersible at the wreck site within sixty hours—normally still a viable window for trapped sailors.

And a region-wide SOS could also rouse the commercial sector: state-of-the-art diving operations working the nearby Arctic oil fields could deploy one of their submersibles, possibly even attempting a little-known "hot tap" penetration of the stricken sub's hull—using a powerful but little-known tool called a "Cox's bolt gun"—bypassing any escape hatch complications. The move would be drastic, but the commercial diving operators have been inclined to boast of their "robust" skills in such cases.

Or . . . if Russian searchers found the stricken *Kursk* and determined there were survivors on board—and if the fleet carried properly equipped divers to submarine exercises as a routine safety precaution—a quick stopgap measure might be employed. Those divers could rapidly descend to the sub and attach air hoses with communications lines through exterior valves traditionally designed for such a purpose.

If, of course, the *Kursk* had not been among the first Russian submarine designs to eliminate such life-saving valves.

Or . . . if the fleet immediately summoned the storied rescue submarine *Lenok*—a 6,800-ton, ninety-four-man diesel sub that could speed to the wreck site at fifteen knots, ready to deploy the two mini-subs it carries tucked into its hull, each submersible capable of carrying twenty-four extracted submariners—life-saving operations could begin before nightfall.

If, of course, a cash-strapped Russia had not scrapped the *Lenok* in 1995 due to budget cuts.

If.

BLAST PLUS TWO HOURS, THIRTY MINUTES

Back in his Severomorsk office by 1400, Admiral Popov contemplates finally sounding the alarm. He considers alerting Russian Navy commander in chief Vladimir Kuroyedov, who could alert Kremlin officials in Moscow and Sochi.

But can he be truly certain that something's wrong? As with the Russian/Soviet military leaders who have preceded him, Popov knows there are no rewards for delivering bad news to superiors. To the contrary, recent decades have witnessed a parade of commanders toppled from their posts for doing just that: former premier Joseph Stalin, taking a page from sixteenth-century czar Ivan the Terrible, shot generals who reported the loss of major battles in World War II. More recently, Soviet general secretary Gorbachev sacked Russia's defense minister and his senior confederates after learning of an amateur German pilot's unchallenged landing of a small aircraft in Red Square. Popov is reluctant to join the tradition. He errs in favor of career caution and does not sound the alarm.

From his metal ledge beneath the *Kursk*'s escape trunk, Captain-Lieutenant Dmitry Romanovich Kolesnikov reviews the names of his comrades at regular intervals, starting from the top each time, calling out each name, trying to gauge each man's level of consciousness from the strength of his response. Kolesnikov's roll call begins with members of the sixth compartment. He has neatly written each name on its own line, sometimes just last names, sometimes with ranks, sometimes including the initials. But one pattern is remarkably consistent: Each has a series of status marks next to his name—hatchmarks and checkmarks in the left margin, plus signs to the right.

Including himself, the list comprises just four commissioned officers. The rest are warrant officers, petty officers, and some very young seamen, a few still teenagers. They settle in uneasily, some preparing their escape suits for a possible buoyant ascent, others nervously fiddling with oxygen masks, some quietly praying.

One of the most able-bodied sailors has been elected to bang on the escape trunk in hopes of attracting searchers. In the confined compartment, the loud clanging only adds to the sailors' discomfort.

Rashid and the eighth-compartment commander, Captain-Lieutenant Sergey Sadilenko, try to remain still in their bunks—Rashid on the lower level, Sadilenko on the upper.

The air is dank and tinged with smoke. The sound of water slowly leaking in from below brings a special torment.

The survivors have collected oxygen plates from the other aft compartments and pooled them. When the sealed packages are torn and the plates exposed to air, the brick-sized wafers "breathe" automatically, extending the compartment's limited air supply. But the plates also bring their own risk: the chemical reaction that helps them create breathable air is volatile. If the opened cartridges are accidentally exposed to seawater or oil, they will explode. They are normally placed only in a confined metal "blower" designed for the purpose, fixed in place within the compartment.

If the survivors can keep the seawater out, their ability to make breathable air could last for more than a week or ten days—some are aware of one case in which trapped Soviet sailors were rescued after three weeks. Their food supply can also last some days—canned meats, peanut butter, potable water, powdered milk, chocolate bars.

One of the more insidious threats is the sheer pressure at their present depth—at slightly above the seabed, about 340 feet. The natural pressure at such a depth is 150 pounds per square inch, ten times the pressure at the surface. If that pressure seeps into the compartment, the inside atmosphere will become compressed, dramatically raising the proportion of nitrogen. The pressurized nitrogen will then enter a submariner's bloodstream at ten times its normal rate, quickly reaching the point of saturation. Submariners exposed to sustained high levels of nitrogen can feel lightheaded, numb, and euphoric. They eventually become confused, uncoordinated, anxious, and scared. The end stages bring convulsions, blackouts, and death.

Flooding magnifies these effects by shrinking the available airspace, and even the most finely engineered submarines suffer small leaks. For the *Kursk*, the ninth compartment is inherently vulnerable: the vessel's propeller shafts run below the deck where Kolesnikov and the other twenty-two survivors now dwell, passing through openings in the stern of the pressure hull before projecting into the sea. The twin propellers' bushings are surrounded by "stern tube glands" to cushion their revolutions while restricting the entry of seawater. Even under normal operating conditions, those glands are designed to allow modest leakage to lubricate the massive shafts. But without power, the seals leak badly and the bilge pumps no longer work.

Seawater can also now leak slowly through tiny openings that normally carry ventilation and wires through the bulkhead. Even the long, trim pipe that runs nearly the entire length of the *Kursk*'s lower decks inside the pressure hull has opened to the sea at the sub's forward end, further compounding the flooding rate.

Once the water level reaches the sailors' feet, their body temperatures will face a losing battle with the Barents's cold. The regeneration plates produce some heat, as do the sailors' collective body temperatures, and nearly all of the sailors have already donned their thermal underclothing. But none of these things will be enough. To buy more time for any rescue effort, the best minds in the *Kursk*'s ninth compartment must now pool more than food and oxygen supplies. They must also bring together their best survival strategies.

As the sailor who knocks the SOS signals occasionally pauses to listen for a response, his comrades strain to hear with him, some pressing their palms to the hull in hopes of detecting meaningful vibration. With the minutes stretching to hours, some talk of attempting the manual ascent through the escape trunk. At the moment, the trunk's ladder lies stowed away, detached from its base.

Rashid Aryapov and Sergey Sadilenko try to assess the gathered emergency escape suits, and soon learn that their country's poverty has even found its way here: desperate metals thieves have pilfered the breathing masks' brass belts. More sad than furious, the men resign themselves to abandoning the manual escape plan. They must hope the fleet's searchers can find them in time.

The ninth-compartment officers try to apportion the oxygen plates for maximum duration, unaware that many of the unopened packages remain hidden beneath the sailors' scattered equipment. Though none have yet worked up an interest in opening the food pouches, many drink the bottled water.

The deteriorating conditions tax the huddled survivors. Nausea has set in. The deepening cold is brutal. Movement is difficult. Some men are moaning in pain. From his upper bunk space, Captain-Lieutenant Sadilenko tries to fulfill his duty as an officer to report on the circumstances. He scrawls a few details on a small piece of paper, including key bits of technical data: "Twenty-three men in ninth compartment," he writes. "Poor health. Weakened by effects of carbon monoxide during damage control. Pressure in compartment 0.6 kg/m2. Running out of V-64 [regeneration plates]. We will not endure compression during an escape to the surface. Not enough brass belts for personal breathing devices. Missing clasps for safety cords. Need to fasten the buoy cable reel assembly [by pulling them in]. We will not survive more than one day."

By later in the afternoon, the trapped submariners still detect no response to their desperate emergency signaling efforts. If any of the sailors has battery power for remaining flashlights, he declines to use it. Still, Dima continues updating his log without the aid of light.

"15:45," he writes in a barely legible scrawl. "It is dark to write here, but I'll try by feel. . . . It looks like there are no chances. 10 to 20 percent. Let's hope at least someone reads [this]. Here are the lists of compartments' submariners, some of them are in the ninth and will try to escape. Greetings to all. Don't despair."

BLAST PLUS FIVE HOURS

Nearly a thousand miles to the south, President Vladimir Putin is still captive of a last-minute Saturday afternoon ministerial meeting at the Kremlin, trying to get a fix on the recent bombings in Moscow. There is still no strong evidence of the "Chechen trace" that could help the Kremlin intensify its campaign against breakaway rebels in the Caucasus. The meeting started at 1400, and Putin tries to hurry it along, itching to escape as soon as possible for his vacation.

Four thousand miles east, U.S. Marine colonel Roy Byrd places an urgent call from the Pentagon to Robert Tyrer at 0830 Eastern Time— 1630 Moscow time—to inform him about overnight reports of a likely downed Russian submarine in the Barents Sea. Tyrer, chief of staff to

Defense Secretary William Cohen, takes the Saturday-morning call on his cell phone at Bethesda's Burning Tree Golf Course, where he's practicing his shots.

Colonel Byrd then calls Secretary Cohen at the secretary's suburban Washington home. Cohen thanks Byrd, but issues no orders.

11

AMERICAN DILEMMA
WASHINGTON, D.C.
SATURDAY, AUGUST 12, 0930 HOURS EDT (1730 HOURS MOSCOW TIME)

BLAST PLUS SIX HOURS

The clay tennis courts in Rock Creek Park are coveted turf in August, and Mark Medish is one of the lucky few with a weekly Saturday-morning doubles arrangement. It's perfect tennis weather—a northerly breeze and seventy degrees.

Medish, thirty-seven, is one of the more avid players among the senior White House people, and he's not happy when his bleating cell phone interrupts the match. He apologizes and steps to the side court.

"Mr. Medish," says the calm voice from the White House Situation Room. "We're following reports of a large underwater explosion in the Barents, possibly involving a Russian submarine exercise." He further tells Medish that top Pentagon officials got the word an hour earlier.

"Okay," says Medish, still catching his breath. "Tell Sandy Berger and get the reports ready. I'll be there in about an hour."

He turns back, telling his partners he'll have to leave after the set. "What can I say, guys?" he says sheepishly. "The NSC never sleeps."

Though Medish's partners tease him that he's got his priorities all wrong, they accept that such interruptions are normal enough.

In minutes the hotel room phone of National Security Advisor Sandy Berger rings in Los Angeles, where it's just past 0630. Berger is attending the National Democratic Convention with President Clinton, where the party is desperately trying to hold on to the White House with the struggling candidacy of Al Gore. Despite his early-morning brain fog, Berger verifies that Medish is on the case and will brief him soon. It is not yet the sort of clearly urgent information that justifies waking the president. Berger hopes that if the Russians have had an accident, they might break from tradition and announce it. But if they don't come out with it soon, Berger might initiate. And if the Russians need U.S. help, the United States will do what it can; it's been a hallmark of the Clinton administration to cautiously embrace a post–Cold War Russia in its rocky journey toward democracy.

Of course, Putin is still an enigma to the Clinton White House, but he already seems the antithesis of Boris Yeltsin. For one thing, Yeltsin used to make a bellicose show of noncooperation with the West in public, then often find a way to acquiesce in private, only insisting that the United States help him save face with the Russian people. Clinton's team liked Yeltsin well enough, even if his boorishly drunken behavior was sometimes hard to swallow. In one incident later recalled by Deputy Secretary of State Strobe Talbott, the visiting Yeltsin lurched about Blair House in his undershorts before stumbling down the stairs. Minutes later, he could be heard shouting "Pizza! Pizza!" Despite his liabilities, however, Clinton, Berger, Secretary of State Madeleine Albright, and Talbott all agreed Yeltsin genuinely shared the Western desire to drive a stake through the heart of the failed Soviet communist system.

The United States finds Yeltsin's successor to be another story altogether. When Clinton's team makes a proposal, the poker-faced Putin typically responds with studied circumspection—"interesting idea" or "maybe" or "let me think about it." The senior Clinton people understand this is Putin's way of saying no, and they've been getting a lot of these responses in the early days of Putin's presidency. Some of the younger members of Clinton's team have taken to calling Putin "Mr. Nyet."

Over breakfast at the hotel, Berger worries about the Russian submarine report. For the moment, this war-game incident could be a benign mishap, but Berger opts not to take any chances, and quickly calls Medish. He wants Medish to find out everything. Berger wants to know how quickly he can reach his counterpart, Russian Security Council secretary Sergey Ivanov. He wants Medish to find out pronto what the United States might do to help; if the United States is going to offer assistance, Berger doesn't want to do so in bad faith. Meanwhile, Berger will update Clinton during pauses in the convention politicking.

News of the unfolding crisis quickly rattles through the American security and diplomatic system, despite the many August vacations of senior officials, bringing into the loop all of the top players before noon on Saturday. Conspicuously absent from the early Saturday intelligence loop is the entire complement of U.S. diplomats at the American embassy in Moscow—or, for that matter, anyone in Moscow's British embassy.

Beyond that, the U.S. leadership is unaware that the Russian leadership is still in the dark. Even ten years after the Cold War's end, there is still no automatic protocol for calling any of them to find out—though assigning the embassy in Moscow to the cause couldn't hurt. But the few senior officials in the U.S. Department of State who've been made aware of the crisis elect not to spread the word beyond a tiny circle of Washington insiders.

It might be different if this were news about any submarine from, say, a European nation. Such an event might bring an international broadcast, an all-points alarm, a bold summoning to quick global action. But it is a Russian sub, a potentially very menacing one, and the Cold War won't really be over until the two sides begin acting as though it is.

12

A WORRIED FLEET
SOUTHERN BARENTS SEA
SATURDAY, AUGUST 12, LATE AFTERNOON

BLAST PLUS SIX HOURS

Russian fleet rules dictate that the vessels in an exercise must report their status at least once every four hours, even submarines. By 1600 hours on Saturday, it's been more than five hours since anyone in the Northern Fleet has heard from the *Kursk*.

By 1635, the fleet commanders have lost patience. Admiral Boyarkin orders the transmission of messages on the underwater telephone system. "Vintik!" barks the system's operator, using the *Kursk*'s call sign in a crude transmission mode that often sounds little better than garbled static. When submarines are well below the surface, the underwater telephone system is usually the only communications option. "Report on your location and status!" The message is the first in a series of urgent attempts—including both voice and typed broadcasts—all of which are met by silence.

Boyarkin quickly relays news of the failed contacts to Admiral Popov in Severomorsk. Popov orders a helicopter to be placed on standby in case a break in the weather allows him back to the *Peter the Great*. He also authorizes his chief deputy, Admiral Mikhail Motsak, to quietly alert the fleet's rescue forces. Motsak relays word to headquarters duty officer Alexey Palkin at 1720: "Rescue ship *Mikhail Rudnitsky* is to be on one-hour readiness to put to sea," says Motsak. "Scheduled report from the *Kursk* submarine has not taken place."

Word then reaches the fleet's rescue chief, Captain First Rank Alexander Teslenko. At 1740, Teslenko reaches the *Rudnitsky*'s commanding officer, Yuri Kostin, at his home near fleet headquarters in Severomorsk. Teslenko tells Kostin to ready his vessel within the hour, but does not explain why. Kostin and the rest of the rescue crew—rounded up one by one through phone calls or messengers dispatched to their apartments—are startled that an apparent exercise would be called now. They passed their practice tests just a month earlier, using three separate rescue submersibles—and weren't expecting another round until this coming Tuesday. Was this someone's idea of finding out how quickly they could deploy?

Aboard the *Peter the Great* about a hundred miles due east, Boyarkin and Burtsev and other senior fleet commanders hand binoculars to a number of sharp-eyed sailors and tell them to look for any evidence of a ship in distress—a buoy, an oil slick, even blown flotsam and jetsam, debris that submariners are trained to eject if their rescue buoys fail to deploy. They are not told of the earlier blast reports, only that the *Kursk* has failed to respond at its scheduled time.

Despite the low clouds, visibility remains high from a blustering wind racing across the cresting wave caps.

At 1814, the Northern Fleet chief of staff, Admiral Motsak, puts the search-and-rescue effort into higher gear, ordering five Il-38 search planes into the air from Severomorsk. He will soon order a series of six helicopters to join a search effort that will eventually include twelve combat ships, twenty-one rescue vessels, and two diving ships. The Il-38s depart for the *Kursk*'s designated sector by 1852, and dip below the low storm clouds. Within a half hour, they widen their search to a twenty-mile radius.

The *Altay* tug lingering near Kildin Island twenty miles west is ordered to prepare for search-and-rescue operations by early evening, but is told first to wait for a rendezvous with the fleet's rescue mothership, the *Rudnitsky*.

Minutes later, land-based Northern Fleet radiomen say they've detected a weak and unstable signal from a vessel using the *Kursk*'s exercise code name, "Vintik." The report prompts speculation that the *Kursk* may have surfaced but can't properly transmit. The radiomen attempt to get a rough fix on the signal's bearing, sending some rescue vessels toward the suspect coordinates.

By late afternoon, Admiral Popov is keeping a tense vigil from his office in Severomorsk, ordering more rescue vessels to the scene even as the weather remains marginal, debating with himself whether it's time to tell Moscow.

He has yet to formally declare a fleet alarm.

Popov opts again not to alert his superiors, instead tapping his trusted Vice Admiral Yuri Boyarkin to head up the informal search efforts from aboard the *Peter the Great*. Boyarkin has been transmitting to Popov in ten-minute intervals for several hours. In one radio exchange, Boyarkin confirms to Popov that there have still been no reports of found torpedoes or any other signs of the *Kursk*. By now, few put much stock in the reports of weak signals from a vessel calling itself "Vintik."

13

WHITE HOUSE SITUATION ROOM

WASHINGTON, D.C.
SATURDAY, AUGUST 12, 1030 HOURS EDT (1830 HOURS
MOSCOW TIME)

BLAST PLUS SEVEN HOURS

"So what have we got, guys?" asks Mark Medish as he arrives at the Situation Room on a lower level of the West Wing of the White House. With no time for a shower and still wearing his tennis clothes, Medish quickly studies the thin stack of white briefing papers. They indicate little more than they did an hour before, and Medish thinks the key concern remains whether the Russian leadership understands the crisis yet. His colleagues can't say for sure, but a new report that Putin has departed the Kremlin for his flight to Sochi suggests not.

What the Americans know is sketchy. Abnormally big explosions. Chief assumption is that a nuclear submarine is down. Survivor prospects unclear. U.S. subs monitoring, but not yet reporting. All information coming from surface assets and some truly remarkable seismographic reports from systems that would normally detect secret nuclear testing. The only new data include radio intercepts, many of them unencrypted, clear indicators of some kind of emergency. Possible signs of a Russian search-and-rescue effort just getting under way. Or could these things simply indicate a state of confusion?

Within minutes, Medish engages in a series of quick exchanges with associates at the Pentagon and State Department. The first question is whether the United States might help. Senior Pentagon policy official

Frank Miller voices his worry: If the Russians don't know what they're facing yet, won't initiation of such information compromise U.S. intelligence-gathering methods? He also mentions the long-standing naval tradition that all of the world's navies are presumed able to take care of their own; aid should be rendered only when requested.

The State Department's Debra Cagan, who directs the office for security affairs with the former Soviet Union and who shares a long and like-minded professional history with Miller, advocates against making an unsolicited offer. She cautions that it would come across as impolite at best, insincere at worst. How would it look for Western surveillance vessels suddenly to offer help to the quarry of their efforts? She suspects the Russians might view such a gesture as an insult or, worse, a thinly masked attempt to gain further intelligence data from an enemy vessel. She suggests a rescue offer is more likely to be greeted with Russian finger-pointing than gratitude.

Cagan also thinks it wouldn't succeed in any case. She says that, in accord with Soviet-Russian history in such matters, senior fleet officials on the scene are likely already misleading their superiors—both military and civilian. Why should the West believe the fleet would shoot straight with foreign rescuers in need of technical specifications required to mate a U.S. rescue submersible with one of their own hatches?

Medish and NSC chief Berger take the cautions into account, but choose to attempt discreet contact with the Russians. Accordingly, Medish turns his attention to finding Russian security chief Ivanov. It's mid-August, when most Russians vacation with a vengeance. Ivanov has always been difficult to raise quickly, so the vacation period can only compound the problem. But Medish instructs Sit-Room operatives to call their counterparts in Moscow in an attempt to find him. Soon Medish learns that Ivanov is also headed for Sochi with Putin, and that he won't be available until Monday. This feels like a growing communications breakdown. Medish is frustrated. Berger almost never calls Ivanov, even during the week. Operating on the assumption that Moscow aides have properly relayed the request to Ivanov himself, Medish is incredulous. *Surely Ivanov and his people know a call on a Saturday would indicate some urgency?*

Medish phones Berger in L.A. with the no-go news about Ivanov.

He knows what I'm calling about, thinks Berger. *Sergey's deliberately avoiding me. He doesn't want to accidentally confirm the Barents problem.* Berger can't imagine that Ivanov would *not* know about the enormous blasts seven hours later.

But Ivanov does not know. Putin does not know. No one in Moscow knows.

Berger asks Medish to determine the status of U.S. rescue assets. Medish turns to a naval officer attached to the NSC staff, Captain Phillip Cullom, to assemble details about what the United States can offer, should they decide that's the way to go.

Before leaving the White House, Medish, Miller, and Cagan agree to develop recommendations for handling any press inquiry, but they make no plan to initiate an announcement that might betray U.S. knowledge of any tragedy involving a Russian submarine in the southern Barents Sea. If such an unprecedented event is to occur at all, it must happen at a higher level—Berger, Cohen, Albright, or the president himself. They will meet again tomorrow, Sunday, to button up the media strategy.

Meanwhile, Medish can collect updates from the secure telephone at his home in nearby Potomac Palisades. He can track Captain Cullom's efforts regarding U.S. rescue assistance. He can push for a breakthrough with Ivanov.

Medish's intimate exposure to the decision-making firing line makes it hard for him to relax. Though one of the Clinton foreign-policy team's youngest members, he is a worthy poster boy for its operating philosophy. Medish comes from the same school of thought as Strobe Talbott, Clinton's most trusted adviser on Russian affairs. Like Talbott, Medish is pro-engagement and unburdened by the hardened Russophobic skepticism that afflicted so many of his NSC forebears. But Medish also comes to the post with more than the academic pedigree of Georgetown-Harvard-Oxford Russian-studies specialist. Medish grew up in Washington as the son of a Soviet émigré. His father was a Red Army prisoner of war captured by the Germans near Stalingrad; he later fled to the West after Stalin's secret police seized *his* father, who died in captivity.

As director of the National Security Council's Russia policy, Mark Medish has become a key White House point man in trying to close the administration's unfortunate distance from the new Russian president. The unfolding crisis presents an important crossroads in a complicated but critical global relationship, and Medish wants to help seize the moment. But as the August afternoon unfolds, no encouraging news arrives from Ivanov's people.

Medish is all too familiar with communications glitches when it comes to contacting the Russians. Though just one year into his NSC post, he's had a series of jobs in the Clinton administration that have kept him close to Russian affairs since 1994. Through all that time, he has been amazed at the primitive barriers that impede East-West contact between top government officials. There are internecine channels, absurd formalities, surprising gaps in communications technology—including a mysteriously broken link with an airborne president Yeltsin the previous year—and the pervasive, insidious no-man's-land of mid-August vacations among developed countries in the Northern Hemisphere.

There is also the occasional willful lack of response, but it's hard to know when this is the case. For the moment, Medish feels stymied.

The handful of other American officials apprised of the unfolding Barents crisis make no attempts to contact their Russian counterparts. No one attached to the Pentagon, including Captain Cullom, contacts key members of the American sub-rescue system. Cullom gets his information from other sources. No one calls the U.S. Navy's head of submarine-rescue services, Commander William Orr. Neither are the sub-rescue crews in San Diego notified of prospects for an international effort to save trapped men from an erstwhile enemy navy.

No one in the U.S. embassy in Moscow is alerted of anything.

The British Ministry of Defence (MOD), normally kept intimately informed of U.S. intelligence developments, is mysteriously quiet. As in the United States, no one from the British MOD's intelligence operations notifies anyone outside their cloistered circle, including their own submarine-rescue forces. Their state-of-the-art rescue submersible—the celebrated "underwater helicopter" known as the LR5—is headed for an exercise in the eastern Mediterranean near Turkey. The *LR5*'s "kit" material is currently on trucks headed across Europe. Its skilled operators are gearing up for their long-scheduled "Sorbet Royale" sub-rescue practice, one of the very NATO events to which the Russians said *nyet*. The British rescue operation's commander, Royal Navy commodore David Russell, could divert the entire rescue package to the Barents at a moment's notice. But on the afternoon of Saturday, August 12, he receives no such word.

14

FLEET BREAKING POINT
MOSCOW
SATURDAY, AUGUST 12, 1928 HOURS

BLAST PLUS EIGHT HOURS

At 1928 Moscow time, Vladimir Putin's presidential jet finally lifts off its runway and climbs, selecting a southerly course for the Black Sea coast. The sun visible from his right-side window is still five degrees above Russia's hazy western horizon. With normal flight time, Putin should reach the airport near the warm beaches of Bocharov Ruchei—the sprawling compound that serves as a favorite presidential dacha—in about three hours.

Meanwhile at fleet headquarters in Severomorsk, an agitated Admiral Popov strides into the command post at 1930 and orders reports from other vessels in the *Kursk*'s designated firing area. "Commander *Leopard*!" the headquarters operative hails by radio, quickly raising the commander of the Akula-class sub that was closest to the *Kursk* at the moment of the mystery blast. "Did you observe K-141's work?" the headquarters officer asks, using the *Kursk*'s numerical designator.

"We did not observe K-141's work," the *Leopard*'s commander replies. The nearest torpedo catcher also reports no meaningful observations. With those two vessels reporting nothing, it does not occur to rescue coordinators to quiz the *Karelia*'s captain, as the *Karelia* was farther away from the *Kursk*'s last-known site. How could the *Karelia* have detected anything if the much-closer *Leopard* didn't?

Popov then orders the *Peter the Great*'s Boyarkin to launch a series of grenade explosions in a more concerted attempt to hail the *Kursk*. The first salvo explodes at 2027, the second at 2042, then 2102, then 2137. . . . All of the grenades are dropped in the *Kursk*'s last suspected operating area, and are intended to forcefully compel the missing sub to respond in any way it can. But Boyarkin and his ship are still not close enough to the *Kursk*'s position to hear any noises that might arise from it.

As daylight begins running out, the Il-38 patrol aircraft receive orders to return to base.

BLAST PLUS TEN HOURS

Just past 2130, the sky over Vidyayevo has broken up, with the departing storm's chaotic fragments catching the waning sunlight. They create a tangled scarlet veil, bathing the hills that surround the garrison town in a warm glow. Irina Lyachina has come to treasure rare northern sights like this, but she can't suppress a vague anxiety that keeps bothering her as the evening wears on. The friends who visited in the afternoon had arrived late, and Irina still finds it silly that the other submariners' wives kept asking if she'd gotten any word from Genna about the exercise. Even if he is the captain, Genna never contacts her from the sea, and Irina has learned over the years to abide his absences patiently.

But now that she's alone, Irina finds it hard to settle down. She tries reading a book, but can't concentrate on the words. Then she drops the book. She looks out her window to see that the sky is still a pleasing red. She tries the TV. She leaves it on for a while, then turns it off again. She wanders into the kitchen and begins pacing.

Just after 2200 hours in his Severomorsk office, Admiral Popov's fears are bubbling over. How much longer can he hold out? The Il-38s have come back to Severomorsk empty-handed. The *Mikhail Rudnitsky* rescue vessel is still tethered to its mooring nearly twenty minutes past sunset, its preparations well under way but not yet ready for sea. Vice Admiral Boyarkin on the *Peter the Great* has still reported nothing from the fringes of the *Kursk*'s operating area—no oil slick, no emergency buoy, no signal responses. Popov radios an order for Boyarkin to maneuver the cruiser directly into the *Kursk*'s designated exercise site, normally a risky proposition. Boyarkin must now carefully watch for any indication that a submarine might be surfacing; he must avoid a collision. Popov directs Boyarkin to try signaling the *Kursk* to surface.

Meanwhile, the *Karelia*'s commander has checked in. When Captain Korablev hears that the *Kursk* is missing, he is forced to rethink the dramatic blast effect he'd felt earlier in the day. Now he wishes he'd reported the event when it happened. He tells his superiors in Severomorsk that the *Karelia* was rocked by an extraordinary underwater blast at about 1130 hours.

With renewed urgency, Vice Admiral Boyarkin orders the *Peter the Great* to proceed on a northeasterly course. While doing so, her sonar and radar operators compare data on the *Kursk*'s last-known position, focusing intently on the intersection of bearings where the *Peter the Great* and other vessels—now including the *Karelia*—detected the enormous blast eleven hours earlier. With a rough approximation of the blast's bearing in hand—but lacking adequate data on its range—the *Peter the Great* begins a slow zigzag pattern along the suspect bearing, her echo sounder searching for anything unusual on the seabed.

At 2300, it has been nearly twelve hours since anyone in the fleet has communicated with the *Kursk*. This is her final scheduled time for communication, but she remains silent. Boyarkin reports to Popov that the *Kursk* has missed another reporting window.

Boyarkin and other senior fleet officers confer on the *Peter the Great*'s bridge, and soon decide to share their best data in a broadcast over the fleet's open communications channel. "At 1130," the *Peter the Great*'s radioman reports, "at a bearing of zero-nine-six from location 69.40 north and 36.24 east, an impact blow was heard."

BLAST PLUS TWELVE HOURS

After hearing further details from Boyarkin, Popov makes it official at 2330, declaring that a formal alarm be broadcast fleet-wide. He's risking his career along with those of many who share the command with him, regardless of the outcome.

With the wind speed settling at ten knots and nighttime visibility good at eighteen miles despite light rain, Boyarkin and the others watch the lights of a seagoing tug combing the site by 2345 for any sign of surfaced *Kursk* flotsam—or floating crewmen.

Popov asks about the progress of the *Mikhail Rudnitsky* rescue vessel. He is dismayed to learn that it still hasn't left its dock. Resigned to the idea that events are now well beyond his control, Popov turns to the landline phone in his Severomorsk office, and places a call to his boss in Moscow, Russian Navy commander in chief Vladimir Kuroyedov.

Fifteen minutes past midnight, Kuroyedov joins his staff at the Defense Ministry headquarters. He tells Minister of Defense Marshal Igor Sergeyev that the *Kursk* is missing. Sergeyev decides not to disturb the president on vacation in Sochi until officials get more information.

At first, the Northern Fleet's alarm is shared discreetly to select locations around the Kola Peninsula—most prominently to key officials in Severomorsk, but also to the *Kursk*'s home garrison in Vidyayevo. Those calls aren't to inform family members that their men are missing, but to request that senior officers from the *Kursk*'s sister sub there, the *Voronezh*, begin preparing their vessel for a possible search effort. At first, they are not told which vessel is missing.

Shortly after midnight, one of the *Voronezh*'s senior officers, Captain Third Rank Evgeny Zubkov, takes a call at his apartment directing him to report to the docks as soon as possible for an urgent deployment. Zubkov asks why, but he is told he will learn more once he arrives at the dock.

Zubkov does as ordered, but doubts the *Voronezh* can be readied very quickly. He knows that, back in the spring, his submarine had been designated to participate in the exercise, but that her commander reported it had too many deficiencies, and so the *Kursk* was chosen instead. Now, given the chronic shortage of spare parts, some systems on the *Voronezh* were cannibalized to prepare the *Kursk*. Zubkov had transferred off the *Kursk* over a year before because of a conflict with one of her officers, but he remained close with many of its sailors—especially Kolesnikov and Aryapov and Lubushkin. He was envious when the *Kursk* was chosen over the *Voronezh* for the Barents exercise, but had grown accustomed to the supporting role. If the *Voronezh* can be coaxed into readiness, Zubkov figures, at least the two vessels and their crews might be reunited in the fleet's mysteriously urgent business.

15

EMERGENCY SEARCH
SEVEROMORSK
SUNDAY, AUGUST 13, 0100 HOURS

BLAST PLUS THIRTEEN HOURS, THIRTY MINUTES

Northern Fleet rescue chief Captain First Rank Alexander Teslenko stands aboard the *Mikhail Rudnitsky* as it finally begins departing from its dock in Severomorsk. Once cleared and under way, *Rudnitsky* Captain Yuri Kostin takes Teslenko's orders to proceed at maximum speed to a rendezvous point near Kildin Island, just east of the Murmansk fjord's mouth, where he will link up with the salvage tug *Altay*. Teslenko declines to tell the *Rudnitsky* crew what their mission is, but their vessel has two rescue submersibles fixed to its decks. Even at a maximum speed of nearly sixteen knots, the *Rudnitsky* will need at least eleven hours to reach the search area.

Not that it matters much yet. As the *Peter the Great* continues to probe the seabed along the suspect bearing, its echo sounder has detected nothing.

But then there is a sound.

At 0120, the nuclear cruiser's chief navigator, Captain Third Rank Evgeny Golodenko, is standing on the bridge, peering through darkness into the turbulent sea, when he detects an emerging pattern to the noises in the sonar track. To keep everyone on the bridge fully informed, the sonar signal continues to be broadcast through loudspeakers. As

Golodenko listens intently, he notes that the faint pulses seem to come in a series of six to seven knocks. After several repetitions, he deduces the noises appear to be in response to the *Peter the Great's* own sonar pings. Golodenko alerts sonar man Andrey Lavriniuk on the bridge, who confirms knocking sounds, and says they could be automated responses from a station on board a submarine. Excited, the men report the signal to Boyarkin and others nearby. Even if it is, indeed, only an automated SOS, officers on the *Peter the Great* suspect they're closing in at last on their target.

As the cruiser maintains course, the knocking sounds become noticeably easier to hear, even over the buffeting winds and rough seas. By 0222, with the *Peter the Great* at 69.37 degrees north latitude and 37.38 east, Golodenko and Lavriniuk join deputy navigator Sergey Vasiliev to fix the signal's origin on a bearing of 281 degrees from their position. And now there's another noise—all agree they hear grinding metal.

At 0315 faint daylight slowly brightens the low cloud cover, and the *Peter the Great* notes three clusters of eight to nine taps, all in response to the cruiser's signals. They detect the sounds again at 0320, this time as five rhythmic taps over an eight-second period. At 0330, the *Peter the Great* straightens its course toward a point immediately above the signals' origin.

With the early daylight, the *Peter the Great's* captain orders more sailors back to the decks to resume their vigil, looking for any trace of the *Kursk*. They are also ordered to look for any sign of a foreign submarine, as speculation emerges from the senior officers that there may have been a collision with a NATO spy vessel. The sailors who begin assembling will soon be joined by men aboard neighboring ships, the destroyers *Admiral Chabanenko* and *Admiral Kharlamov*.

Minutes before 0400, sailors aboard the *Peter the Great* alert to a comrade's shout. They cluster near him as he points excitedly into the murky waters at a large blue and green object submerged well below the surface. Perhaps a buoy tethered to a sub in distress? But the Russian Navy's emergency buoys are red and white. Who uses blue and green? A more senior sailor tells them that even the colors red and white appear blue and green when submerged.

The men quickly lower a small vessel from a surface deck, and the sailors on the smaller launch try to cope with their rocking boat while attempting to hook the mysterious submerged object. But as they watch, the object appears slowly to go deeper, beyond the reach of their grappling devices.

Meanwhile, the persistent knocking noises continue to come from the earlier bearing, still some distance away, still in seeming response to their locator's signals. It would seem the submerged buoylike object cannot be from the *Kursk*, and the *Kursk* is the searchers' top priority.

But soon the "mystery buoy" rumors circulate throughout the fleet. If it is not from the *Kursk*, could it be from a foreign vessel that collided with her? One senior captain who studied the submerged blue-green object from the deck suspects it was simply one of the larger jellyfish that frequent the Barents in late summer. Yet he is reluctant to argue against the growing consensus that the purported buoy signals the presence of a foreign sub.

Then, at 0413, a sailor on the nuclear cruiser spots a bright orange glove floating on the surface. Such bits of floating garbage are commonly spotted on the sea surface, but the ongoing search makes some of the sailors worry about this item's origin.

By 0430, Lavriniuk, Golodenko, and others note that the recurrent tapping is "similar to an SOS," but they can't say for certain that the signal is human in origin. Sonar man Lavriniuk certainly has a more personally vested interest in hoping it's human; he went to naval college with many of the *Kursk*'s midlevel officers, and they have remained close. If the *Kursk* is on the seabed, he'd like to think his friends are alive and preparing for an evacuation. In any case, the group narrows the signal's source to 69 degrees 37.89 minutes north, 37 degrees 32.43 minutes east. Within eight minutes, the *Peter the Great*'s echo sounder detects an "anomaly" on the seabed at 69-37.8 N,

37-33.3 E. It picks up an abrupt fifty-foot rise in a normally featureless area of the Barents.

Nearby vessels in the search flotilla quickly train their sonar equipment on the coordinates. Fifteen radiomen on various ships near the scene agree that the knocking sounds like an SOS signal. But the men disagree on whether the signal is automated or made by sailors trapped aboard the sub.

Vice Admiral Burtsev already believes the worst, but he doesn't share his dark thoughts. He doubts there is any life at all on the *Kursk*, and interprets the various sounds as "the sound of a perishing ship." He hears random rattling, cracking, whacking noises.

Back in Moscow, naval commander in chief Admiral Vladimir Kuroyedov is alerted to the new developments, and at 0500 he orders a plane placed on standby for a flight to Severomorsk. But Defense Minister Sergeyev orders the flight grounded; he wants Kuroyedov in Moscow.

More reports trickle into the Ministry of Defense. At 0507, sonar men report "wailing and grinding" noises arising from the seabed. At 0530, another series of suspected SOS signals. At 0624, the report of an oil slick.

Popov tells Moscow that he strongly suspects that the *Kursk* has been found on the seabed, but that no rescue vessels are yet on the scene to make an approach. And without any deep-diving support equipment, summoning deep-water saturation divers from St. Petersburg would be pointless. Meanwhile, the *Mikhail Rudnitsky* is still more than five hours away.

By 0715, Defense Minister Sergeyev reluctantly places a telephone call to the president on vacation in Sochi. Putin initially responds to Sergeyev's news with several seconds of awkward silence. "What is the situation with the reactor?" he finally asks. "What is being done to save the people on board?"

Putin offers to fly to the Northern Fleet headquarters, but Sergeyev assures the president that his arrival on the scene would have too little practical effect to warrant breaking off his vacation. Sergeyev tells Putin that Northern Fleet rescue officials have everything they need, and that the situation is under control.

Out on the Barents Sea, rescue chief Teslenko orders the *Mikhail Rudnitsky* to approach the shore near Kildin Island, where the *Altay* salvage tug awaits. But the *Rudnitsky* errs on the coordinates and misses the scheduled rendezvous entirely, easily costing ninety minutes.

16

RUMORS COME ASHORE

VIDYAYEVO

SUNDAY, AUGUST 13, 0720

BLAST PLUS EIGHTEEN HOURS, FIFTY MINUTES

Shortly after boarding the *Voronezh* submarine at its dock in Vidyayevo, Captain Third Rank Evgeny Zubkov learns from fellow officers that the *Kursk* has missed a scheduled check-in time. Zubkov now realizes that his friends are the object of his mission. At first, news that the *Kursk* is in trouble is only mildly alarming. But as Zubkov assists with heating up the *Voronezh* reactors, it begins to dawn on him: If fleet officials are concerned enough to attempt deploying the long-tethered *Voronezh* for the search, things with Captain Lyachin and his former *Kursk* comrades must be serious. Though he applies his best skills to aiding in the *Voronezh*'s preparation, Zubkov seriously doubts this heavily cannibalized sub will be leaving its pier any time soon.

Aboard the *Peter the Great*, the exhausted sailors who'd kept the overnight vigil yield their posts to the new watch. Just after 0800, two of the men assuming the sonar post—Captain-Lieutenant Yuri Ostryanin and Seaman Oleg Zyryanov—detect a new series of tapping sounds. They hear three successive knocks, then a pause, then three slower successive knocks, then a pause, then three successive knocks. The purposeful SOS code seems unmistakable.

A slight ray of hope arrives with the report that the *Mikhail Rudnitsky* has finally entered the exercise range's edge at 0839. Its revised estimated time of arrival to the suspected wreck site: 1200.

Frustrated at the agonizingly slow pace of the seaborne rescue vessels, other senior officers at the scene quietly request the services of a small secret submarine commanded by officers who report to Russia's Main Intelligence Department in Moscow. The top-secret AS-15 normally operates independently of the Northern Fleet, oftentimes monitoring fleet activities on behalf of senior Moscow officials. Admiral Popov has requested its assistance in assessing things with the *Kursk.*

The AS-15 is a thirty-six-man Kashalot design whose side thrusters give it dynamic maneuverability for seabed exploration. All of its crewmen are officers, and it is equipped for sabotage operations, including disruptions of NATO's secret system of underwater hydrophones. Its operators can also transmit images back to intelligence officers at the surface. The AS-15 makes its way toward the coordinates of the suspected wreck, and is soon transmitting disturbing images for the few senior officers allowed to view it. Amid the murk at a depth of over 350 feet, the submersible's light beam reveals dark shards of metal on the seabed.

Soon the whalelike black hull of a submarine comes into view, and the AS-15 continues to gather up images that shock all who see it. The Russian Navy's single most powerful underwater gladiator lies crippled and helpless on the seabed, a "terrifying hole"—as one official would later describe it—gaping from the top starboard space where the torpedo compartment is supposed to be.

The senior Russian officials now have a glimpse of the enormous tragedy that has befallen their country. But for the time being, at least, this reality will be their secret.

Before departing the site, the AS-15 intelligence sub gathers up other bits of data that can aid in the eventual rescue attempt. The *Kursk* is on a heading of 285 degrees. Visibility at the site is an adequate ten feet, and the current is between 1.2 and 1.4 knots, about what would be expected. The intelligence sub also detects no externally visible evidence of a human presence in or near the *Kursk.*

At 0920, still hours before the long-awaited arrival of the *Rudnitsky*, another flurry of excitement arises over the apparent sighting of a second submerged buoy. The observers see a greenish obelisk, over twenty-five inches across, about fifteen feet beneath the surface. But again, the object slowly sinks before anyone can hook it. Within minutes, the *Peter the Great*'s fathometer detects an abrupt shallowing in the vanished object's vicinity. The combined data fuels intense speculation that a second sub lies stricken near the *Kursk*, perhaps the other party in a collision.

BLAST PLUS TWENTY-ONE HOURS

When Captain Evgeny Zubkov visits the garrison headquarters building on a midday lunch break, the other officers look grim and know little. They tell him they believe the *Kursk* has been found, and that it's "lying on the seabed." At first, Zubkov doesn't believe it. *Such a mighty vessel lying on the seabed?* He wants desperately to deny that the *Kursk* has suffered an accident, but "lying on the seabed" strains his disbelief.

After determining that the other officers know little else for certain, Zubkov wanders back into the dirt-covered streets of Vidyayevo, instinctively adopting the steely reserve of an officer who doesn't want to needlessly alarm anyone with incomplete information.

But other sailors based in the garrison are beginning to return from the exercise, some of them released from the overnight search for the *Kursk*.

One of them joins a line of residents waiting for a delivery of fresh bread to a Vidyayevo shop, and casually complains of his exhaustion. "I'm about to collapse," he says, drawing the attention of residents hoping for early results of the exercise.

"Why?" asks one of them.

"Because we've been up all night looking for a sub," he says. "The *Kursk* is lying at the bottom of the sea."

One of the women faints, and the ensuing commotion spreads quickly.

Olga Lubushkina soon hears the story from some visiting girlfriends. At first she dismisses it entirely, then decides the problem can't really be that serious. No one is sure of anything. Olga tries to busy herself by letting out the cuffs of Sergey's pants.

Irina Lyachina finishes initial cooking preparations for her son's birthday, and steps outside her apartment with a shopping list.

"Irina!" shouts one of the *Kursk* officers' wives from across the street. "When will our men be back?"

Irina smiles at her. Some of the younger wives take a long time to get accustomed to even the shortest absences. The commander's wife says she expects Genna and the boys to return no later than tomorrow, then offers a maternal tease: "So you are missing him already?" She turns to walk away.

"Don't you know anything?" the woman asks plaintively.

"No," says Irina. "Why?"

"Our men are lying on the seabed."

Irina instinctively turns expressionless, saying she has heard nothing of the sort. But even as she says this, her stomach twists. She instantly links it with her strange feelings from the previous evening. Still, she has trained herself not to panic over rumors, and she urges the young wife to do likewise. As Irina walks away, she begins bracing herself. If such rumors are running through Vidyayevo, then she will handle them with the professionalism that Genna would expect of her.

As she heads home, Irina is stopped by a cluster of other wives, all of them apparently unaware of the rumors. Like her, many have just returned from vacations, which dominate the small talk. Normally, the warm weather that so briefly graces Vidyayevo makes these spontaneous outdoor gatherings a welcome respite, but today Irina finds it torturous. Feeling trapped, she goes through the motions of the conversation while looking for the first opportunity to retreat to her apartment.

Finally breaking away, Irina hurries home, shielding her eyes from Vidyayevo's bright afternoon sunlight as she struggles against a chilly wind toward her apartment. She spots Dasha, her teenage daughter, in the window, and worries Dasha may have also heard the rumors. Her worries seem confirmed when she sees Yura, a close family friend for twenty years, who joins Dasha at the window.

As Irina enters the apartment, a grim-faced Yura rushes to help with her bag of groceries. "Something's happened," he says.

Irina comes to an abrupt halt, refusing to hand over the groceries. "Either you tell me everything right now," she commands, "or you tell me nothing at all."

Yura nods, ushering her into the kitchen. Irina tells Dasha to wait in her bedroom, and closes the kitchen door. "Genna and the men are on the seabed," Yura says flatly, acknowledging that this is all he knows.

Irina tries to compose herself, stifling sobs. She enters Dasha's bedroom and is reassured at the sight of her daughter also keeping her emotions in check. "Nothing is known," Irina says, encouraging Dasha to maintain hope. She tells Dasha it's best to stay inside for the time being, to avoid the flow of rumors.

"Mama," says Dasha, her eyes suddenly welling up, "they say that everybody is dead."

"Not true," Irina admonishes. She reminds her of their larger responsibility to the community. As the commander's family, they cannot break down in public. "Watching us," says Irina, "people will know how to react."

Norwegian admiral Einar Skorgen is relaxing at his home on the northern coast of Norway on Sunday afternoon, even as some of the men who report to him keep watch over the Barents exercise from their radar stations, signals-tracking units, Orion aircraft, and the *Marjatta* surveillance vessel. He and his wife are just finishing up a midday bite of smoked salmon and salad when two intelligence officers pull into the driveway.

Admiral Skorgen greets the pair—a major who is chief of Norwegian Intelligence from Oslo and a lieutenant who serves at Skorgen's own base in nearby Bodo—and ushers them into his living room for coffee. The young officers tell Skorgen that it appears to be nothing urgent. They just thought he should be aware that Norwegian surveillance assets have noticed a sustained "search-and-rescue pattern" of Northern Fleet vessels, and thought he might want some of the details.

"Is there any reason to believe this is a live situation?" Skorgen asks, suspecting it might be a part of the exercise routine.

"No," one of the intelligence officers says. "There's no indication that this is not an exercise."

The officers are also aware of blast reports picked up in the Barents before noon the previous day, but their local analysts have not provided intensity levels. Those reports do not yet seem significant to the intelligence officers—especially in the context of a weapons firing exercise—and so they don't mention them to Skorgen.

Toward the end of the half-hour visit, Skorgen tells the officers to keep him informed of any significant changes, and to be prepared to render assistance if the Barents activity appears real.

As Admiral Skorgen sees the men to the door, he worries whether his friend Russian admiral Vyacheslav Popov would be reluctant to initiate a request for help from Norwegian forces. But Skorgen can't imagine such a case, not this long after the Cold War's end, not after their warm exchanges in recent years.

Just a few years earlier, Skorgen himself took the risk of proposing to his own Defense Ministry that the Soviet Union's collapse should herald warming relations with the Northern Fleet. God knows the cat-and-mouse naval games both sides played had created misunderstandings over the years. Why can't the region's two top admirals have a direct line to each other, like neighbors just helping neighbors?

In that spirit, Skorgen invited Popov to Norway so they could talk through mutual security concerns and share ideas. Popov accepted, opening up a series of cross-border visits that gave both men a new level of comfort. They had regaled each other with great sea stories while emptying bottles of vodka and sharing the rituals of the Russian sauna. On one such visit the two admirals joked about the unfortunate political posturing that came with their jobs, where they were sometimes forced to say and do things because higher authorities demanded it of them. Of course, both agreed, Popov had more than his share of such demands. "Between us sailors," Popov joked, "we need to forget about what I say in Moscow."

The friendship had progressed to the point where Skorgen genuinely liked and respected Popov. Like Skorgen himself, it seemed, Popov had a healthy disrespect for politics when it came to the things that really mattered. *Surely,* Skorgen thinks on this Sunday afternoon, *Vyacheslav would not hesitate if he needed something.*

Just after sunrise reaches the American East Coast, the phone rings in Admiral Harold W. Gehman Jr.'s home at the naval base in Norfolk, Virginia. Vice Admiral John Grossenbacher, who commands the U.S. Navy's Atlantic submarine fleet from Norfolk and lives on the same naval base, is on the line. For security reasons, Grossenbacher doesn't want to risk talking over the phone. He asks Gehman, who heads up the larger network of submarine operations throughout the Atlantic that are covered by NATO countries, if they can meet somewhere along the sidewalk that links their homes.

Once the pair meets face-to-face, Grossenbacher tells Gehman that an American sub has just transmitted a remarkable text report from the Barents. The commander of the USS *Memphis* believes he and his men witnessed the catastrophic death throes of an Oscar-class Russian nuclear submarine. Grossenbacher says the report helps clarify other data collected by signals intelligence, seismograph reports, and radio intercepts gathered the previous day. All of this is news to Gehman.

Grossenbacher adds that the *Memphis* captain made clear his vessel was not involved.

Gehman is a patrician fifty-eight-year-old navy man finishing up thirty-five years of distinguished service that has earned him the highest honors and a reputation for integrity, judgment, and policy smarts. He chews over the information for the briefest moment. He knows Russian military tradition all too well. He knows that the Russians are disinclined to blame themselves when things go wrong. He knows that they are still lathered up over the Kosovo bombing, and that the United States is still the main target of their ire. Finally, he says: "They're going to blame this on us."

Gehman knows that the checkered history of NATO activity in the Barents would support such Russian charges on the merits, even if this case didn't fit the pattern. And Gehman is willing to entertain his own doubts; his years of leadership have taught him to "never believe the first report" when it comes to incidents at sea. And there's another thing: Unlike so many of his American peers, Admiral Harold W. Gehman Jr. doesn't automatically trust the claims of U.S. sub captains just because they're in his own navy.

Concerned that U.S. leaders might too hastily dismiss Russian collision charges out of hand, Admiral Gehman immediately contacts army general Hugh Shelton, chairman of the Joint Chiefs of Staff. "Listen, Hugh," says Gehman. "This is gonna be blamed on us, and we're going to have to prove a negative." Gehman advises Shelton to proceed cautiously, until Gehman can further verify the U.S. sub commander's precise position relative to the Russian sub. He also needs to hear from the other U.S. sub in the area, the *Toledo*. Gehman wants to protect defense chief Cohen from making hasty public remarks: "Tell the defense secretary not to go too far out on that limb before I get back to you." Gehman says his process will "move quickly," but not so quickly as to compromise the U.S. subs' positions by making them beam signals from the exercise area. Shelton quickly agrees.

Soon after hanging up, Gehman's mind goes to work crafting the questions he wants posed to the commanders of the *Memphis* and the *Toledo* when they next surface for communications sessions.

17

DISHEARTENING SIGNS
SOUTHERN BARENTS SEA
SUNDAY, AUGUST 13

BLAST PLUS TWENTY-SIX HOURS

The *Altay* tug slowly combs the apparent wreck site, scooping up a disheartening mix of flotsam. Odd packages, bottles, bits of garbage, none of it truly proving a disaster.

At 1327 hours, while finding a place to anchor, the *Rudnitsky* reports the sighting of an oil slick. Russian pilots in Il-38s say the oil slick is almost a thousand feet long, and also say they've spotted a rope, a three-foot-diameter piece of turquoise-colored material, a larger piece of plastic-looking material, and an oblong red object nearly twelve feet long. They drop two buoys from their aircraft to mark the coordinates, thirty-five nautical miles southwest of the wreck site.

Shortly after 1400, Admiral Popov's helicopter deposits him on the *Peter the Great* as he quickly assumes on-site command over the rescue operations. Within the hour he is informed that the *Rudnitsky*, too, has detected underwater tapping, and has marked its relative bearing. The reports are confirmed by sonar men on the *Peter the Great* and the *Admiral Kharlamov*.

Optimists still believe the knocks are human in origin. They believe an untold number of trapped submariners are sending out signals to indicate their position, and also using their designated code tables to signal a rising water level within the stricken supersub. In the coming days, this growing conviction will circulate around the world.

The *Admiral Kharlamov* reports a steady tapping of twenty consecutive rhythmic beats on a bearing of 129 degrees at 1557. Nearby, the rescue crew aboard the *Mikhail Rudnitsky* is still wrestling with its AS-34 submersible, still unable to get it into the water. Wind gusts up to thirty knots play havoc with winching efforts, as the rescue crew struggles to keep the submersible from striking the mother ship.

At 1614, the *Rudnitsky* finally deploys its AS-34. Within six minutes, it detects an automatic signaling response from the "anomaly" that the AS-15 has already quietly confirmed is the *Kursk*. The formal detection constitutes "technical contact" for the Northern Fleet's rescue crew. The submersible pilots, Alexander Maisak and Sergey Pertsev, gauge the target at a distance of 1.3 nautical miles. Their progress will be agonizingly slow: at an underwater speed of two knots and pressing against an opposing underwater current—the AS-34 will require over ninety more minutes to close with the target.

Shortly after 1800, the AS-34's Maisak reports a blip on his sonar screen. He maneuvers closer over the next fifteen minutes, and finally sees the motionless twin screws of an Oscar-class submarine, which can only be the *Kursk*. He spots the large bright seating ring of the ninth compartment's escape hatch, his primary landing site. The shiny-smooth ring should allow him to attach and mate with the *Kursk* by forming a pressure seal. He maneuvers AS-34 until it briefly touches against the giant sub's rubber coating. At approximately 1820, the Northern Fleet has established physical contact, of sorts, with its billion-dollar submarine.

It has been nearly thirty-one hours since the mysterious explosions from the previous morning.

The AS-34's sensors detect no internal activity. The rescue experts hold on to the idea that any trapped submariners are now confident that rescue is at hand, and are therefore conserving their strength.

Sensing their own vessel's progress, the AS-34's Maisak and Pertsev begin maneuvering again. But the current is working against them, slowly sweeping them aft. Suddenly their tiny vessel strikes the giant submarine's rudder at a speed just under three knots. Worried about their sub-mersible's watertight integrity, they quickly blow ballast, bobbing to the surface at 1832.

The rescue team has also deployed the AS-32, but that submersible fails even to spot the *Kursk* despite repeated attempts that will last until well past midnight, when its battery power is spent.

Frustrated and fatigued, the rescuers talk of bringing to the scene a third submersible, the more robust *Bester*, currently on shore for repair. Fleet rescue chief Teslenko soon determines that it can be quickly made ready, though it lacks a viable mother ship.

At 1955, with another wave of low pressure moving in from the North and with the reported aerial sighting of a new oil slick, Popov orders search aircraft to return to base. He radios word to Moscow that he is 99 percent sure that the object on the seabed is the *Kursk*.

With the rescue process stalled, fleet authorities move the *Rudnitsky* closer to the site, where she drops anchor again by 2048. The commander of the *Altay* salvage tug orders his men to prepare at least eighty rescue kits.

The AS-32 is deployed again just after sunset, and her commander, Captain Pavel Karaputa, reports renewed SOS tapping. But some of the rescue officials now suspect this could be wishful thinking—especially the select few who are aware of the larger damage already evident from the AS-15 intelligence sub's earlier images. They now believe these sounds are coming from metal chains slapping the sides of the gathered rescue vessels as they rock in the blustery wind. Still, some acknowledge, they can't rule out the possibility of survivors aboard the *Kursk*.

18

WESTERN PARALYSIS

WASHINGTON, D.C.

SUNDAY, AUGUST 13, 1100 EDT (1900, MOSCOW TIME)

BLAST PLUS ONE DAY, SIX HOURS, THIRTY MINUTES

After a restless night with continuing silence from Moscow, Mark Medish prepares for the planned Sunday telephone meeting. This time, Strobe Talbott joins in on the four-way talk along with Frank Miller and Debra Cagan. As a light morning rain falls on Washington, the group focuses on Cagan's lingering question of whether the Russian military brass may be misleading the Kremlin about the Barents problem; the two parties can be surprisingly coy with each other. How much does Putin really know? The submarine has been down for nearly thirty-two hours, and the Russian officials have yet to tell their own people. Putin still hasn't said a word, but maybe he's operating in Soviet-era mode, when the Kremlin never announced submarine accidents. Meanwhile, continuing U.S. surveillance shows little progress on the rescue efforts, and the Northern Fleet's dearth of equipment and training have been well known for years.

All of yesterday's questions still apply: What should the United States do? Should it act on humanitarian impulse, or politely wait for a request? If it waits, shouldn't rescue assets be put on standby immediately? But then how would it look if the Russians *did* ask, only to find American rescue assets suspiciously suited up and ready to go? *Meddling spies-cum-saviors?!*

The dilemma is a poignant one for the Clinton administration, which considers U.S.–Russia relations a foreign-policy centerpiece. The inner circle wants to distinguish itself from the previous Republican regime by more actively aiding the former adversary's path to democracy, but all agree that Russia's military culture remains hard-wired to Soviet-era thinking; its leadership can barely contain a seething resentment for the rising tide of capitulations to Western interests. In such a climate, even the most earnest gestures might be viewed with deep suspicion, and the Clinton administration's even-keeled relationship with the Russian president doesn't seem to help much; the Clinton team recently witnessed a prime display of the Russian military's habit of making up its own foreign policy—independently of the Kremlin.

The dramatic display unfolded just the previous summer, when Russian army troops joined an international peacekeeping force in Kosovo, at NATO's invitation. Yeltsin's Kremlin welcomed the role, but top Russian general Anatoly Kvashnin and his senior confederates chafed at the notion that their presence would serve as mere diplomatic gingerbread; Kvashnin and his comrades thought it made Russia look inappropriately supportive of NATO's actions. The moment seemed right for a show of Russian displeasure.

Just as the NATO brass in Kosovo began debating which forces should take the airport in Pristina, Kvashnin ordered two hundred Russian Army paratroopers to race ahead and seize the airfield—much to the surprise of everyone, including key senior officials in Yeltsin's government. Russian foreign minister Igor Ivanov instantly branded the stunt an "unfortunate mistake" ordered by a rogue general. Even Russian defense minister Marshal Igor Sergeyev said he'd been kept out of the loop. Yeltsin later claimed in his memoirs that he had secretly authorized the Pristina surprise—a statement many saw as a cynical face-saving ploy.

Russia's new president appears closer to his military establishment, but conflicts loom. Putin has signaled his preference for the Russian military eventually to answer to civilian authority, which means that the next defense minister might not be a military man at all. With ambitious generals like Kvashnin eyeing the post—and with most of Russia's military establishment skeptical of civilian management altogether—this is not a confidence builder.

With Clinton, Berger, and Albright away from Washington, Talbott assumes the senior chair in Sunday's strategy session, the top man among the foreign-policy team's "deputy dogs" of August. Talbott is one of the West's most seasoned Russophiles, with long stints as a Russian correspondent for *Time* magazine and six policy-smart books on U.S.-Soviet relations. When Clinton became president, his friend Talbott seemed a natural choice for the foreign-policy team. He was quickly named deputy secretary of state, with a heavy focus on Russian affairs.

Talbott had distinguished himself as an advocate for warming relations, and once sharply criticized Ronald Reagan's portrayal of the Soviet Union as the "evil empire." Though Talbott believed Reagan's characterization may have been correct on the merits, he considered the former president's grand declarations of the pithy catchphrase harmful. Such criticisms by Talbott later won him derision from Senator Jesse Helms's Senate Foreign Relations Committee, the conservative members of which grumbled colorfully as Talbott's appointment won confirmation. Talbott's critics broadly viewed him as a Russia dupe.

Cagan is more cynical about the U.S.-Russia relationship. She believes that Russia has never been friendly toward the United States, and that the Americans should feel no great need to go out of their way to help them. And Cagan doesn't come by this view casually—in her long diplomatic career, she has built a reputation for quietly forging cooperative relationships with the Russians in areas like space exploration and nuclear threat reduction.

Cagan feels a growing sense of doom over reports of a slow-moving Russian rescue initiative. It seems obvious to her that men have already lost their lives. But she also thinks that there are clear political considerations to be observed. If the United States plans to respond, Cagan favors a by-the-book approach—formal, diplomatic, strictly business. And the initiative *must* come from the Russian side.

The Pentagon's Frank Miller generally agrees with Cagan. More than others in the discussion, he's mindful of what this submarine's true purpose really is. Miller is a career navy man with deep expertise in submarines, and he's acutely aware that the *Kursk* was designed to blow American navy men to kingdom come. Hell, it was *actively practicing* for just such an event. Of course, Miller feels the natural bond that all submariners share across ideological boundaries, but he'd still feel better letting the Russians make the first move.

As for Medish, he remains philosophically closer to Berger and Talbott, and wants to assist in reaching out to the Russians. But he also can plainly see that Ivanov's continuing refusal to come to the phone is a bad sign. Medish says he feels like U.S. hands are tied. With Talbott's assent, the Sunday brain trust settles on the media plan just in case questions come. They also agree to advise Berger and Clinton not to initiate any announcements on the Russian crisis.

For the second day, the Pentagon opts not to put its sub-rescue assets on standby. Nor do either of the other informed NATO countries. For their own reasons, each of four key countries aware of the *Kursk* crisis — Russia, the United States, the United Kingdom, and Norway — maintain a Cold War silence.

Meanwhile, the entire U.S. embassy in Moscow is still kept in the dark.

As the Sunday evening darkness descends over Russia, a state-owned television network broadcasts the prerecorded footage of Admiral Popov proclaiming the success of the Barents exercise. But Vidyayevo is now coursing with frightening rumors, its residents increasingly agitated and bewildered. Popov's TV broadcast only makes them more confused. What is Popov saying? Does this mean everything is okay now?

A distraught Olga Lubushkina calls her parents, who live in the Northern Fleet headquarters town of Severomorsk. They tell her they've heard nothing, and try to reassure her that everything will turn out all right. She tries hard to sleep.

19

LYING TO THE PEOPLE

MOSCOW

MONDAY, AUGUST 14, 0930 MOSCOW TIME

BLAST PLUS ONE DAY, TWENTY-TWO HOURS

On state-controlled radio, a Russian Navy spokesman gently informs his countrymen that a submarine involved in the Barents Sea exercises has suffered a technical malfunction just the day before, Sunday, and that her captain has descended to the seabed to assess the situation. The spokesman, Captain First Rank Igor Dygalo, tells the Russian people that rescue vessels have established contact with the crew and are supplying air. He says no casualties have been reported.

The broadcast awakens Moscow's increasingly bold independent media outlets, conditioned since the fall of communism to question the government's version of events at every turn.

At the U.S. embassy, an assistant to naval attaché Captain Bob Brannon interrupts a morning meeting to deliver the news alert. In minutes, Brannon is working the phones to learn what he can from his counterparts at the Russian Ministry of Defense.

In the United Kingdom, British navy commodore David Russell arrives in the office of Royal Navy headquarters at 0745 London time, as an officer from the overnight watch rings his line. "We're following some unusual activity in the Barents," says the officer. "It looks like a possible submarine rescue." He tells Russell it could be an exercise, but might also be the real thing. There is nothing in the statement to indicate to

Russell that British intelligence has been following the unusual activity for the better part of two days.

As head of the United Kingdom's submarine-rescue service, Russell gets an adrenaline jolt. He asks the watch stander to monitor the situation closely, and notes that it's still before 1100 in Moscow.

In Vidyayevo, Khalima Aryapova ventures from her apartment in midmorning, still unaware of the rumors. She stops by to see Olga Lubushkina in the passports office. "Have you heard?" Olga asks. "They say the *Kursk* is lying on the seabed." Khalima thinks Olga is joking. Olga tells her she's not, then quickly adds that officials have assured everyone that it's just a technical problem.

A brief television update in late morning is only slightly more alarming. Khalima tries to assure herself that her husband's magnificent submarine can certainly manage its way through technical problems.

Watching the news from his brother Dima's Vidyayevo apartment, twenty-two-year-old Sasha Kolesnikov is convinced that something is seriously wrong. Though he's just beginning in the submarine service, even amateurs know that a nuclear submarine never lies on the seabed because of "technical malfunctions." *Why are these officials saying such nonsense?*

In Estonia, Dima Kolesnikov's parents are planning another spa day when Irina Kolesnikova answers the phone at her family's holiday cottage. It's her brother on his cell phone. "Something has happened to the *Kursk*," he blurts. "Turn on the TV." The TV reports strike Dima's parents as mild, but when they tune in to the U.S.-funded Radio Liberty, the information in the latest reports takes an ominous turn. The *Kursk* is at the bottom, nose down, filling with water. Momentarily panicked, Irina tries to place her faith in the rescue effort. Retired submariner Roman knows the situation is deadly serious, but tries to reassure Irina just the same as they make plans to catch the first bus out of Estonia at 0600 on Tuesday.

In the farming village of Boksitogorsk near St. Petersburg, Olga Kolesnikova is puzzling over why the birthday telegram she sent to her Mitya has been returned with a note saying it was "unreceived." It makes no sense and it makes her worry. Later, she hears a grim statement from television that the *Kursk* is down for unknown reasons. She makes immediate plans to depart for Vidyayevo.

In the United States and around the world, Russia's pre-noon radio flash gets picked up by CNN, which runs the first global reports at 0335 EDT, while the American political establishment sleeps.

The cluster of new broadcasts serves as an update for U.K. sub-rescue chief Russell, who pauses over the Russian report's detail that all of the trapped submariners are okay. Russell's skepticism regarding Russia's military culture tells him otherwise. As he would later put it, "straight talk is not prevalent" in official Russia.

Russell's mind races. Elements of his remarkable *LR5* submersible and its "kit" are now divided between the British mainland and France. Its crew is booked for flights to the Mediterranean exercise off Turkey. At 0810 U.K. time, Russell decides instantly to order the *LR5* and its components to hold up and stand by. By 0850, Russell calls Admiral Sir Nigel Essenhigh, the Royal Navy's commander in chief. "We are ready to offer the Russians our services," says Russell. "We'll have our report ready by 1000."

On his small farm in Devon, Royal Navy captain Geoffrey McCready—the United Kingdom's current naval attaché to Moscow—is talking with a friend out in a field when his wife brings him the cordless telephone. "It's Beach," she says, using the nickname for McCready's assistant at Moscow's British embassy. McCready already has plans to catch a flight from Heathrow Tuesday morning back to Moscow, ending his summer leave for an easygoing mid-August workweek. But the Barents alert from Lieutenant Commander Patrick "Beach" Seakins puts him into much higher gear. Seakins reports that the United Kingdom has a diplomatic note in the pipeline to offer help. McCready tells Seakins he'll be in Moscow tomorrow to help finesse the offer with his Russian counterparts.

Royal Navy captain Simon Lister—who has been tapped to replace McCready as naval attaché in the coming month—is also home in England on leave. He's been trying to build a new wall on an old house to keep the garden at bay. "Have you heard the news?" his caller says, then provides details. The caller suggests that Lister may want to get in the loop in advance of assuming his Moscow post. Lister calls the Royal Navy headquarters to get the latest. After the briefing, Lister signs on to any efforts at assistance. "Consider me available," he says.

In Norway, the scientific director of the NORSAR (Norwegian Seismic Array) seismology center in Oslo, Frode Ringdal, has been puzzling all morning over some remarkably strong tracings recorded during his weekend absence. These occurred before noon on Saturday. Ringdal's station is part of a global network established to monitor underground nuclear tests, and his system can even pinpoint the event's location. But the Saturday tracing doesn't look like a nuclear test, and the Barents is geologically much too stable for this level of earthquake activity. When Ringdal hears the reports out of Russia about a submarine accident, he has his answer. Ringdal alerts officials at his Defense Ministry that his tracings show a violent explosion occurred in the Barents before noon on *Saturday*—a day *before* the date given by Russian military officials.

Alarmed, Norway's Defense Ministry urges Admiral Einar Skorgen to use his hotline to Admiral Popov. Skorgen picks up the red phone. One of Popov's senior aides answers and relays word to the Northern Fleet commander aboard the *Peter the Great*. The answer comes back in minutes: *Thanks, but no thanks; we've got the situation under control.*

But Skorgen knows the Northern Fleet doesn't even have deep-sea divers. He suspects Moscow is doing the talking, not his friend Vyacheslav. Skorgen calls Oslo to say he is alerting Norway's naval rescue services, just in case. Meanwhile, Skorgen wants to find out what's up in the Barents with his own surveillance assets. From his northern Norway headquarters in Bodo, the Norwegian admiral orders his P-3 Orion patrol planes into the air to update him on Northern Fleet activity.

Now that the Russians have gone public, Western governments feel freer to offer help.

By 1100 London time—1400 Moscow time—U.K. Ministry of Defence duty minister John Spellar faxes a formal rescue offer to Russian defense minister Marshall Igor Sergeyev.

"I was very concerned to hear about one of your submarines currently experiencing difficulty in the Barents Sea," Spellar's fax begins. "I am sure that your own Navy is extremely capable of resolving the incident and rescuing all those involved," he continues. "I would however like to offer assistance in the form [of] the use of our rescue vehicle *LR5* and the ROV [remotely operated vehicle] '*Scorpio*' and advice and assistance on the handling of casualties. The UK submarine rescue system is about to be transported to an exercise in the eastern Mediterranean. It would be no trouble at all to divert the equipment to assist your submarine in the Barents Sea and we would be happy to do this should you so wish. If we can be of any assistance, my Defence Attache in Moscow stands ready to relay any messages back to London."

Commodore Russell and his men are keyed up, expecting an imminent call to action. But the U.K. offer is met with a bewildering silence.

NATO similarly offers its services as a bloc, a proposal initiated from its submarine division commander based in Norfolk, Virginia, Admiral Gehman, who is "double-hatted" to serve as NATO's Supreme Allied Commander Atlantic. The NATO offer comes simultaneously with the U.K. offer, but it, too, is met with silence.

Out on the Barents Sea, the Northern Fleet's *AS-34* submersible suffers the effects of its mother ship's vulnerability to a rough sea state. While suspended by two cranes between deployments, the *AS-34* is violently rocked back and forth, repeatedly striking structures aboard the *Mikhail Rudnitsky*. The blows eventually destroy the submersible's navigational equipment. The damage will later be valued at 1.6 million rubles, or $58,000.

BLAST PLUS TWO DAYS, SIX HOURS

Within hours of the U.K. and NATO offers, U.S. National Security Advisor Sandy Berger succeeds at reaching Sergey Ivanov in Sochi. Berger tells Ivanov the U.S. sub-rescue service is at his disposal. If Russia just says the word, Berger tells him, U.S. assets could arrive on site within twenty-four to forty-eight hours. Though the figure is unrealistic because

U.S. assets had not been alerted over the weekend, the point is moot; Ivanov's answer is about the same as the silence that greeted the offers from Norway, the United Kingdom, and NATO: *Thanks, but our military men assure us they can handle it on their own.*

Most of the countries that maintain relations with Russia know that its leaders nearly always prefer to work with them one by one, and not as groups. Separately, offers from other countries arrive and are similarly deflected—from France, from Germany, from the Netherlands, from Italy, from Sweden, from Israel, from Canada, from Japan.

Amid the rising tide of offers, Russian Navy commander in chief Admiral Vladimir Kuroyedov makes an evening TV announcement implying a foreign cause to the incident, and he doesn't sugarcoat the prospects. "There are reasons to believe there has been a big and serious collision," he intones gravely.

On learning of Kuroyedov's unsubtle allegation, U.S. officials instantly detect the very accusation they'd expected. The Pentagon's Frank Miller can barely conceal his fury. "Let's not even dignify this with a response," he advises in an afternoon White House meeting. The sentiment is echoed in other quarters of Clinton's administration. "We are ripshit!" says the normally diplomatic Strobe Talbott, invoking a bit of New England vernacular.

At the NSC, Medish reminds his colleagues of a Soviet-era maxim: "Russians have three main reasons for lying. One, because they have to. Two, because it's convenient. And three, just to stay in practice."

President Clinton appears unfazed by the Russian stunt, but Berger has a more pragmatic reaction. He knows that American subs are in the Barents. He knows U.S. subs have collided with Russian subs—in the Barents. Though Frank Miller and others assure him that none were involved in this case, Berger wants to hear it from the sub operators themselves.

Submarines avoid sending signals from surveillance sites unless they believe U.S. security faces imminent danger, but they do receive messages at pre-arranged intervals—without transmitting responses that could risk detection. Miller and other sub-smart senior officials strongly urge Berger not to solicit premature reports from the *Memphis* or the *Toledo* until they have fully cleared the area. But Berger declares this an exceptional circumstance. Over navy objections, Berger orders the submarines to transmit radio reports on their status ASAP.

One indignant Pentagon official calls it "Berger's panic attack," unaware that Admiral Gehman had already demanded the exact same information from both the *Memphis* and the *Toledo*.

20
THE GLOBAL WHIPSAW
KOLA PENINSULA
TUESDAY, AUGUST 15

BLAST PLUS THREE DAYS

With the world's media suddenly flocking to a remote Kola Peninsula long conditioned to Soviet-style secrecy, Russian officialdom is caught unprepared. Even the domestic journalists have lately picked up the disturbing foreign reporters' habit of posing impolite questions, forcing officials to improvise. The reporters also find no shortage of victims' families willing to talk, giving unprecedented vent to a deeply agitated citizenry.

Out on the Barents, the would-be rescuers begin fighting thirty-knot winds and bouts of rain that will last through the night. No rescue subs are deployed, but Moscow's AS-15 intelligence submersible makes a four-hour second survey of the *Kursk*'s wreckage. Its operators report that the *Kursk* is flat against the seabed, and that it has a mild starboard list of five to ten degrees. They can see pipes jutting from the giant hole in the upper part of the forward hull, along with occasional emerging bubbles. They report air bottles and ballast tanks broken and scattered on the seabed. Such details are still withheld from reporters.

The reporters are also barred from the "closed" garrison at Vidyayevo, and compensate by interviewing its residents in Murmansk, where many are arriving by train. Inside Vidyayevo itself, the residents are broadly numbed in the hellish limbo between shock and disbelief. Irina Lyachina wants to hide from the parade of concerned neighbors who gather at her apartment door, but she continues to maintain a brave front in the presence of witnesses. She is comforted by the return of her young son, Gleb, and marvels at the way her daughter, Dasha, has insulated herself in front of the television, where she is videotaping the rising tide of reports. "When Papa is back," Dasha says sweetly, "he will see all of it."

To Khalima Aryapova, the garrison town feels unreal. She walks through the streets mechanically—dazed, denying, detached. She receives a telegram from one of Rashid's Uzbekistan siblings: "Urgently report to me what happened. How is my older brother?" Olga Lubushkina tries to maintain telephone contact with Sergey's parents as well as her own, veering painfully between hope and despair, morosely clinging to TV and radio reports, grasping at every trace of optimism.

The media pick up word of the rejected stream of foreign rescue offers, even as the world tracks the disheartening reports of the Northern Fleet's faltering efforts. The first reports of rebuffed bids come from Radio Liberty and the BBC, then more shrilly from the private Russian station NTV—the one owned by anti-Putin oligarch Vladimir Gusinsky—and the independent radio station Ekho Moskvy.

Soon even the state-owned media operations are infected with the same indignation, many braying over their president's invisibility and the inexplicably discarded offers of help. *Kursk* relatives gain enough confidence to question the tragedy's handling. Even everyday Russians express their disgust, while their country's liberal social critics hold forth on the trenchant Soviet impulse to value machinery over men, pride over men, secrets over men.

These domestic critics go beyond the oft-repeated accounts of historical repressions and purges of millions of their fellow citizens. They cite lesser-known cases that evoke a deeply rooted national character trait for treating Russian citizens as disposable commodities. They tell stories of army officers using young conscripts as human mine detectors, ordering them into suspect zones where their ultimate sacrifices will make the fields safe for other slightly less expendable men. They lecture on the persistent failure of the non-Russian thinkers to grasp the deeper nuances of how the popular term "apparatchik" describes Soviet people as "apparatus," inanimate objects harnessed to the will of the state. They remind outsiders how the few remarkable houses of worship that survived communism's official atheism—the ones spared by Stalin's church-wrecking crews—are only now serving higher purposes as more than architectural curiosities. They joke about how Russian pilgrims still worship at the Red Square "altar" of Lenin's tomb—where his preserved corpse lies displayed behind glass—as if he were a saint, and of how Stalin's profound brutalities are casually brushed off by many older Russians as the occupational hazard of keeping a once-restless population under control; many of the nation's elders stubbornly revere him.

In their more philosophical moments, Russia's social brooders even wonder whether the widespread genetic weeding out of their more passionate forebears has congenitally condemned latter-day Russians to abject compliance with the dictates of all authority.

But the images of the more emotive Northern Fleet families belie such dark proclamations. The open wailing of submariners' wives and mothers and children are beamed around the world in an instant, showing a Russian face rarely witnessed by the outside world. The most expressive faces are those of wives and mothers and children—never the submariners' fathers, who appear stoically resigned. The unfolding human tragedy resounds, as camera crews pour into the Kola Peninsula. A race to rescue the Russian submariners soon unfolds, quickly dominating the late summer's global conversation. Emerging reports of desperate tapping from the icy depths touch a universal nerve.

It is as if the aggregate character of the new Russia is visible to the world for the first time—the people on one side, the government on another—each side perplexed at the other's view of what matters most when human lives are on the line.

The dramatic face-off provokes a virtual international referendum regarding the enormous nation's course, as it lurches violently between democratic yearnings and the traditional Soviet desire for social control.

And still, the new Russian president remains invisible. Who is Putin? Which way to the New Russia?

Cloistered in his vacation dacha, Putin invisibly summons his deputy prime minister, Ilya Klebanov, to Sochi, where he delegates the crisis to him.

Also beyond public gaze, aging senior members of Russia's Ministry of Defense—still obsessed with delusions of fighting the Cold War—are winning the debate on the foreign assistance question. They would sooner see trapped submariners die than let loathsome foreigners defile their national pride with an internal inspection. If only their Soviet-era counterparts up north would cooperate and keep the unseemly scream-ing of distraught family members away from the TV cameras.

But the families and TV cameras and world opinion conspire against the hard-liners, forcing some to break ranks with their xenophobic com-rades. Just two hours after Russia formally notifies NATO of its rebuff on Tuesday at noon, Brussels time, comes the first sign of possible thawing: Russia politely reiterates its official *nyet*, but wants an exploratory chat. NATO instantly agrees. The Russians tap two military men, both army colonels, from their embassy in Brussels. Five hours later they are linked in a teleconference with a British vice admiral, along with U.K. sub-rescue chief Commodore David Russell. The linkup gives Russell a cau-tious optimism.

Russell and his team try quizzing the two Russian officers about the actual conditions of the *Kursk* and her crew. The U.K. rescue chief wants hard-to-get technical info like the *Kursk*'s hatch characteristics, her angle on the seabed, the water current, visibility, the estimated internal pressure at depth. But the army colonels are poorly informed on details. Dismayed, Russell expresses his sympathy for the crew, then quickly outlines for the Russian intermediaries his ongoing preparations with the United King-dom's *LR5* and her team.

The Russian colonels sense Russell's frustration, but they are author-ized to talk only about possibilities. Higher authorities must give their permission. *Thanks*, say the Russians. *We'll get back to you.*

Troubled and mystifyied, Russell continues his full-court press after the conversation's conclusion. This is no time to stand on ceremony.

Despite the opening of talks, Moscow refuses to authorize any foreign assistance. Russell and the United Kingdom must gamble that Moscow's position will change, as they continue their unsanctioned moves.

As reports of the ongoing failure of Russian submersibles to attach to the *Kursk* circulate ever more intensely around the world—one state TV journalist has even been cleared to broadcast live updates from the *Peter the Great*—the United States suspects Russia may be ready to yield. Naval attaché Captain Brannon presides over a draft offer from the American embassy in Moscow, quickly sending it to the Pentagon. Just before 1100 Eastern Daylight Time—1900 Moscow time—U.S. defense secretary William Cohen's office faxes the signed version back to the U.S. embassy, addressed to Russian defense minister Sergeyev.

Dear Marshal Sergeyev,

I must extend my deepest thoughts of concern to you and your valued crew members aboard the *Kursk*. I know I speak for the entire U.S. Department of Defense in expressing our sincerest hopes for the best possible outcome. In the meantime, our thoughts are with you and the crew's families; we wish them strength during this most troubling time.

My department stands ready to provide any assistance you may need: please do not hesitate to ask.

Sincerely, [signed] Bill Cohen

Brannon tucks the folded sheet into a standard diplomatic envelope and leaps into a Moscow embassy staff car headed for the Ministry of Defense. Once there, he can see instantly that the young duty officer is taken aback at the sudden presence of an American naval captain in full uniform, especially amid the growing Russian assertions that the *Kursk* collided with a "foreign submarine."

To Brannon's surprise, the Russian lieutenant rebuffs his delivery. Brannon protests, using his best Russian to persuade the man to allow him to present the offer to Sergeyev's staff. The Russian officer refuses to budge, forcing Brannon to begin keeping a vigil in the foyer. And the U.S. captain isn't passive about it: Brannon pleads with the lieutenant to consider what really matters, that fellow Russian military men may be dying as they speak, that the United States can summon the latest rescue equipment quickly, and that the lieutenant's refusal could be blocking their only hope.

"There are one hundred eighteen lives at stake," says Brannon. "They're running out of air. Could you live with that for the rest of your life by refusing to let me through the door? I don't care if you like America or not; I'm the only country that can help you right now. Don't slam the door in my face."

Eventually, Brannon's impassioned pleas bring the young officer to the point of tears. Both men find the moment awkward, but the Russian lieutenant relents. Brannon is escorted into an area where members of Sergeyev's inner office staff are gathered, and the American navy captain at last places the formal offer in the hands of a ranking official of the Ministry of Defense.

BLAST PLUS THREE DAYS, TEN HOURS

As he departs, Brannon feels a brief sense of victory, but he has a vivid sense of the obstacles still ahead. He can read the signals; Sergeyev and his men probably have no intention of accepting the offer, but just wanted Brannon to go away. Unsettled, Brannon embarks on an energetic series of telephone calls with his Russian military counterparts that extends into the early-morning hours.

But during the course of Brannon's charm campaign, Washington complicates his job. The Pentagon insists on a hardball quid pro quo: The Russians must retract their specious collision allegations, they say, or U.S. rescue assets won't budge. Brannon heatedly objects that this is the wrong time to punish Russian suspicions—they have yet to specify their belief that it was an *American* submarine—but he is defeated by higher authority. The defense secretary is "pretty hot" about the allegations, a

Pentagon captain tells Brannon. Though hobbled by the rigid directive, Brannon places a call to the Russian Defense Ministry and dutifully conveys the offer's new conditions.

Sergeyev and his senior staff passionately debate the conditional American offer. The argument pits Old Russia against New Russia, and the American government's strident condition helps Old Russia's resurgent Cold Warriors to prevail. For the time being, the Cold Warriors also bring Putin's Kremlin with them.

But there is an odd concession: While maintaining the aloof posture with the United States, Minister Sergeyev dispatches Russian vice admiral Alexander Pobozhy to NATO headquarters in Belgium to advance the exploratory discussion. Pobozhy will not fly to Brussels until Thursday.

At the same time, the Northern Fleet finally declares that the *Kursk*'s first three compartments are flooded, piquing the torment of families whose men work in those compartments.

Beseiged Russian officials try to defend their actions. In one of many televised interviews with officials throughout the evening, Deputy Prime Minister Klebanov touts the unparalleled excellence of Russia's own rescue service. He argues that foreigners are not necessary.

But the nation's popular opinion presses the argument, probing about how much longer trapped submariners might hold out. A spokesman from Vice Admiral Motsak's office insists rescuers can still hear tapping. Navy commander in chief Kuroyedov boasts of the strength of Russian submarines, and claims the *Kursk*'s aft compartments will hold enough air to last until Friday, August 18.

In an evening press conference in Severomorsk, the *Kursk*'s designer lists the stricken ship's survival supplies. There is food, says Rubin Design Bureau chief designer Igor Baranov, and water supplies, and oxygen-regenerating equipment—enough to last another "five or possibly six days."

The series of official reassurances restores a thread of hope to desperate loved ones gathered in Vidyayevo, whose population swells, as far-flung family members migrate to the tiny town for collective support. Many of them must pay for their own transportation. Others receive travel funds from private donors, or from their regional governments. A significant number of families aren't even sure their men are aboard the *Kursk* at all: the Russian government has yet to provide an official crew list.

The appearance of such mounting indifference sharpens the Russian public's rebuke. In a midweek radio call-in poll on Ekho Moskvy radio, an overwhelming 85 percent of callers urge the Russian hierarchy to let the foreigners help.

Even as he is kept duly informed of the growing public pressure, Putin remains on the Black Sea coast, still officially invisible to his nation's people. Nevertheless, Russian television stations ORT and NTV show video footage of the athletic Russian president racing across the mild waters on a Jet Ski.

Some Russian pundits familiar with Putin's past can't understand his rejection of the latest Western rescue equipment. Despite Russian officials' loud proclamations that Western technology offers no advantage over homegrown know-how, Putin should know better. When he was a KGB agent in Dresden, the major's primary mission was to recruit East German students and businessmen who had good cover stories for traveling to the West and secretly transferring sensitive schematics and other information to help reduce his motherland's technological deficit. Similar activities demanded the time of his other colleagues in espionage, most of whom fretted over the persistent lag. To many throughout Russia and around the world, Putin seems surreally disconnected.

One world leader successfully reaches out to Putin at his dacha compound. Israeli prime minister Ehud Barak personally implores the Russian president to accept outside help, placing Israel's rescue assets at his disposal. Thanks, says Putin, who confides to the Israeli leader that he's been informed that the *Kursk* crew's rescue chances are now considered "extremely small." Putin tells Barak it is most likely "already too late" for the *Kursk*'s trapped seamen.

21
OPENING THE GATES
MOSCOW
WEDNESDAY, AUGUST 16

BLAST PLUS FOUR DAYS

Day four of the crisis brings no letup in international pressure. Russian Navy spokesman Igor Dygalo renews his defense of the rebuffs, saying that coordinating foreign help would require too much time, "and we cannot afford to waste it." He then resorts to a series of shocking deceptions, inexplicably claiming the *Kursk* is listing to port at sixty degrees, that visibility is unacceptable at just a few inches, and that a strong underwater current prevents mating by a rescue submersible. The implication is that the conditions would defeat *anybody*'s best technology.

Though none of these details is true, commentators in Russia and those throughout the world take them seriously. Even the hardened Western cynics find it hard to fathom why these kinds of details would be fabricated. TV broadcasts and newspaper artists craft their illustrations in accord with the Russian descriptions. Even the United Kingdom's Commodore Russell calculates his early strategy based on some of the falsehoods: though he strongly doubts the alleged current and visibility problems, the reported angle-on-the-seabed issue is genuinely worrisome—if it turns out to be true.

But zealous reporters soon begin chipping away at the early falsehoods, and Russian newspapers wax vitriolic. Popular daily *Komsomolskaya Pravda* publishes a "chronicle of tragedies and lies," prominently playing up the inconvenient reality that Western observers forced Russian officials to acknowledge the tragedy occurred twenty-four hours earlier than first announced. Centrist *Nezavisimaya Gazeta* bitterly opines that "the morally obsolete ideology of the Soviet era still dominates the mentality of the bosses." The reformist *Segodnya* mocks the anti-foreigners faction with a quote from an unnamed navy source: "Admirals believe that if even one Russian seaman is rescued from the Russian submarine with foreign aid, this will definitely end in political disaster."

Amid the storm, U.K. commodore Russell participates in an early-morning teleconference with Russian vice admiral Pobozhy, in which several of the Russian lies are dispelled. The visibility is fine, says Pobozhy. The currents are fine. The *Kursk* suffers only a modest list on the seabed. *At last*, thinks Russell, *a real breakthrough. The LR5 can handle this.*

Russell tells Pobozhy that the United Kingdom is ready to start loading the *LR5* for air transport to a port in either Norway or Murmansk, where it could link up with a suitable mother ship.

The Russian vice admiral is taken aback. "You made these preparations ahead of the politicians?" he asks.

"Yes," says Russell.

Next, says Russell, the *LR5* needs an aircraft big enough for an oversized load. Pobozhy pauses over logistics and costs, but Russell interrupts. "Let's just charter it anyway," he says, "and worry about the money problem later."

Pobozhy is in no immediate position to further aid the United Kingdom's efforts; he still carries no authority to sanction any foreign country's rescue efforts. Russell's bid remains a gamble.

In the southern Barents, one of the struggling submersibles' pilots describes the sight of air bubbles escaping the *Kursk*. Admiral Popov orders a temporary halt to all extraneous inter-vessel communications in an attempt to detect any sounds of human activity, but the radio silence is met only in kind from the stilled submarine on the seabed. No one has reported tapping from the *Kursk* since yesterday, a detail not yet publicized.

As maintenance men aboard the *Mikhail Rudnitsky* struggle to repair a submersible damaged during a wind-rocked launching effort, they send a telegram to the *Peter the Great*. "To repair AS-34," the telegram begins ominously, "we need: monkey wrenches, (5) socket wrench sets (5-24 mm), (2) sets of two manual drills (with bits of 2-16 mm), (10) sheets of consumable paronite [a rubberized asbestos fabric] (0.5-5 mm), (10) sheets of rubber (0.1 mm or thicker), a 100 kg PGV-2 (vertical hydraulic press), (2) sets of charging stations for the REYA radio set."

The list is an enumeration of standard repair materials normally carried by the *Mikhail Rudnitsky*. With living conditions so dire among Northern Fleet sailors, valuables not welded down disappear faster than naval supply depots can stock them.

BLAST PLUS FOUR DAYS, SIX HOURS

The United Kingdom's *LR5* lifts off in a giant Russian cargo plane from the British mainland at 1230 London time on Wednesday, bound for the northern Norwegian seaport of Trondheim. A suitable mother ship has been found in the commercial oil sector that can handle the submersible's complicated ocean-transport needs. Of course, Russell would have preferred a closer point of access from Russia's Kola Peninsula, but even without a Russian invitation, Russell and his team are striving to shave every precious minute.

In a separate move, Norwegian admiral Skorgen's men have commandeered a diving support vessel and assembled a dive team under the guidance of a multinational commercial oil operation, Stolt Offshore. The Norway and U.K. efforts will coordinate loosely with each other while under way, but are otherwise independent.

On the Black Sea past midday, President Putin pauses after entertaining a group of scholars from Russia's Academy of Science. Tanned and wearing a golf shirt, he indulges some questions from a small group of Kremlin pool reporters until one journalist abruptly changes the topic from the country's brain drain to the events in the Barents Sea. The situation is "beyond critical," says Putin calmly. "But all possible efforts to save the crew have been carried out."

The electronic media further detail Putin's work activities from Sochi, including the appointment of Russian ambassadors to Jamaica and Chile, along with a birthday call to a beloved Russian actress.

In the United States, President Clinton continues to find Putin's Barents strategy perplexing. Now ensconced in the Oval Office, Clinton hopes to apply some persuasion in an early-morning phone call.

Putin had requested a non-urgent telephone conversation the previous week, wanting to share thoughts with Clinton over his Kremlin meeting with Arafat. That call could wait, but other topics are building up, including the U.S.-Russia agenda for a planned U.N. summit meeting slated for early September in New York: The United States fervently hopes to dissuade Russia from aiding Iran's nuclear capabilities; Russia just as strongly wants to convince the United States not to proceed with a national missile defense shield. Clinton also plans to press an ongoing campaign to win the release of jailed U.S. businessman Edmund Pope, arrested in the spring after purchasing what he says he thought were unclassified design plans for Russia's shadowy super-fast Shkval torpedo. The NSC's Mark Medish is Clinton's point man on the Pope issue, and will also serve as the conversation's translator. Before the exchange is through, Clinton hopes to bring up the *Kursk* debacle.

Clinton and Medish have become accustomed to Putin's trademark calm, a trait Putin himself has acknowledged as both a liability and an asset. But Clinton and his foreign-policy team also have sensed for some time that Putin is giving the American president the lame-duck treatment, with the Russian leader delaying the bigger bilateral decisions until he learns in November who he'll really be dealing with. By the time the conversation arrives at the *Kursk* saga, Clinton proceeds cautiously; he and Medish still consider it an open question as to whether Putin's men in the Barents are informing the Russian president candidly about their own rescue capabilities. Still, Clinton beseeches Putin to open up to help in any case—if not from the United States, then from closer European countries.

Thanks, says Putin, adding that he's open to continuing the dialogue about such a prospect, but that his experts have assured him that they have everything they need.

Clinton hangs up the phone, trying to take some satisfaction in the idea that Putin has at least left the door open.

Within an hour, Putin dramatically reverses course on blocking the international rescue offers, ordering his military men to accept help "wherever it comes from."

Some in the Northern Fleet see the acquiescence to foreign rescuers as a humiliating defeat. Admiral Popov is among those who feel betrayed by the Moscow reversal. He reluctantly places the red-phone call to Norway's Admiral Skorgen in Bodo. To Skorgen's ear, the Russian admiral sounds exhausted. "Einar," says Popov, "we have had an accident, and I need your help." Skorgen instantly says that he's at his friend's disposal. "I mostly need divers who can go down to one hundred meters," says Popov, "to help connect with the rescue vehicle."

Other Russian officials simultaneously open up to David Russell's ongoing bid with the *LR5*, clearing him to fly straight to Northern Fleet headquarters in Severomorsk, from where he can immediately helicopter to the Barents scene. Once there, Russell hopes to assess the rescue obstacles while awaiting the U.K. and Norwegian rescue vessels. Even as he is airborne, Russell calculates his vessel's arrival time to the site. He hedges back and forth with unknown variables, since little reliable information has come from the Russians regarding diver-support vessels and viable ports. Though *LR5* is now committed to a mother ship off Norway's west coast—which means it's already too late to wonder about closer ports and runways on the Russian mainland—Russell's focus shifts to crafting a comfortable working chemistry with the Northern Fleet's search-and-rescue chief. He imagines helicoptering onto his Russian counterpart's own boat, working closely, side by side, through a translator.

But his thoughts are interrupted by the flight crew just before the aircraft sets down in the Norwegian town of Bodo for refueling. Russian

Defense Ministry officials have withdrawn the invitation. The British and Norwegians may continue their long pilgrimage from the Norwegian ports, but no foreign rescuers will be deploying from the Kola. There is no explanation. Russell receives this news poker-faced while on the aircraft, but after debarking at Bodo and setting up a makeshift headquarters operation with satellite phones in a motel room, he and his teammates vent over this seemingly homicidal xenophobia. "For God's sake," says Russell, "we're not coming in B-52s. We're here to help."

Even well past one hundred hours, none of Russia's senior authorities publicly voice flagging hope, though nerves continue to fray. In an emotional evening news conference in Moscow, Russian Navy spokesman Igor Dygalo confirms growing rumors that there has been no reported knocking from the *Kursk* for the past day, but quickly insists that this does not mean that the submariners are dead. One interviewer then hits a nerve by asking Dygalo how much longer the oxygen can hold out. Losing his composure, Dygalo holds up a religious icon and, in a shaky voice, urges people to pray.

In a separate proclamation, the *Kursk*'s chief designer Igor Baranov suggests the submariners could last "another two days." From the United Kingdom, Paul Beaver, a naval affairs expert for *Jane's Defence Weekly*, suggests that well-equipped deep-sea divers can descend onto the wreck site using parachutes. And in a Pentagon press conference at midday in Washington, D.C., Pentagon spokesman Rear Admiral Craig Quigley confirms that U.S. assets remain unrequested by the Russians, but that its submersibles are "always ready." He details how the well-equipped *Avalon* and *Mystic* mini-subs are on standby in San Diego, each capable of diving down to two thousand feet to bring back twenty-four sailors at a time. He says a C5A Galaxy aircraft based at nearby North Island can fly the U.S. mini-subs to Russia, and guesses they could be on site within two days.

22
GOING INTERNATIONAL
RUSSIA
THURSDAY, AUGUST 17

BLAST PLUS FIVE DAYS

By Thursday morning, the *Kursk* has been stranded on the Barents seabed for five days, untouched by any rescue divers, its interior temperature steadily dropping, the condition of its silent occupants unknown.

Public information is still sparse, even for the submariners' loved ones. "We've been calling the hotline every day," Ludmila Milyutina tells one reporter on an overnight train to Murmansk. "They are telling us they have no information. They say 'Go to Murmansk and ask journalists.'"

Angling to end the mystery of the *Kursk*'s official occupants, an editor at the Murmansk bureau of Russia's biggest daily newspaper, *Komsomolskaya Pravda*, accepts a furtive offer from a high-ranking naval officer who will provide the official crew list for 18,000 rubles, about $650. The exchange occurs at a bus stop outside the Northern Fleet headquarters in Severomorsk.

In Brussels, Belgium, Russian vice admiral Pobozhy participates in a four-hour afternoon videoconference from NATO headquarters. In the group exchange, U.S. admiral Gehman agrees to contribute his best sub-rescue experts from Norfolk and the Pentagon. NATO officials in the United Kingdom and the British embassy in Moscow learn what they can. Much of the key information is then funneled into David Russell's makeshift rescue headquarters in a Norwegian motel room. His team's

LR5 is already loaded onto its mother ship on the nearby central coast, preparing for a nine-hundred-mile race to the Barents.

Pobozhy and his men provide some faxable technical drawings, but they are unable to persuade their superiors in Moscow to clear Russell's aircraft to land on Russian soil.

In the annals of Russia-NATO relations, Pobozhy's visit is unusual. Russia's power elite has demonstrated clear reluctance to engage in multilateral exchanges like this, always preferring bilateral talks with individual countries. Still, the Ministry of Defense reserves its deepest dislike for NATO's American element, considering the broader alliance the lesser of two evils. And within NATO, better to accept help from the Brits and Norwegians, the Norwegians the least odious of them all.

After the Brussels session, the Russian vice admiral walks a gauntlet of international media, looking decidedly uneasy. In every sense, Pobozhy's in an awkward spot: Russia still nurses an enduring bitterness toward NATO for a litany of offenses—from the Cold War to the Kosovo bombing, from continued spying activities against Russia to openly "aggressive" plans for the alliance's expansion to countries on Russia's western borders—and now to the more chillingly active suspicions that a NATO sub may have hit the *Kursk.* It is a perfectly unpleasant moment to serve as Russia's supplicant, especially while standing at the center of NATO's universe, and even more so since many see the entire gesture as mere window dressing aimed at stanching popular criticism at home and abroad.

Which, in many respects, it is. When the Russian Ministry of Defense selected Pobozhy, they chose one of the men with whom most of the Western diplomatic community were quite familiar. Pobozhy had become a regular favorite for whenever Moscow wanted to send a "duty admiral"—someone inoffensive and good at small talk—to ceremonial functions. Diplomats at the American embassy had even taken to fondly calling him "Admiral Priomnik," which translates as "Admiral *Reception*-nik."

In Brussels, Pobozhy strikes his NATO hosts as little better than a traveling duty admiral. Many are left wondering if Pobozhy and his team have actually come in the hopes of gathering Western scuttlebutt about a collision. The NATO officials feel their aid efforts are being offered in good faith, and they resent the notion that Russia might be willing to waste their time.

Despite the extraordinary pressures, Vice Admiral Pobozhy remains poised. When the gathered journalists pepper him with questions about whether delaying foreign aid may have further imperiled the submariners' lives, Pobozhy responds calmly. Trapped submariners, he says, have been known to hold out for surprisingly long periods of time. "From our experience with Soviet submarine forces, it can be as long as two to three weeks."

As he speaks in Brussels, one of the Northern Fleet's submersibles makes a series of bold landings on the *Kursk*'s aft hatch, none of which succeeds in sealing before the struggling vessel's batteries run out.

Despite the Northern Fleet's official request for help the previous day, Norway's Admiral Skorgen continues to face serious obstacles. On mid-Thursday, he finds himself impatiently vexing over the new fax of a poorly hand-drawn sketch of the *Kursk*'s hatch specifications. Skorgen suspects this may be the result of intermediaries who've been communicating on Admiral Popov's behalf since the initial call. Annoyed, Skorgen picks up the red phone and insists on speaking directly to Popov, not through an intermediary.

Once Popov comes to the phone, the Norwegian admiral implores him to deliver the proper information. Popov demurs, proposing to deliver better details when the foreign rescuers arrive. Skorgen turns up the temperature, insisting the delay is just a time waster. "Vyacheslav," says Skorgen, "I can't accept waiting until we are in the diving position to get this kind of information! You and I know that every minute, every second, counts."

After a long pause, a deeply wearied Popov finally relents. "Einar, I understand you," he says. The Russian admiral explains that the rear hatch offers the best chance. Though the Russians suspect it's damaged, the Norwegians or Brits might be able to achieve a seal. Popov promises better information. Despite the late stage, Skorgen and his men get their first meaningful dose of optimism. Maybe the *Kursk*'s clever sailors have found some lifesaving air pockets.

Admiral Skorgen wants more, of course, but considers Popov's about-face a small victory. He remains mystified by his Russian friend's obvious reluctance. *Isn't saving trapped men the only thing that matters at a time like this? Of what possible intelligence value are the rescue hatch specifications? And why are such details more valuable than young men's lives?* Skorgen tries to convince himself this must be what his friend warned about in the Russian spa those months ago. Certainly this was "Moscow talking," not Vyacheslav Popov.

And then this: Skorgen's radar men report the sighting of Russian aircraft rapidly approaching Norway's airspace, proceeding south along his coast. Skorgen hasn't seen such a brazen approach from his neighbors in four years. Alarmed, the Norwegian commander scrambles his F-16s to meet the unannounced visitors, then summons Popov again on the red phone, asking what this is about.

Popov's response is all business. "I have information that there has been communication between Western submarines," says Popov, inferring that a Western sub has reported an emergency from the exercise region. "We have reason to believe there has been a collision."

What's so suspicious about Western subs communicating while departing the site of an exercise? wonders Skorgen. And if an American sub has collided with the mammoth *Kursk*, the much smaller U.S. vessel clearly would be lying on the seabed beside it. Popov's assertions make no sense. The Norwegian admiral thinks Moscow is still calling the shots, and that they're probably even listening in on Popov's every exchange.

But then the picture becomes even clearer to Skorgen. Later in the day Russia's Northern Fleet reports that it has spotted a Los Angeles–class attack sub moving south along Norway's west coast at a surface speed of eight knots. They describe it as "limping" toward Bergen "for repairs," stoking the already roused anti-American sentiment among Russia's unrepentant Cold Warriors. The report is circulated globally, lending apparent substance to Russia's loudly proclaimed theory that the tragedy has a Western cause.

•   •   •

Aboard the USS *Memphis,* now heading south along the Norwegian coast, Captain Breor and his men are looking forward to their first port of call since departing Groton, though they are a day behind the long-planned call date for their arrival north of Bergen. They already consider their Barents mission a success, though many strongly suspect they suffered a counter-detection when their masts may have been spotted above water. Their generally ebullient mood is also blunted by knowing that they may have "witnessed" fellow submariners from another country meeting a horrifying fate. And on that count, Captain Breor and his sonar men have serious work to do before they dock: they must prepare and extract all of the acoustic data related to the *Kursk* blasts, ASAP. Tapes and other records will be unloaded outside the Haakonsvern Naval Base just north of Bergen and flown to the United States for study.

As the Northern Fleet's rescue efforts continue to falter through Thursday night and into Friday morning, Russia awakens to reports that *Komsomolskaya Pravda* has a list of the *Kursk's* crew, sensationally headlined across the front page: "18,000 Rubles for Names of *Kursk* Sailors." The paper describes the unholy bribe exacted for the list, which was stamped "Top Secret." The paper's editors don't mince words about the list's profiteering provider: "We have lost all faith in the honor of our commanders."

The account is picked up by Russia's similarly indignant broadcast media—many of which deplore the withholding of such naturally public information in the first place—deepening the rift between the people and their government. The list devastatingly confirms the worst fears of some loved ones, while providing shattering news to others who never knew their men made transfers onto the crew just before the exercise.

Along Norway's northwestern coast shortly before 0900, Norway's chartered *Seaway Eagle* makes a much-needed refueling stop in the port city of Tromsö, simultaneously upgrading herself into a full-fledged diving-support vessel. The *Eagle* takes on its quickly assembled team of twelve deep-sea specialists plucked from Norwegian oil fields and the British military. It's the prospect of military divers that will most concern officers of the Northern Fleet, since they are trained in intelligence gathering and could conceivably do so even amid a rescue operation. Sensitive to this, Skorgen lays down strict orders that the divers are not to gather any information beyond what's needed for rescue efforts.

After a remarkably efficient three-hour turnaround in Tromsö, the *Eagle* departs at midday for her thirty-hour sprint to the wreck site, playing tag team with the U.K.-chartered *Normand Pioneer*, which carries the United Kingdom's *LR5* and her crew.

Still holed up in his hotel room in coastal Norway, Commodore Russell finally surrenders any delusions that Russian officials might yet reverse course and let him fly to the site for preparations ahead of the *LR5*. With the *Normand Pioneer* well under way, Russell and Captain Simon Lister—who has joined the mission to serve as a translator—board a helicopter for a high-speed flight through Norway's coastal fiords and out across the Norwegian Sea for a rendezvous with their submersible and her mother ship.

In Sochi, Vladimir Putin can no longer escape his nation's unhappy media, whose barbs now target the absentee president himself. "The sailors dying in the Barents Sea couldn't interrupt the summer vacations of our statesmen," declares the normally Kremlin-friendly *Izvestia* in a thinly disguised reference to Putin's Sochi activities. "They have a picnic on the shore with a view of the drowning men." Moscow business daily *Kommersant* runs a front-page photo of Putin taking a salute from a young naval conscript. The headline above it: "Whose Honor Is Drowning in the Barents Sea?" *Komsomolskaya Pravda* seizes on the reports of discontinued tapping. "The Sailors on the *Kursk* Fell Silent Yesterday," the paper headlines. "Why Has the President Been Silent?" The *Moskovsky Komsomolets* is most pointed: "Damn You, Do Something."

The relentless assaults finally score a direct hit. Vladimir Putin—stilted scion of one of the world's most relentlessly anti-democratic cultures, a professional chameleon long proud of his ability to avoid the spotlight—is facing one of the most brutal tests of a would-be democratic leader in a would-be open society. Is Putin a man of the people, or the natural product of an unfeeling Soviet bureaucracy? As the whole world watches, Putin is forced to learn on the job. He took the advice of Defense Minister Sergeyev and others, who suggested his presence up north would serve no meaningful value, that the Northern Fleet had all it needed. The advice initially made sense to Putin, who still sees himself as a quietly effective senior bureaucrat with instincts for modesty in times of crisis. *This problem is best handled by professionals,* he tried to convince himself, *by military men and skilled rescuers. Everyone should stay in his place.*

But within minutes of boarding a vessel on the Black Sea that will carry him to a planned summit meeting in Yalta with key leaders from the region's former Soviet states, he can't hide an apparently deep state of agitation. As his aides try to avert their gaze, Putin begins pacing nervously back and forth on the deck, his body language conveying to all that he is not to be disturbed.

What would the world have him do? NATO still spies on Russia. East and West may no longer be active enemies, but deep disagreements persist. For the time being, NATO and the West are still Russia's most likely opponents. Do Russian citizens really want to suffer the humiliation of inviting them in?

Then again, how much faith to place in the candor of his own military men? Did it really happen as they say? Is the rescue effort as good as it can get? Does the Northern Fleet truly have everything it needs?

If the young leader casts about for a Soviet-Russian role model at this moment, he finds little inspiration from his nation's recent history. No Soviet or Russian leader has ever had to say a word about submarine problems if he didn't want to, and the public never had a voice to challenge the silence. But this is different. Of all his recent predecessors, Putin most unapologetically admires Yuri Andropov, the former KGB chief who led the country for fifteen months before his death from kidney failure in

1983. Andropov left heavy thumbprints throughout the communist era, firmly establishing himself as a legendary xenophobe skilled at suppressing popular dissent, including the artful use of psychiatric commitment for citizens who resisted the Soviet order. Because of his short time in office, historians were left to debate whether Andropov might have emerged as a reformer. But how would he have handled an angry population roused by an unleashed media?

Gorbachev's example is little better. His mishandling of the Chernobyl nuclear power plant disaster in 1986 is a textbook case of what *not* to do; Gorbachev's response was a perfectly absurd attempt to keep the Chernobyl disaster a secret—giving the lie to his famed glasnost proclamations—a plan that backfired when European countries downwind began reporting alarming levels of deadly radiation descending from the skies two days after the blowup.

Yeltsin's example seemed just as dubious; Putin quietly disagreed with his political godfather's free-for-all philosophy, seeing it as one of the underlying causes of post-Soviet decline. If anything, Putin wants to reverse the Yeltsin-fomented chaos.

He could look toward the democratic Western leaders, of course, but Putin's courtship with democracy remains deeply ambivalent. He fancies himself as a bridge between the U.S.S.R. and an as-yet-ill-defined New Russia, in which he hopes to wed a free market economy with a resurgent central authority based in Moscow. He's also acutely sympathetic to Russia's restless senior cadre of unrepentant Cold Warriors. Like them, Putin yearns for a return to some semblance of the former bipolar world, in which Russia might once again emerge as a great power that can act as a check on U.S. hegemony. But of course, the proximate demise of his navy's most formidable warship clearly throws another wrench into those plans.

Amid his lonely pacing, Russia's president is forced to turn the day's most popular question on himself. The chameleon must at last display his truest colors.

•   •   •

A trim and fit black belt in judo, a "man of action" long trusted for solving problems noiselessly, a beige persona only modestly interested in alcohol—Vladimir Putin never planned on ruling his country. But he's patriotic to the marrow, and has long taken personally his nation's decline.

When Yeltsin tapped him as his surprise successor, Putin's advisers produced a quick biography introducing him to the Russian people in advance of the March elections. Published under the title *First Person: An Astonishingly Frank Self-Portrait by Russia's President*, one of its most revealing chapters detailed his anguish over the Soviet Union's collapse.

According to the book's account, the low point came during Putin's final KGB years in Soviet-controlled East Germany in 1989, when a thirty-six-year-old Major Putin watched helplessly as Eastern Bloc countries began their breakaway with the breach of the Berlin Wall. An angry mob had already sacked the Dresden headquarters of the despised East German secret police, the Stasi. Then word circulated that Putin's KGB station was next. True to the reports, an enraged crowd gathered outside Putin's gray villa office at number 4 Angelikastrasse, with apparent plans to seize the files the KGB and Stasi had secretly amassed about their country's own citizens.

Alerted to the looming seige, Putin and his colleagues had been furiously burning sensitive intelligence documents round-the-clock, such volumes of material that the office furnace actually burst. Given that he and his colleagues had only a handful of light arms, Putin called for the support of a nearby Soviet regiment to quell the furor; surely a timely display of Soviet-style resolve would dissuade the uprising. But the answer that came back would shake Putin to the core: "Moscow is silent," said an officer at the garrison, making it clear they would not mobilize until cleared from the top. Feeling betrayed at this news, Putin gathered his wits.

The young major went outside to meet the crowd. Some people were already attempting to break into the security offices. A woman in the crowd shouted: "Look for the passageway under the Elba! There are prisoners there being tortured in water up to their knees!"

Summoning the trademark cool that came from years of KGB training combined with his nearly religious devotion to judo, Putin calmly faced the frenzied group and assured them there were no meaningful documents at all in his building, only dull and common administrative papers instructing him and his associates in how to best support their East German "friends" in their business efforts. Of course, Putin's perfect German aided him in finessing this silky smooth lie, and the belated arrival of a small Russian military force found the quieter crowd easier to disperse.

When Putin described this rite of passage to his intimates, according to lifelong friend Sergey Roldugin—godfather to Putin's older daughter and lead cellist in St. Petersburg's Mariinsky Theater Symphony Orchestra—all understood his pride in the masterly deceit. They had long made peace with the reality that skillful lying was their "Volodya's" patriotic duty, much the way some people in the West admired the high-stakes deceits of U.S. Marine colonel Oliver North. Roldugin and other Putin intimates felt sure Volodya would always tell them the truth whenever it was possible.

In childhood, Putin was virtually weaned on the romantic accounts of the KGB's clever cat-and-mouse spy games in service to the motherland. Tormenting the country's independent thinkers wasn't what first drew him to the agency. The Stalinesque legacy of employing the KGB in the brutal exterminations of 10 million fellow citizens was a virtual invisibility; the books of his youth barely mentioned such unpleasant details.

But the Dresden experience affected Putin in a very profound way. "That business of 'Moscow is silent,'" he would later tell his biographers. "I got the feeling then that the country no longer existed. That it had disappeared."

Disillusioned at the grand unraveling of so much of what he believed in, Putin backed away from his life as a full-time spy. He took his wife, Ludmilla, and their two young daughters and moved back to St. Petersburg, slowly weaving his way back into civilian life—all the while still meaningfully tethered to the splintering KGB.

He considered becoming a full-time cab driver. But when some of his more influential friends learned of Putin's return to St. Petersburg, opportunities sought him out. In short order, Putin commenced a breathtakingly rapid succession of political operative positions in St. Petersburg's city government and then senior executive posts that took him to Moscow, even making a brief stop as the civilian director of the latter-day remains of the KGB (renamed the FSB) and later serving as Russian prime minister for all of five months before an ailing Yeltsin tapped the quietly competent fixer as his acting successor.

Just a decade after the dispiriting ruin he witnessed from Dresden, Putin suddenly found himself atop a reeling nation yearning for the "powerful man" ideal of the Soviet era.

But now, as he nervously paces about on the ferry to Yalta, it is Putin who is supposed to be that "powerful man"—not merely a skilled operative waiting for a superior's orders—and it is he who is now headed across a balmy Black Sea to a political gathering while his nation is facing one of its darkest hours. Now *Putin is Moscow*, and it is *he* who is silent.

Out on the Barents Sea, Northern Fleet rescuers finally bring out their best hope, the more robust AS-36 submersible, also known as the *Bester*. Between the hours of 1345 and 1750, *Bester's* operators make five promising contacts with the stricken *Kursk*, achieving brief periods of suction over the aft hatch three times. But on its last try, the *Bester*—which hadn't seen deep submergence since 1996—suddenly begins leaking through her aging seals. Her operators automatically blow ballast for a quick ascent to the surface. Once there, it bobs for a few moments before beginning to sink; a quick-thinking crewman aboard the *Mikhail Rudnitsky* manages to hook the mini-sub, winching her back to safety.

23

DEMOCRACY, UP CLOSE AND PERSONAL
VIDYAYEVO
FRIDAY, AUGUST 18

BLAST PLUS SIX DAYS, SIX HOURS

By the evening of Friday, August 18, Deputy Prime Minister Ilya Klebanov prepares to face the submariners' families on Putin's behalf. As he enters the simple officer's auditorium in Vidyayevo, he senses the crowd is piqued in a way utterly unfamiliar to him. In Soviet times, displays of grief and distress might manifest, but this is a people he barely recognizes.

Taking his position at the podium, Klebanov is flanked by Murmansk regional governor Yuri Yevdokimov along with Kursk regional governor and popular Russian war hero Alexander Rutskoi.

Rutskoi's presence serves as a key touchstone. He was at the center of the 1991 coup attempt to oust Mikhail Gorbachev, a bold effort essentially intercepted by Yeltsin. It is also Rutskoi's region in western Russia, Kursk, which gives the great submarine its name. The region became deeply etched into the Russian psyche as the site of history's biggest tank battle, in which the Red Army decisively turned back the Nazi advance in Russia's "Great Patriotic War." The region has been so enamored of its namesake submarine that its citizens have routinely supplied it with supplementary foodstuffs, and have held annual competitions for local young men to win slots on her crew. Seven sailors from the Kursk region are among the 118 who sailed out to the exercise, their fates now unknown.

But the support of such officials offers little protection for Klebanov against the pent-up fury of a hall filled with stricken relatives who have seemingly lost all fear of a government they now see as increasingly deceitful, incompetent, and inhumane.

Some of the young wives are in the auditorium, clinging to the idea that here is a Kremlin official who might have better news. Khalima Aryapova has spent long stretches alone in her apartment all week, but is now supported by her brother, who has just arrived. Olga Lubushkina yearns for any official information. Olga Kolesnikova has also arrived, along with Dima's parents. Dima's young wife is stoic, but more functional than her two stricken girlfriends.

Deputy Prime Minister Klebanov's plan is to assuage the families with a confident description of how Russia's greatest assets have been brought to bear to rescue their relatives. Perhaps that is the information they lack, so he will show them. But no sooner does Klebanov begin listing the numbers of vessels involved in the effort than he is abruptly halted with a primal shriek.

Nadezhda Tylik shoots to her feet. "You're swine!" she screams, as a TV camera furtively pans away from the podium to her location in the crowd. Tylik has spent the better part of her adult life in this desperate garrison town, and she had grown accustomed to Moscow's official neglect. This is the first time in her memory that such a senior government official has seen fit to pay a visit to her forgotten little community, whose people forgo even basic necessities to guarantee their country's security. They'd trusted their government to be there when the chips were down, but these feeble mutterings are more than she can bear. "They're dying down there in a tin can for $50 a month!" she thunders. "And you don't care! Do you have children? Do you? I will never forgive you! Take your medals off and shoot yourself! *Bastards!*" As she speaks, a number of officers swarm around her. With Tylik in midscream, a female medic plunges a syringe filled with a sedative into her thigh, and the distraught mother's cries diminish as she sinks to the floor, guided by the officers who surround her. As the crowd watches the Tylik incident unfold, another outraged mother quietly approaches the podium.

A shaken Klebanov tries to regain his composure, only to find the

middle-aged mother of eighth compartment commander Sergey Sadilenko reaching out to throttle his neck. She is slow to loosen her grip on
the deputy prime minister's collar as officers move to restrain her.

Klebanov fumbles through the remaining announcements, and a number of the gathered women remain hysterical, some bolting the hall for the
nearby medical clinic. These women *want* the government's sedatives,
which are liberally dispensed in the form of pills or injections. Nothing in
Klebanov's presentation has raised their hopes that their men might still be
saved. Government counselors have been bused into the settlement, where
they try to offer comfort in any way they can. The town's hospital ward is
filled to capacity.

Staggered by the outbursts, Klebanov and his fellow delegates retreat,
unsure of how to prepare the Russian president for such unruly emotions.

Olga Kolesnikova's arrival in Vidyayevo completes an emotional circle
for the three young wives. As the eldest of the trio, it falls to her to administer maternal support. Kolesnikova finds Olga Lubushkina sedated, her
mood swinging between confusion and anger at the displays of official
weakness. Despite her own torment, Kolesnikova finds herself shuttling
between Lubushkina and Khalima, who cannot cry and refuses to eat.

At one gathering in the Lubushkina apartment, Olga Kolesnikova
posts herself close to the television, tracking rescue images and trying to
direct her thoughts toward giving her husband strength. *Mitya,* she
thinks, *you have to breathe. I'm with you.*

Out on the nearby Barents, desperate fleet rescuers feel a looming humiliation at the news that foreign rescuers are bearing down on their site.
The top brass presses its struggling Russian submersible crews to give it
all they've got.

The *Seaway Eagle* expects to round Norway's Northern Cape at
around midnight before heading southeast for the Barents. Many of its
crew keep an eye on broadcasts from the BBC and CNN, and feel

moved by Russian families' increasing grief. The divers and support crew sense the world is galvanized by the image of 118 young men standing below the trapped submarine's escape hatch, hoping. Many of the Western rescuers are unaware of the senior-level East-West standoff, and anticipate a warm welcome from the Northern Fleet, convinced everyone will be on the same page, comrades in arms in a shared rescue effort.

The *Eagle*'s dive supervisors begin splitting the divers—twelve British and four Norwegian—into three-man teams. Supervisor Mark Nankivell knows he wants one of his most cool-headed men on the first team to dive, and he approaches Brit Tony Scott on the *Eagle*'s deck. "You're going team one, diver one," says Nankivell. "Okay then," says Scott, and resumes making preliminary adjustments to his gear—even though the target is still many hours away.

In Yalta, members of Vladimir Putin's summit staff notice that their president remains restless and distracted throughout the attempted pleasantries. Soon he signals that he has no plans for returning to Sochi. He will fly to Moscow at the earliest opportunity.

In Moscow, word circulates that CIA director George Tenet has made a sudden appearance in the Russian capital, entering closed-door meetings with senior officials of the Russian security services. When quizzed about the visit's timing—in light of the growing claims of an American-caused collision—Russian officials and a spokesman for the U.S. embassy say Tenet's visit was planned long ago. His previous stopover was Bulgaria. U.S. attaché Brannon even shared dinner with him Thursday evening, noting that Tenet displayed only the mildest interest in the *Kursk* issue. All parties describe the CIA chief's visit as "routine," yet the development still adds one more suspicious detail for the conspiracy theorists. In short order, some Russian pundits claim they can now see the connections, even if their "facts" are actually based on thinly sourced rumors and distorted half-truths. To wit: The suspect U.S. sub was detected sending an "emergency" radio message to Bergen for "repairs"; President Clinton's twenty-five-minute call to Putin in Sochi included a clandestine offer of political concessions in exchange for keeping the tragedy's true cause a secret; CIA chief Tenet has arrived to button up the details of the unholy deal.

While tracking the fulminating collision rumors, American officials make little formal attempt to elaborate on their denials. Privately, Clinton's foreign-policy team is deeply frustrated; all their handiwork at trying to build new bridges is being undone in the final days of their administration, and they feel sure the Russian officials are cynically selling out the warmer relations for the sake of domestic consumption.

Over a dinner conversation with Russian ambassador Yuri Ushakov at La Chaumière restaurant in Georgetown—ostensibly scheduled for other routine matters—the NSC's Medish tries to turn up the diplomatic temperature over the widening *Kursk* rift. "This collision speculation is really not helpful," Medish pronounces firmly. "It's counterproductive." While Ushakov tries to change the subject, Medish comes back to it later in the evening, hinting that President Clinton's pending decision on the Nuclear Missile Defense program "might be deferred." The issue is critical to the Russians, who are vehemently opposed to the idea of such a nakedly unilateral abdication of the balance of power that held sway throughout the Cold War. Medish knows the subject is dear to Ushakov's heart.

24
KEEPING THE WEST AT BAY
SOUTHERN BARENTS SEA
SATURDAY, AUGUST 19

BLAST PLUS ONE WEEK

The United Kingdom's *LR5* is approaching the Barents Sea at 1100 Moscow time aboard the *Normand Pioneer* when David Russell takes a helicopter to Norway's *Seaway Eagle*. Royal Navy captain Simon Lister joins him as an interpreter. The *Eagle*, now some hours behind the *Pioneer*, will host the first "summit meeting" between the inbound rescuers and the beleaguered Russian rescue chief, Rear Admiral Gennady Verich.

Verich and his small delegation also helicopter to the *Eagle*, and in minutes the group gathers in a small conference room. The Russian Navy's rescue chief looks deeply unslept, making Commodore Russell all the more eager to tell him how quickly his *LR5* can assist. First, of course, Russell feels the need to immediately disarm the Russian military's natural anxieties regarding the protection of its technology.

"I understand your security concerns," Russell says. "We'll do everything we possibly can to show you what we're up to. You can come on board for the operation and see what we do." Russell is on edge, speaking in an urgent staccato, ready to lay out plans immediately.

But Verich appears to be on a different timetable. He begins a formal round of introductions, including a laborious expression of gratitude at the foreigners' willingness to help. . . .

As the Russian admiral continues for several minutes, the members of the inbound rescue crew grow impatient. To them, Admiral Verich is behaving as if it's already too late for a rescue attempt. He wants to talk about recovery of bodies, clearly at odds with Popov's latest assurances.

Verich's position poses instant conflict. Both the British and Norwegian rescue teams' missions are sharply confined to a rescue effort only; a recovery operation is beyond their scope. Most of the would-be rescuers keep their confusion bottled up, but the moment provokes a flood of questions. *Are the Russians playing tricks here? Is there something they're not telling us? Is Popov's assurance of a viable rescue bid just a charade? And if so, toward what end?*

Then Verich defines the impasse more forcefully. He thanks the British for bringing along their *LR5*, but says flatly that it will be of no use to the Russian efforts.

Taken aback, Russell interrupts, hoping to sell Verich on the *LR5*'s remarkable capabilities.

Verich interjects. "We really only want the divers," he says, implying that all he needs is to confirm that the entire submarine is flooded, that all of the submariners have perished.

Dismayed, Russell tries to maintain a diplomatic decorum. "I don't think this is correct," he says firmly. "I hope you'll reconsider. We're ready. We can do this."

But Verich stands his ground. No *LR5*. No rescue. Only divers, and there will be limits on where they can go: no one may explore points forward of the aft escape hatch.

Russell reluctantly demurs. But as Russell and Captain Lister board their helicopter, Russell begins planning to team up with Norway's Admiral Skorgen in trying to sway the Northern Fleet's course. Russell hates to politic when lives might be on the line, but if politicking is required, then so be it.

Back onboard the *Pioneer*, Russell's associates are aghast at the Russian rescue chief's mystifying obstinacy. "What a complete idiot," one crew member says.

Minutes later, men aboard the *Pioneer* rouse to the sound of helicopter blades slicing through the Arctic air. *Aha,* thinks Russell. *Verich has changed his mind.*

But the Northern Fleet naval officer who emerges from the aircraft onto the *Pioneer's* helipad is not Verich. Through an interpreter, a red-eyed Vice Admiral Oleg Burtsev introduces himself to Russell. The portly Burtsev says that the *Kursk* is from his flotilla, and that he and *Kursk* commander Gennady Lyachin are friends. Burtsev tells Russell he wants to assist the effort in any way he can, and is especially interested in seeing the LR5.

In the course of small talk, the Russian vice admiral learns that his daughter and the daughter of a senior British officer on the team were recently married just a day apart. The conversation proceeds on a personal tack, and soon Burtsev's eyes are welling up, as he talks emotionally with Russell of the need to exhaust every last effort to bring any possible survivors out alive. Before departing, Burtsev embraces Russell in a bear hug and pledges his intent to cut through any remaining obstacles to a speedy final rescue effort. As Burtsev's helicopter lifts off from *Pioneer,* Russell hopes this new man has the clout to break the deadlock.

By 1910, the *Normand Pioneer* informs the *Peter the Great* that it expects to arrive at the wreck site no later than 2100. But given Verich's initial rebuff of the *Pioneer's* LR5 cargo, the point might be moot. Officials on the *Peter the Great* order the *Pioneer* to stop fifteen miles from the site. Russell and his men are beside themselves at the news. They are still hoping Admiral Burtsev will prevail on their behalf. But when a frustrated Commodore Russell presses for a better explanation for the holdup, Northern Fleet officials vaguely claim they need to "prepare the area."

BLAST PLUS SEVEN DAYS, THREE HOURS

The Russians want one last chance to open the *Kursk's* aft escape hatch on their own. They hope to repair one of their three on-site submersibles for this final bid, but their mini-subs stubbornly defy the urgent maintenance efforts. The unfolding failure raises the ante in what many on the scene—on both sides of the emerging standoff—are beginning to see as a perverse game of chicken. To the British and Norwegian rescuers, men's lives might still hang in the balance, and matters of national pride are a luxury no one can afford. To most senior officers of the Northern Fleet, the men's lives are already long lost; now they just want to protect what's left of their military secrets and battered dignity.

With this latest bid thwarted, senior Northern Fleet officers debate face-saving prospects. Some think it wisest to publicly declare what nearly all of them actually believe, even before the foreigners make any attempt. Others argue to wait and see if the foreigners might indeed possess technology that can remove all doubt.

Vice Admiral Mikhail Motsak is among those deeply convinced that the "optimists" are toying with everyone at the expense of people's emotions, and he volunteers to put a stop to it. In a Saturday evening broadcast from Severomorsk on Russian national television, Motsak shares the fleet's prevailing conviction: "Our worst expectations have come true," he says, calling it "the gravest disaster in the history of the Russian fleet." He says the *Kursk's* entire front end is flooded, and that most of the men died within minutes. He says men in the aft sections knocked on the hull for at least two days, signaling rising water and pressure, along with decreasing oxygen. "Regrettably," he concludes, "in effect we have crossed the critical boundary of assuring the life of the crew."

Though surprising to many, even this televised declaration has little effect on the British and Norwegian hopes. With the *Seaway Eagle* that carries the Western divers also now nearing the site, the idea of giving up on a last-ditch rescue bid without any rock-solid confirmation that all of the submariners have died is quite nearly unbearable for the foreign crew. But then the *Seaway Eagle*, too, is ordered to maintain some distance from the wreck site, just outside a four-mile limit.

Soon after learning of the Motsak statements via their television monitors aboard the already "parked" *Normand Pioneer*, David Russell declares to the British media that he and his team will be "fighting on" until they are ordered to depart.

After the *Eagle* comes within sight of the Russian destroyer *Admiral Chabanenko* nine miles away from the wreck, Russian rescue chief

Admiral Verich boards a small launch and heads for the Norwegian diving platform just before 2300.

Crew on the *Eagle* carry mixed expectations with this second onboard arrival of Verich and several other Russians, but they generally keep their game faces on, hoping to sell the wary guests on the worthiness of a genuine new rescue bid.

Verich assures them that rescue diving might still be an option, but he first needs to understand their plan.

Graham Mann, who is overseeing the diving operation on Norway's behalf, elects first to sell the Russians on the *Eagle's* state-of-the-art systems. In moments, several of the *Eagle's* experts are escorting Verich and his men through the *Eagle's* three decks, past a dizzying array of consoles and survey screens that can guide and track the activities of remotely operated vessels and divers working at depth. "Jesus Christ," one Russian mini-sub pilot confides to a comrade in his native tongue, "we're twenty years behind."

The five-year-old *Seaway Eagle* carries eighty crew, comes fully equipped with its own dynamic positioning system to hold its place in an angry sea, and normally leases out to commercial oil interests for $175,000 a day. The men who typically use it consider its facilities vastly superior to any military-purposed diving vessel. The *Normand Pioneer* and her *LR5* cargo are similarly expensive, yet none of the foreigners plan on billing the Russians for their services; they see the event as the universal seafarer's obligation to aid fellow sailors in distress.

Western dive supervisor Garry Ball guides his Russian counterpart through the *Eagle*, trying to explain how the Western divers use a dramatically different diving approach from that employed by the Russians. The Russians work on the seabed in short bursts, in a "bounce-diving" technique that relies on frequent breaks in pressurized chambers to avoid decompression problems. The Western divers, Ball explains, rely on equipment that can support round-the-clock saturation diving—his boys can operate on the seabed for up to a month, if necessary, even in heavy seas, stopping only for food and sleep. Though such capabilities shouldn't be necessary for this operation.

Anticipating that Verich will finally approve the diving operation, *Eagle* diving supervisor Mark Nankivell orders Dive Team One into the vessel's saturation chamber to be conditioned for a pressure equivalent to over three hundred feet. Lead diver Tony Scott settles in with his two fellow divers for the nearly three-hour process, periodically clearing his ears by clamping his nose and mouth shut while forcing air into his sinuses as the warmed helium-gas mix flows into the sealed chamber.

Then Graham Mann meets with Admiral Verich and others in the vessel's conference room. Mann optimistically tells Verich that the divers will soon be ready, but that the *Eagle* must first deploy a remotely operated vessel to perform a general video survey of the wreck site. They need to map out objectives, obstacles, safety threats. Verich pauses, and delivers an emphatic *nyet*: There will be no video snooping forward of the aft escape hatch mounted over the *Kursk*'s ninth compartment.

The conflict is only the first of many, as the Russian admiral spells out a series of restrictions on any foreign diving operation. Mann refuses to compromise the safety of his men, and presses for his key requirements past midnight, making no progress against Verich's constraints. The standoff finally breaks sometime near dawn at 0355, when Verich relents. The protracted debate has cost another eight hours.

The *Eagle* finally proceeds to the *Kursk* wreck site at 0430 on Sunday, August 20.

Remote Posting: The site where the *Kursk* went down, marked here with a star, is just off the coast of Russia's Kola Peninsula, where the Northern Fleet maintains dozens of naval sites. The peninsula's main civilian population resides in Murmansk, the largest city in the Arctic Circle. The area is just east of the northern fringes of Finland, Sweden, and Norway.

Cold War Hot Spot: The Barents seabed, shown here in an image specially prepared by a scientist at the National Oceanic and Atmospheric Administration, is a relatively shallow and featureless basin whose average depth is just 750 feet. (For reference, the deeper Arctic Ocean is indicated by a steep drop-off in this image's upper left corner.) During the height of the Cold War, this area was a key playground for American and Soviet submariners engaged in a high-stakes game of blindman's bluff, a contest popularized in the book of the same name. Some of this activity continues to this day.

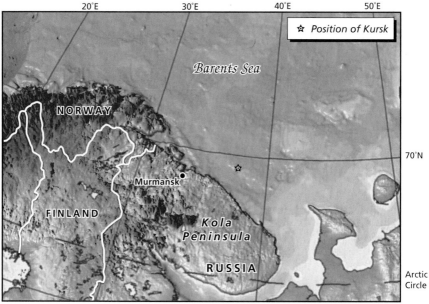

(Map prepared by Dr. Peter Sloss, NOAA)

Modest Mooring: The *Kursk*'s home base was Vidyayevo, which shelters several other subs along its docks. The garrison town where the sailors and their families reside lies a short bus ride from this site. *(AP)*

Deadly Prowler: Docked at her Vidyayevo pier prior to the August 2000 exercise, the *Kursk* had helped Russia hold on to its tenuous place in the international pecking order. For the two years before she set out for the fleet-wide war game, her home garrison had no operational weapons-loading cranes. *(AP)*

Mission Accomplished: In October 1999, *Kursk* commander Gennady Lyachin triumphantly announces the successful completion of the *Kursk*'s finest moment—the seventy-six-day patrol in which she'd tracked and harassed an American aircraft carrier conducting operations near Yugoslavia. A chagrined American admiral later testified before a U.S. congressional panel about the disquieting episode. *(Getty Images)*

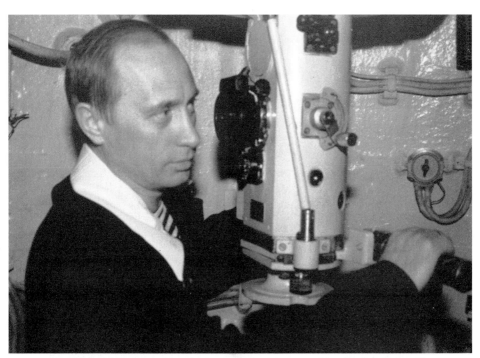

Presidential Interest: Soon after becoming Russia's new president, Vladimir Putin paid a visit to the Northern Fleet and promised to revive his nation's navy. In this photo from April 6, 2000, he tries one sub's periscope. *(AP)*

Birthday at Sea: Dmitry Kolesnikov and friends aboard the *Kursk* in August 1999, celebrating his twenty-sixth birthday. His best friends, Sergey Lubushkin *(top left)* and Rashid Aryapov *(top right),* crafted a *Kursk* T-shirt for the occasion. *(Photo courtesy of the Kolesnikov family)*

Wife Meets Mistress: After introducing his wife to his "great steel mistress," Dmitry Kolesnikov poses with Olga Kolesnikova in front of the *Kursk's* sail, July 2000. *(Getty Images)*

Before the Exercise: All three couples celebrating at a pre-exercise outing in the hills above Vidyayevo, July 2000. *(Photo courtesy of Olga Lubushkina)*

One Last Favor: Captain Third Rank Murat Baigarin *(left)* with wife, Svetlana, had returned briefly to Vidyayevo to pack up his young family for transfer to St. Petersburg. But a series of *Kursk* crewmen informed Baigarin that his old commander had a worrisome torpedo onboard for an imminent exercise, and they needed Baigarin's expertise. Baigarin responded to the call of his longtime crew. *(Photo courtesy of Svetlana Baigarina)*

Silent Stalker: During its exercise in the Barents, the American spy sub USS *Memphis*—a *Los Angeles*-class attack sub similar to the one shown—closely tracked the *Kursk*. The American sub felt a shudder from the blast from 25 miles away. *(U.S. Navy handout photo)*

"Attention Prowlers!": Captain Mark Breor, commander of the USS *Memphis*, frequently used this phrase to alert his crew to announcements. On the Barents mission, Breor did not break radio silence regarding the mysterious sensations his vessel had experienced until many hours had passed and he had safely cleared the area. *(Photo courtesy of Breor family)*

Periscope Sweep: At one point during their surveillance, officers aboard the *Memphis* worried that their periscope may have been spotted above the sea surface. It wasn't. *(U.S. Navy handout photo)*

Where the *Kursk* Lived and Died

First, a Detour: Before the *Kursk* could join the Barents exercise, it had to sail from its home port in Vidyayevo to a parallel fjord so it could accomplish some last-minute torpedo loading. But complications at the loading dock in Zapadnaya Litsa Bay made the *Kursk* hours late for her scheduled arrival. *(Illustration by Robert Snyder, adapted by Chris Robinson)*

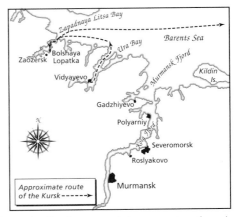

Blast Positions: At the moments when the *Kursk* suffered its two explosions, a number of vessels were close enough to feel the effects. In this schematic, two details can be fixed—the positions of the *Kursk* itself and of the Russian surface warship that was to act as its torpedo target, the *Peter the Great*. The other vessel positions are the "best guesses" of the author and chief advisor Lars Hanson, based on extensive original reporting and known Russian torpedo-exercise procedures. When Russian officials became worried over the coming hours, they asked the commander of their closest vessel, the *Leopard* (marked 5 in this diagram), if he had heard the *Kursk*'s torpedo work. The *Leopard* said it had not. Officials later surmised this was because the *Leopard* was facing away from the *Kursk* at the moment of the fatal blast, allowing its shock wave to wash over it undetected.

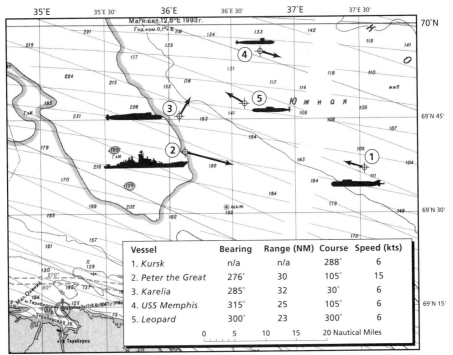

Vessel	Bearing	Range (NM)	Course	Speed (kts)
1. *Kursk*	n/a	n/a	288°	6
2. *Peter the Great*	276°	30	105°	15
3. *Karelia*	285°	32	30°	6
4. *USS Memphis*	315°	25	105°	6
5. *Leopard*	300°	23	300°	6

(Graphic adaptation by Chris Robinson. Nautical chart provided by East-West Cartographic. Final vessel positions, bearings, courses, ranges and speeds mapped out by Lars Hanson. Same elements reviewed by retired Rear Admiral Thomas Evans.)

The *Kursk* at the Moment of Its First Blast

Last Refuge: The *Kursk*'s ninth compartment is normally occupied by just three men. After the sub's second, and mortal, blow, twenty-three survivors from the aft compartments gathered here together, sealing the watertight door behind them and using a metal object to knock out SOS signals. A flash fire ignited by a dropped oxygen regeneration cartridge killed most or all of the twenty-three before rescuers could latch onto the sub eight days later. At least four sailors left notes here.

Faulty Hatch: Some of the *Kursk*'s twenty-three blast survivors tried to open this ninth compartment hatch, hoping to escape by a dangerous buoyant ascent. Though scratches were found on the bottom hatch's lower surface, no sailors were able to enter the tube and equalize pressure. Similarly, when a Russian rescue submersible tried to attach to the hatch's exterior, it failed to budge. A team of British and Norwegian divers freed the hatch shortly after arriving over one week later.

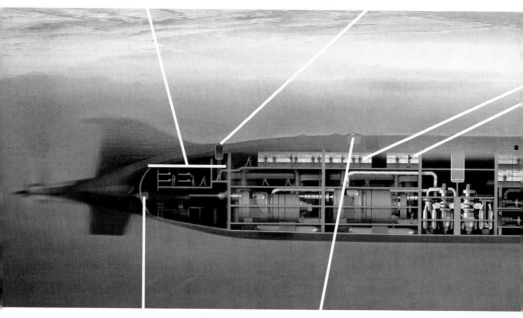

Deadly Design: The *Kursk*'s stern tube gland—which conveyed the propeller shafts through the aft end of the sub's pressure hull—was known to leak excessively when the vessel idled. The design weakness allowed a slowly rising level of 38-degree seawater into the ninth compartment while sailors there awaited rescue.

Broken Buoy: When submariners tried to deploy the *Kursk*'s emergency rescue buoy—which would have risen to the surface to mark their location and provide a communications link—they found it stuck. An investigation revealed its transport packaging had never been removed. It also had never been tested, as required.

(Illustration by Doug Stern, with guidance by Lars Hanson)

Three Friends: Capt.-Lt. Dmitry Kolesnikov commanded the *Kursk*'s turbines, Capt.-Lt. Rashid Aryapov was the main propulsion assistant, and Capt.-Lt. Sergey Lubushkin an engineer specializing in remote control of the reactor plant and other systems. All three shared a tight bond born in naval college in St. Petersburg ten years earlier. After the *Kursk*'s second blast, Lubushkin was trapped in his compartment. Kolesnikov and Aryapov successfully retreated to the ninth.

First Blow: The *Kursk*'s faulty torpedo exploded in the tube at 11:28:27 Moscow time—instantly killing several torpedo men and many of the senior officers in the adjacent command and control post—and sending a storm of projectiles throughout the torpedo room. The blast also penetrated the forward pressure hull through the broken torpedo tube, allowing water to flood in, but failing to quench the fire. The catastrophic second blast arrived two minutes and fourteen seconds after the first, when live warheads on some of the remaining weapons detonated almost simultaneously.

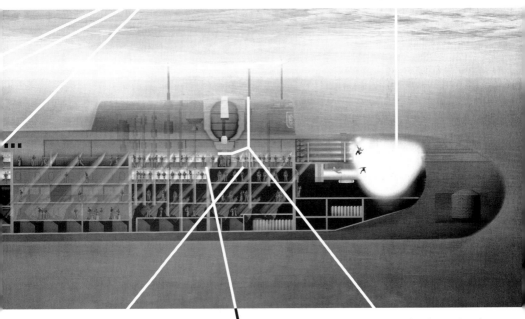

Worried Commander: *Kursk* captain first rank Gennady Lyachin had a lot to worry about when setting out for the August 2000 exercise. He was planning to fire a rarely used and notoriously volatile torpedo with a weapons crew that had almost no experience with it.

No Way Up: Many Russian submariners placed confidence in the *Kursk*'s sail-mounted escape capsule, designed to carry up to 115 sailors to the surface in an emergency. After the first blast, *Kursk* sailors queued for the chamber but failed to gain entry.

Knowing Navigator: Senior Lt. Sergey Tylik, who served as the *Kursk*'s navigator, told his mother before departing that the sub had "death onboard." Though Sergey's mother never knew if he was referring to a troublesome torpedo, she reassured herself that the *Kursk* was thought to be indestructible. She was later infamously injected while shouting at a government minister over the handling of the disaster.

First Alerts: American officials learned of the unfolding submarine disaster hours before the Russians did. The first member of the Clinton administration's foreign policy team to get the call was NSC Russia specialist Mark Medish *(top left)*, who quickly brought into the loop his boss, National Security Adviser Sandy Berger *(top right)*. Deputy Secretary of State Strobe Talbott *(bottom left)* presided over the weekend strategy discussions. The only attempt at initiating contact with the Russian leadership that Saturday came from Berger. *(Medish photo courtesy of Mark Medish; Berger photo courtesy of his consulting company, Stonebridge International; Talbott photo by the AP)*

On the Spot: Northern Fleet admiral Vyacheslav Popov presides over a faltering Russian rescue effort. *(AP)*

Rusted Rescue: It took the Northern Fleet's primary rescue vessel, the *Mikhail Rudnitsky*, over thirty hours to arrive at the rescue site. Its design makes it top-heavy, and its shallow keel adds to its instability in heavy seas. For the *Kursk* rescue effort, its submersibles were also found to be missing many basic tools, crippling any prospect of repairing them. *(AP)*

Attaché in Action: The American embassy in Moscow's naval attaché, Capt. Robert Brannon *(here on the left, welcoming Secretary of Defense William Cohen at a Moscow airport earlier in 2000)*, only learned of the Russian sub disaster when the Russians announced it two days after the fact. Many diplomatic figures in both the U.S. and British embassies expressed dismay over this late notice. Brannon's team quickly swung into action, crafting a formal offer on behalf of Cohen on Tuesday, the fifteenth. Brannon kept a vigil at the Russian defense ministry headquarters until its duty officer allowed him to present it. Like other foreign rescue offers, it was rejected. *(Photo courtesy of Capt. Robert Brannon)*

Western Resources: Amid rebuffs from the Russians, Norway chartered this state-of-the-art diving support vessel, the *Seaway Eagle*, to rush deep-sea divers to the scene. Britain made a parallel advance move, chartering a vessel to bring its modern rescue submersible to the scene. *(AP)*

Disengaged: Even as his nation faced one of its darkest moments in the Barents Sea, Russian president Vladimir Putin remained on holiday at the Black Sea resort of Sochi. Here he is seen conferring with Security Council Secretary Sergey Ivanov after meeting with Russia's top scientists at the resort on Wednesday, August 16, 2000, hours before ordering his navy to accept foreign help. *(AP)*

The Press Swarms: Vice Admiral Alexander Pobozhy faces close questioning at NATO headquarters in Brussels during his visit on August 17. *(NATO photo)*

No Bodies to Bury: A number of grieving relatives begin the long process of saying good-bye, in this case, at sea. Olga Lubushkina is pictured at far right. *(AP)*

First Recovery Effort: In October 2000, the *Regalia* deep-sea diving complex lingered over the wreck site for weeks while divers recovered the *Kursk*'s first twelve bodies from the vessel's ninth compartment. *(AP)*

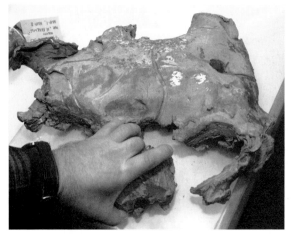

Telltale Artifact: Among the forty tons of material brought up in one phase of the recovery was this molten shard, which hinted at the dramatic firestorm that raced through the Russian supersub. *(Reuters)*

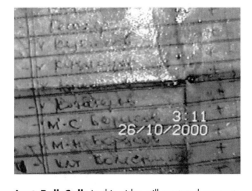

Last Roll Call: In this video-still captured moments after the papers were removed from Kolesnikov's body, the names of his comrades and status marks in the margins are clearly visible. *(Photo courtesy of a member of the recovery-diver team aboard the* Regalia*)*

The Kolesnikov Note: This was among the package of written pages that Capt.-Lt. Kolesnikov left for posterity. The note's discovery on October 26, 2000—and its timely release to the public—sent instant headlines around the world: Russian officials had convinced most relatives that all of their loved ones had died aboard the *Kursk* nearly instantly. *(Photo courtesy of Nikolay Cherkashin)*

Graveside Anguish: Kolesnikov's widow, Olga, and his mother grieve together at his interment in St. Petersburg. *(Reuters)*

Kursk **Probe Glasnost:** After raising the *Kursk* from the Barents seabed in the fall of 2001, naval officials declared the wreck's image off limits to journalists. In this video image from Russian national television, Russian prosecutor general Vladimir Ustinov—shown here in front of the *Kursk* wreck in dry dock outside Murmansk—declared the investigation would be as visible to the public as possible. *(Getty Images)*

Last Man Recovered: Among the very last remains identified were those of *Kursk* commander Gennady Lyachin. He and seven other crewmen were buried alongside Kolesnikov and two dozen other comrades on March 23, 2002. In this photo, widow Irina Lyachina is comforted at the graveside by her son, Gleb. *(Reuters)*

Whose Legacy? In February 2001, Rashid Aryapov's wife, Khalima, gave birth to the couple's son, Ilgiz. Mother, son, and Aryapov's parents have all moved to be closer to his gravesite in Russia's Samara region. *(Photo by Ramsey Flynn)*

25
DOWN TO BUSINESS
SOUTHERN BARENTS SEA
SUNDAY, AUGUST 20

BLAST PLUS SEVEN DAYS, TWENTY-ONE HOURS

Shortly after 0800, the *Eagle* deploys one of its ROVs for the site exam. In one of the *Eagle's* video-monitoring rooms, Admiral Verich watches intently as the ROV slowly homes in on the stricken black giant, as if the Russian admiral is seeing the sunken vessel's image for the first time. The British dive supervisors track the visual exam of the reportedly damaged aft escape hatch, and react with surprise when Verich suddenly begins pointing excitedly at some apparent irregularities near the hatch. Verich says the image vindicates his mini-sub pilots' claims that the hatch is damaged. *Eagle* dive supervisors Mark Nankivell and Garry Ball study the same details but are skeptical; they see what appears to be simply a poorly joined seam in the vessel's outer layer of protective rubber, an anomaly of little or no consequence. They see nothing indicating hatch damage.

Just before 1100, the *Eagle* lowers the diving bell with three men onboard—Tony Scott, Norwegian commercial diver Paul Dinesson, and Jim Mallen—suspended slightly above and to port of the *Kursk's* aft outer deck.

Tony Scott leaves the bell minutes later, as Dinesson guides Scott's support cable from just outside the bell. "You're going to do some tapping," dive supervisor Nankivell reminds Scott through their communications link. "Four taps, four times."

Scott does as requested, striking a small mallet to a fixture welded to the *Kursk*'s hull. Scott then leans his dive helmet onto the hull, hoping to pick up the vibration of any interior response. He holds his breath to reduce audio noise.

Nothing. Another try; more silence. A third try; silence again. After a fourth unanswered try, Nankivell asks the obvious: "No response then?"

"No response," Scott confirms.

Still, the *Eagle*'s crew refuses to accept the silence as a death sentence. The trapped submariners could be unconscious.

Paul Dinesson departs from the bell to join Scott. As he comes into contact with the enormous vessel, Dinesson begins his own tapping. "C'mon, boys," he whispers, "talk to me."

More silence.

Soon, Scott and Dinesson begin examining the aft escape hatch. They describe only superficial scratches in its surface, apparently caused by docking attempts from the Russian mini-subs. Scott probes the separated seams of the outer rubber layer near the hatch with his diving knife, confirming that it poses no threat to the hatch's ability to open. Dinesson applies a metal straight edge across the hatch to ensure it has suffered no distortion from the catastrophic blast.

To all appearances, the *Kursk*'s escape hatch should be working. How had it defied the Russian mini-subs?

The *Eagle* team next moves to the upper hatch's pressure valve, hoping it can tell them if there is still air in the escape trunk. Diver Scott swims to the exterior valve, holding a packet of milky dye to aid him in visually detecting any inflow of water. He carefully tries to turn the valve, only budging it slightly. He expels a small amount of the dye into the surrounding water around the valve stem, but the dye just floats like a decaying jellyfish.

Suspecting the valve might open more easily with some leverage, a welder aboard the *Eagle* fashions a makeshift key at the end of a rod that can be inserted into the valve handle's finger guides. A crane operator aboard the diving vessel soon lowers it close to Scott's position, and the diver applies it to the valve, counterclockwise as ordered by the Russians, again achieving only the slightest movement. And again, the small squirt of milky dye hovers inertly.

Aboard the *Eagle*, the crew wonders if the escape trunk might already be flooded, a prospect that lowers the odds of a rescue. But there is another possibility they have to consider: *Could the trunk have been deliberately flooded by the trapped submariners during an escape attempt?* Such a procedure requires at least one submariner to enter the escape trunk and to close its lower hatch before deliberately flooding up the trunk itself. This would equalize the pressure between the trunk and the exterior seawater, allowing the escaping submariner to easily open the trunk's upper hatch before rising to the surface.

If this is indeed the case, the *Eagle*'s diving experts quickly understand, a dead submariner could be stuck inside the escape trunk. His body would also be buoyant, which would mean that opening the outer hatch could send him hurtling toward the surface, an image that might be captured on television. The operation pauses while trying to devise a solution.

During the pause—which eventually produces a mesh net that can smartly trap an ascending body—the Russian dive advisers briefly step away from the control room. Diver Tony Scott uses the moment to pose an impolitic question to Nankivell: What if Scott made just a *modest* attempt to turn the valve *clockwise*? It would go against the Russians' insistence to the contrary, but Nankivell gives him the green light. The clockwise move works, and the valve easily surrenders. Scott tries the milky dye test again as he opens the valve more fully, but sees only the slightest flow toward the hatch.

Now there is no doubt: the trunk is flooded. *Which still doesn't mean the refuge below it is also flooded.* And yet, the hatch itself continues to defy any attempt to open it. Flummoxed, the team decides to tie a bag filled with air to the hatch. The bag's buoyancy will establish a constant upward tug while rescuers aboard the *Eagle* plan their next move.

But Admiral Verich has had enough of planning, and he feels the foreigners are simply delaying the inevitable. He stridently urges *Eagle* head Graham Mann to use the vessel's crane to forcefully yank the hatch. Mann just as stridently refuses the request.

Just as this new impasse appears, Admiral Popov visits the *Eagle* and dramatically reverses Verich, even inviting the foreign dive supervisors to come and quickly study the hatch mechanisms on a similar vessel docked in Severomorsk. Within the hour, dive supervisors Garry Ball and Mark Nankivell are tucked into a Norwegian helicopter for a three-minute flight to the *Peter the Great*, from where they will take a Russian helicopter to the *Kursk*'s sister sub.

As he debarks from the helicopter onto the *Peter the Great*'s deck, Ball is instantly impressed with the Russian warship's array of missile silo hatches. He and Nankivell are proceeding toward the vessel's stern when Ball looks up to see two Russian sailors on an upper deck, one of whom nods toward the foreigners and taps his hand over his heart, a traditional Muslim gesture of gratitude. Ball silently nods back.

Ball and Nankivell's flight to Severomorsk will take an hour, during which time the *Eagle*'s Graham Mann mounts one last full-court press for the Russians to unleash the United Kingdom's *LR5*. True to form, Verich nixes the idea, reiterating that he just wants the escape trunk hatches opened to finally confirm that the entire vessel is flooded. Moments later, Northern Fleet chief Popov places a radio call to the *Eagle* and again reverses Verich. After some discussion with Commodore Russell and his men still waiting aboard the *Normand Pioneer*, all parties agree that the *LR5* will make its attempt at noon the next day, Monday, August 21—nine days after the *Kursk* hit the seabed.

No one is watching when the outer hatch spontaneously swings open sometime around dawn on Monday. When the *Eagle*'s diving team resumes operations at about 0700, they discover the buoyant air bag has done its job—perhaps from a combination of neutral pressure in the aft escape trunk and the overnight low tide.

The development constitutes progress, but it poses a new dilemma: How to confirm whether there might still be air in the human space below the trunk's lower hatch? But after some discussion, experts aboard the *Eagle* finally come to share Verich's convictions that no one is still alive inside the *Kursk*. The foreign rescuers take some moments to reckon with this new information, and eventually agree to comply with the wishes Verich seemed to express from the beginning. They decide to blow the lower hatch, using a mechanical device attached to one of their ROVs.

When the ROV punches open the lower hatch by 1003, a torrent of bubbles spews up. Observers on the *Eagle* watch their video consoles in resignation, their faces set. Some of them note that the glistening bubbles have very dark interiors, implying a higher level of carbon dioxide than human beings could possibly generate—usually a sign of fire.

Watching the live television footage from an apartment in Vidyayevo, Olga Kolesnikova sees the bubbles surging toward the surface and imagines them as the liberated souls of her young husband and his comrades, freed from their earthly metal coffin, soaring heavenward at last.

Less than an hour later, Russian Navy commander in chief Admiral Vladimir Kuroyedov invites the United Kingdom's senior man on the scene, Commodore David Russell, for a formal visit aboard the *Peter the Great*. The Russians would like to express their gratitude for the foreign rescuers' efforts. As Russell and interpreter Captain Lister fly twenty minutes by helicopter to Russia's only seaworthy nuclear cruiser, Lister turns to the commodore. "You know," says Lister, mindful of the Russian indulgence of spirits at all social gatherings, "we may have to do the vodka thing."

Once on board and ushered into the *Peter the Great*'s dining room, however, it's clear the occasion has defeated even this most persistent tradition. "Normally," says Admiral Kuroyedov apologetically, "we would drink at this time. I don't think that would be correct right now. But maybe sometime in the future."

It is an intimate three-hour gathering, with Russell and Lister sharing the company of Kuroyedov, Deputy Prime Minister Ilya Klebanov, and a very taciturn Admiral Popov. The British and Russian officers compare notes on the tragedy and its outcome. Kuroyedov and Klebanov do most of the talking with their Royal Navy guests; Popov is resolutely silent and downcast. Commodore Russell senses the emotionally battered Northern Fleet admiral might be in shock.

At one point during the candid lunch, Ilya Klebanov—the Russian official so ingloriously displayed on international television suffering the furious screams of Nadezhda Tylik in Vidyayevo only days earlier—confides to Russell that the *Kursk* families' emotional outpourings caught him completely off guard.

Navy chief Kuroyedov has bigger concerns. "As a senior Western submariner," he asks Russell, "what do you think caused the disaster?"

Russell tells Kuroyedov that he believes the *Kursk* suffered an internal explosion in its torpedo room, and proceeds to field Kuroyedov's questions about how Western submariners would handle such an event. Though Russell is aware of Kuroyedov's public allegations that the *Kursk* was rammed by another submarine, the Russian makes no mention of a collision.

Kuroyedov summarizes the tragedy as "the blackest day for the Russian Navy for many years."

Back on the *Pioneer,* Russell gathers his men on the deck and says a few words to the memory of the *Kursk* submariners, their bodies now silently entombed 350 feet below them. Russell and some crewmen cast a wreath onto the Barents surface and prepare to depart.

Later in the afternoon, Norway's Admiral Skorgen places a call from his Bodo headquarters to his friend Admiral Popov. He finds Popov in his Severomorsk office, sounding beaten, even physically sick. Skorgen gently offers his condolences. "*Spasibo,*" Popov thanks him weakly.

They agree to talk later, once the political smoke screens have faded. "Let's hope this never happens again," offers Skorgen, but he senses that Popov is beyond comfort.

By evening, Popov has summoned the strength to make a statement on national television. "Great misfortune has opened the doors of your homes," he tells the submariners' families. "The crew is not to blame for what happened. The circumstances were so catastrophic that after the collision—I am sure it was a collision—most of the crew did not survive even for three minutes.

"The Northern Fleet has lost its best submarine crew," he continues, and then makes a pledge to "seek for the rest of my life to look into the eyes of the person who has organized this tragedy." Then he does something that breaks with Russian military tradition. Popov looks into the camera, eyes swollen and red, takes his hat from his head, and apologizes to the Russian people. "Forgive me," he says, "for not saving your men."

Nearly sixty fathoms down in the Barents Sea, the *Kursk* sailors' refuge has become pitch-black. Empty air cartridge packages lie scattered at the submariners' feet, beneath several feet of water. Other cartridge packages remain intact, unopened, floating on the bilge-darkened surface. Eighty water bottles also remain, with only fifteen of them emptied. A hose snakes chaotically among the men. Near the body of one submariner floats a complete set of instructions for emergency escape.

Some of the sailors are reclined, as if asleep. Several of them have been burned, from a fire that ignited when a regeneration cartridge fell into the oily water. The incendiary reaction quickly consumed the remaining oxygen. A number of submariners donned their masks and fought the fire, then found the masks provided their last breathable air, their last link to consciousness, as the atmosphere of the compartment turned brutally poisonous.

Dima Kolesnikov is slumped below the escape trunk, his head and upper body severely burned from his close proximity to the initial flare-up.

One sailor's body floats lower in the compartment, facedown, also heavily burned, his abdominal wall seared away. Other sailors who dove beneath the water succeeded at protecting the front half of their bodies, but their backs are scorched.

Quickly sapping the last traces of breathable oxygen, the flare-up didn't last long. The men without masks gasped wildly on an acrid black smoke thick with burning oils and the naturally toxic by-products of carbon dioxide and carbon monoxide.

Rashid Aryapov lies shrouded in his bunk below the water, an oxygen mask clamped tightly to his face. One of his pockets contains the short letter written by his comrade in the upper bunk, Sergey Sadilenko. Sadilenko's elevated position left him exposed to the fire, but Aryapov was able to don his oxygen mask and slip below the waterline. On realizing what had happened to his upper-bunk comrade, Aryapov dutifully retrieved the note from his friend's pocket.

Another sailor has written a dying note to his wife and son, and has stuck it into a water bottle for posterity. "My dear Natasha and Sasha!" Chief Warrant Officer Andrey Borisov has written. "If you are reading this letter, it means I am no longer with you. Natasha, Sasha—I love you so very much. Sasha, become a real man. —A. M. Borisov."

A separate line appears to be a broad reproach to Russian authorities as Borisov resigns himself to his fate: "We did everything according to the instructions."

26
PUTIN MEETS THE FAMILIES
MOSCOW AND VIDYAYEVO
TUESDAY, AUGUST 22

On the morning of Tuesday, August 22, Vladimir Putin issues a decree. Effective tomorrow, Wednesday, August 23, 2000, the Russian people will observe an official day of mourning for the lost crew of the *Kursk*. Then the Russian president flies north to meet with the grieving families, many of whom are still too overcome with grief to fully absorb the harsh truth.

By early afternoon, at Northern Fleet headquarters in Severomorsk, Putin is greeted with a sober round of salutes for senior naval officials, including Navy commander in chief Vladimir Kuroyedov and Northern Fleet commander Vyacheslav Popov. A small retinue gathers to escort the president to an ongoing session of the official fact-finding group, led by Deputy Prime Minister Ilya Klebanov. Klebanov's panel is already mulling how the reports of carbon-darkened bubbles rising from the *Kursk*'s interior might give the government an opportunity to retake control of the public message. *Wouldn't fire that far back mean that all of the sailors had died within minutes, making the thwarted foreign rescue offers moot?*

Finding meager solace in these developments, Putin cuts short his meeting with the panel. His government officially pronounced all of the *Kursk* sailors dead only the day before. His higher priority now is to console the families in Vidyayevo, where many of them—including Olga Kolesnikova and Dima's father, Roman—are gathered in a hall awaiting him. They'd been told he would arrive by 1800, and the president is already well behind schedule. Putin's motorcade forms up, and slowly begins snaking through the Kola Peninsula's rocky landscape—first south along the Kola Bay, then curving north through the modestly bustling port city of Murmansk, then westward into the remote rolling slopes that engulf the tiny garrison settlement.

The motorcade is waved through Vidyayevo's two guarded perimeters by 2000, and Putin is bustled off to a private meeting at the apartment of the *Kursk* commander's widow, Irina Lyachina. While expressing his condolences, the president tells her how much Gennady had impressed him during their meeting in Moscow after the *Kursk*'s great Mediterranean adventure. He also asks if the traumatized settlement needs any special support, but Lyachina finds it difficult to respond, citing the most basic things, like food supplies. She struggles to maintain her composure.

Departing Lyachina's apartment, Putin surveys the village's deplorable conditions—the peeling paint, the boarded-up buildings, the exposed utility wiring, the crumbling stairwells reeking of urine. He does not find the conditions shocking; they remind him of the apartments he grew up in. He passes the chapel that has been filled with prayerful wailing for over a week. A sheet of paper is tacked to the door: "0900 Liturgy, sacraments, prayer. 1400 Prayer. 1800 Prayer. 2100 Prayer."

A number of townsfolk greet the president in the streets, many shaking his hand and politely speaking their minds.

By the time Putin enters the officers' headquarters, it is 2115. Five hundred of the submariners' relatives are gathered. Of the 118 dead sailors, sixty-two were married, with sixty-five children among them, including nine infants. At least four of the wives are pregnant, including Khalima Aryapova and the *Kursk*'s torpedo compartment commander's wife, who has also made the long pilgrimage from Dagestan to Vidyayevo.

The diminutive Putin steps to the podium and begins speaking, but the crowd strains to hear his remarks. "We have a meeting planned at fleet headquarters," he begins, "but I thought that I should see you first. . . ."

"We can't hear you!" shouts a man from the back.

Putin begins again, this time by expressing condolences, when a woman's voice interrupts.

"Cancel the day of mourning immediately!"

Caught off guard, Putin comes to understand that many in the room still refuse to accept that their men are all dead. "A day of mourning has been announced because it has been established beyond doubt that people have died," he explains, avoiding a reaffirmation that *all* of the men have died.

He tries to shift to the big picture, hoping to get the families to see the tragedy in the context of Russia's history. "There have always been tragedies," he says. ". . . You surely know that our country is in a difficult position and that our armed forces are as well. But I, too, never imagined that they were in such bad shape. . . . We must live within our means. . . . They should have life-saving equipment."

Another shout, this time about the departing foreign rescuers: "Why did they go?"

"You know," Putin says, "I asked them the same question: 'Are you sure it's all over? Can you prove it's all over?'"

"Why didn't they call foreign specialists immediately?" a woman cries out. "Why?"

"I can answer that," Putin says firmly. "Because we know we have rescue services and divers. . . ." He tries to describe the fleet's response to the tragedy as swift and competent—mentioning that he was first alerted at 0700 Sunday, provoking a new torrent of shouts.

"Just a second," he says, louder, but with growing uncertainty about how to navigate through the many lies that members of his government have told. "I will answer. Contact was lost at 2300 on the twelfth. They began a search. At 0430 they found it. On the thirteenth. In other words, I knew nothing about this. Nothing about what was going on."

The admission that their president was kept in the dark only fuels more outrage, and the shouts rise again, and Putin recounts Defense Minister Sergeyev's early assurances that the rescue effort was well in hand. "As soon as foreign aid was offered," he continues, "on the fifteenth—" he says, before being shouted down again by people who aren't about to accept his revisionist timeline.

Frustrated at last, Putin raises his voice. "It is true, true!" he says. "Television? They're lying, lying, lying." He reminds them that some of the men who control the independent media are the same despised oligarchs who pillaged state assets through Yeltsin's clumsy giveaway plan—a grand depletion of resources that exacerbated the nation's current military decline.

Then he tries a different tack. The fleet's rescue services "broke down," he admits. "There's not a damn thing left. There's not a damn thing left in the country! It's as simple as that."

"[You] pledge your life to defend your homeland, Russia," says one man, "and we can't even understand what Russia is!"

"They're deceiving us!" a woman shouts. "They're still deceiving us!"

"Where is my son?!" another woman wails. "Where is my son?!"

After listening to the outpouring, Putin tries to shift the focus to the future. "As far as money is concerned," he begins, eliciting a new round of shouting.

"It's our relatives we're talking about, not money! When will they give us our children?!"

"I'm talking the truth," Putin intones. "I didn't come here to talk a bit and clear off. I'm telling you how it is. It is a hard truth, but it is the truth."

"Now," he says, "I want to talk about the material side of the matter. . . . We will take the average officer's salary—*an officer's!*—and we will pay each family for ten years in advance."

More shouting. "He got two and a half thousand [rubles per month]!" shouts one woman. "What kind of money is that? For an officer, that's a disgrace!"

"Yes, it's a disgrace," agrees Putin, now sounding more like the son of the submariner his father once was. "Officers must not be thrown off buses because they can't pay for the journey. . . . It is impossible to live on one and a half or two thousand rubles."

"RIGHT!" say several voices in unison, and he begins winning them.

Moments later, a woman in the aisle faints and is carried over the heads of others, and off to the nearby medical clinic.

Hoping to wrap up the meeting, Putin says, "I am prepared to answer for the one hundred days I have been president. For the fifteen years before, I would have been sitting on one bench with you and asking these questions of others."

But the families aren't through. "They believed in the state," a woman shouts, "that the state would save them! You don't understand how they *believed!*"

Putin falls back on his first impulse: "We invited all the specialists who—"

"You could have saved just five!" a voice interrupts. "Bastards!"

And suddenly, fearlessly, one man dares ask the question of the moment: "Why have you come only now?"

"I had to decide for myself from the very start whether I should fly here or not," Putin says mildly. "I asked the military: 'Can I be of help there?' They said firmly, 'No!'"

"Do you believe them?" one woman asks, referring to Putin's military advisers. "You should put them behind bars! They have tricked you, the president, tricked you!"

Alarmed at the apparent insult to the president's dignity—and the insinuation that senior military officials would purposely mislead the president—a uniformed man moves in to make the woman sit down. Putin makes no protest.

"Don't make her sit!" shouts another woman. "Let her speak!"

"Tricked!" the seated woman yelps.

A wearied Putin begins again, as the hours-long meeting wends way past midnight, "They said they had the equipment. . . ."

"In the 1950s!" someone brays.

Putin tries to answer. "Well, we were ready to—"

"Well, it's too late now!" one man shouts in a rage, citing the humiliation of the foreign divers' efficiency.

"The Norwegians," Putin says—referring to the *Seaway Eagle* crew's ability to weld a new tool on the spot—"worked simply by hand. . . . They simply came along and . . . made a key. . . ."

"And we couldn't do that," says the man. "My God . . ."

27
FACING THE NATION
MOSCOW
WEDNESDAY, AUGUST 23

Vladimir Putin sits somberly in a black suit against the backdrop of the Russian tricolor flag, as an interviewer from state-controlled RTR TV gently guides him through a conversation broadcast to the people. It's the official day of mourning for the *Kursk*'s lost crew. Russian flags across the nation's eleven time zones fly at half-mast. The Russian president knows his people are deeply disappointed in his government's latest performance. Like never before, he knows, these new Russian people demand answers, and they now have the world's ear. They are most suddenly a people to contend with.

How will a man raised on professional deception pursue the truth about the *Kursk*? Veteran Russian cynics expect platitudes that will veil the same kinds of lies they've come to expect from their government. Younger Russians striving for a more "normal country" take a wait-and-see approach. Vladimir Putin wants to win both generations—without overly capitulating to Western-style democracy.

He allows long pauses in the interview, conveying an eerie sense of informality rarely displayed by Soviet or Russian premiers. At one point he dwells morosely over his meeting with the families in Vidyayevo. "Words are not enough," he says. "They are difficult to find. I want to wail."

Putin acknowledges that many of his top advisers believe quick sackings would be appropriate. Three senior military men have already submitted their resignations—Defense Minister Sergeyev, navy chief Kuroyedov, and

Northern Fleet commander Popov. "The letters will not be accepted," Putin says, explaining that he believes this is the easy way out. "If anyone is to blame, I must be punished. But we must get an objective picture of the accident and the course of the rescue efforts.

"I will remain with the army and navy," he continues. "Together we will revive the army, the navy, and the country. . . . We will get through this grave tragedy. But these events should unite the nation and people."

Putin pauses on this last point, displaying some ire toward the behavior of the purportedly "free and independent" media that helped fan the Russian fury against the government's handling of the tragedy. Putin talks sarcastically of how the oligarchs who own these media operations have posed as white knights to the stricken families—helping to establish bank accounts in the families' names for donations, covering some of the families' transportation costs to Murmansk. Putin suggests these same oligarchs have inappropriately lined their pockets with Russia's state assets—arguably the Russian people's natural inheritance—helping to cause the very financial neglect that has so dramatically drained the nation's military. The Russian president says these selfish hyper-capitalists should have "sold their villas on the Mediterranean coast of France or Spain. . . . But in that case they would have had to explain why all this real estate was registered in the name of figureheads and dummy legal companies. And we would have probably asked where the money had come from."

While Putin appears to remain above the fray in the coming weeks, many officials in his government rely on age-old instincts, trying to hold their country together by focusing the blame on the Americans. Russian defense minister Sergeyev leads the charge, sharing an especially intriguing pro-collision detail. He announces the sighting of the purportedly foreign buoys near the *Kursk* during the search efforts. He also announces that searchers detected a second seabed anomaly near the *Kursk* site, and declares that all of these things mysteriously "moved away" as Russian rescuers focused their attention on finding the *Kursk*.

Reports also soon circulate that at least one Russian submersible is scouring the seabed around the wreck site in search of foreign sub parts.

Though few authorities allege that the foreign submarine acted with malice, some aren't so sure. One independent nationalist group likens the incident to an outright attack, moving to seize the moment as a call to arms. They publish a manifesto, of sorts, under the heading "In the Hour of Trouble." It reads, in part: "It was not any accident with the ship's equipment, nor a miscalculation by the crew, that caused her death. She went down in the battle. . . . The mystery of the loss of the Kursk has not yet been solved, but within it is hidden, as if inside a 'black box,' the terrible fact that it is Russia that was rammed." Among the document's signatories is the former Soviet Navy's commander in chief, Admiral Vladimir Chernavin.

A tabloid in Murmansk, Komsomolets Zapolarya, echoes the sentiment with a more blunt headline: "America Wins First Round of World War III."

Other explanations for the tragedy's cause emerge, including the idea that the Kursk struck a stray sea mine left over from World War II. Some adventurous theorists even allege that the Peter the Great accidentally struck the Kursk with an errant missile, and posit that the "foreign sub" scenario is part of an elaborate cover-up aimed at deflecting attention from the Russian fleet's own bungling.

Meanwhile, Defense Minister Sergeyev forwards a formal request to the United States to share any intelligence data it may have gathered regarding the Kursk's demise, including a no-restrictions inspection of the hull of the USS Memphis at its temporary berth on the Norwegian coast. Though the U.S. Navy fears the precedent of allowing a foreign power to perform a hands-on study of one of its most secret vessels, they seriously consider sharing the relevant acoustic and seismographic data.

Shortly after his return from vacation to Washington, D.C., in the week after the Kursk tragedy, U.S. Undersecretary of Defense for Policy Walter Slocombe meets with Frank Miller in Slocombe's office on the

Pentagon's fourth floor. There, senior U.S. Navy officials make a presentation using ship tracks and charts showing the precise relative positions of the U.S. vessels in the Barents at the time of the *Kursk*'s two explosions. Slocombe and Miller easily satisfy themselves that the United States kept an adequate distance. Miller will later publicly declare as much in a letter to a retired submariners' club in St. Petersburg, not that it will quell suspicions.

But the East-West relationship remains chilled by the persistent allegations, so much so that it gives rise to a moment of black humor when Russia soon experiences another catastrophe. On August 27, Moscow's soaring Ostankino television tower—which carries the signals of all of the city's major broadcasters—suffers a three-day fire that kills four people and blanks out millions of TV screens. While the U.S. embassy in Moscow offers condolences, some in the diplomatic community murmur with a dark cynicism that there were no U.S. submarines in the tower's vicinity at the time of the conflagration.

An emotional pall hangs over Vidyayevo in the tragedy's aftermath, as many young *Kursk* families cling to the remains of their community. The small chapel can barely contain the bereaved. Some people feel haunted as they walk through the garrison town's streets. *Voronezh* officer Evgeny Zubkov repeatedly catches himself pausing over fleeting glimpses of other sailors—perhaps the man's profile or manner of walking—that briefly give the sense that it's all been a bad dream; his former mates from the *Kursk* are still alive. Sometimes he worries he is hallucinating.

Widows form spontaneous support groups. Khalima Aryapova and Olga Kolesnikova and Olga Lubushkina initially cling to one another, though Lubushkina soon withdraws to the comfort of her family in Severodvinsk.

The widow of *Kursk* torpedo commander Abdulkadir Ildarov lingers in Vidyayevo through September, giving birth to a baby boy on September 6. This is the event Abdulkadir had promised to return for. The widowed mother names her child Abdul.

That same day, Deputy Prime Minister Ilya Klebanov announces one of the initial findings of his investigatory panel. He declares that the persistent reports of trapped submariners knocking were all in error; preliminary analysis strongly suggests all of the sailors died nearly instantly. "Almost certainly," he proclaims, "once it was on the sea floor, no one was left alive."

While some relatives take modest comfort in the idea that their loved ones suffered mercifully quick deaths, government officials find an even greater comfort in how it removes the spotlight from their rescue operation.

Putin publicly echoes the quick-death conclusion, but he keeps a conspicuous distance from the collision theory. Western observers believe this is because Putin knows it's a lie, convenient for deflecting attention from the actions of a Russian military culture that the Russian president increasingly distrusts.

28

SUMMIT MEETING
NEW YORK CITY
SEPTEMBER 6, 2000

In a thirtieth-floor suite of Manhattan's Waldorf-Astoria, Bill Clinton consoles his guest. "I am genuinely sorry for what you've been through," he says to Vladimir Putin. "When something like this happens, people around the world identify with the victims and their families. . . . My heart went out to the people at the bottom of the sea, but it went out to everyone else as well."

The Russian president thanks Clinton, and tries to explain his dilemma. "There was no good option for me here," he says. "I was caught between bad options and worse options. Some people told me that if I'd let a small submarine go in there right away and at least make a try at rescuing the guys, my ratings would have gone up. You can't let something like this be driven by public relations. You've got to give priority to actually saving people."

While Strobe Talbott takes notes of the exchange, the two world leaders linger on the subject. "We operate in a different environment now," offers Clinton. "If a building blows up in Moscow, it's as though our own relatives were involved. Or if people in Mozambique are driven by flooding to take shelter in trees. In many ways this is a good thing. It reminds us of the humanity of others. It makes it harder to hate. . . ."

"We felt impotent during this whole disaster," Putin adds, and then echoes the same claim that his deputy prime minister broadcast to the Russian people only hours earlier. "It now looks as though all the crew died within sixty or ninety seconds. We couldn't tell the relatives, but it looks like there was a hole about two meters wide blown in the hull that flooded the first three sections of the sub. I'm not even sure how we can get the bodies out. There are a lot of cod in those waters, and there may not be any flesh on the bones."

Putin then shares with Clinton the universal frustration common to all political leaders subject to the ire of an independent media. "We tried to apply the brakes to all this furor," says the Russian leader. "But some people are strange, and they just keep feeding it. That's just a fact of life."

The exchange opens a ninety-minute talk between the two presidents. They move on to the scheduled topics of the day—the lingering Balkans conflict, nuclear nonproliferation, troubles with both Iraq and Iran. Clinton wraps up with a personal appeal for Putin to consider releasing American businessman Edmund Pope, still ailing in Russia's Lefortovo Prison as a suspected spy.

Talbott departs the presidents' meeting and takes a hotel elevator twelve floors up, where he sits at a luncheon table arranged amid the white sofas and grand piano of an apartment suite normally occupied by Richard Holbrooke. He spots Stephen Sestanovich, a fellow senior official at State, and slips him a note: "Get a load of Ivanov's teeth!"

Talbott glances across the room at the newly arrived Russian national security advisor, Sergy Ivanov, who hails Talbott with an unusually broad smile that reveals an ambitious dental upgrade. Talbott nods to Ivanov in recognition and returns the smile, then turns back to Sestanovich and mouths, "Wow."

The occasion is the long-planned work session of U.S. and Russian delegations in town for the United Nations' Millennium Summit. Sestanovich and Talbott are hoping to dissuade Russia from increasing its technological aid to Iran, but an air of cynicism hangs over the meeting from the mounting collision allegations. Catty whispers about dental work only hint at the American mood regarding Russia's new leadership. Putin may not be spouting the allegations himself, they say, but he's obviously made no effort to muzzle his many senior comrades.

The gathered members of Clinton's foreign-policy team gamely suppress their irritation over the pointed claims. Russia's deputy minister of foreign affairs, Georgi Mamedov, has already needled his assembled American counterparts—pointing out to Talbott and Medish that the United States had initially denied two previous Barents collisions, then later retracted the denials.

But in a side room, security chief Ivanov is about to confide an entirely different view during a discreet exchange with his U.S. counterpart, National Security Advisor Sandy Berger. As promised ahead of the meeting, Berger plans to deliver a summary of intelligence data that the United States gathered about the *Kursk* incident. The United States believes the data will demonstrate that there was no collision, and that instead the *Kursk* exploded from within.

With Mark Medish translating during the handover of intelligence documents, he and Berger note a dramatic shift in Ivanov's body language—he's visibly "radiating a furious humiliation" during the exchange—and in moments Ivanov makes his thoughts clear. He tells them that he and close friend Putin already believe their military has lied to them about the collision claims. Such a treacherous deceit from Russia's own military leadership has brought Ivanov to this discomfiting imposition. "We know that we have been misled," Ivanov says tersely. He adds that the Kremlin "might have responded differently if we had known these things earlier." He shares his hope that the data "will help quell suspicions."

Berger and Medish view Ivanov as favoring transparency in U.S.-Russian relations, despite his long association with Putin in the KGB. But Berger and Medish share their sense that the new intelligence information won't affect the Kremlin's posture regarding the odious collision claims. If Ivanov is shooting straight, then he and Putin have known this for some time, but they haven't felt compelled to share it with the Russian people just yet. Still, it would be nice if Putin and Ivanov would show some leadership. . . .

After returning to Moscow, Putin and Ivanov revert to Russian affairs as usual. Neither man declares an end to the spiraling collision allegations.

Ivanov tells the Russian media that the American intelligence package reveals "nothing new."

As the anti-American allegations rage unabated in Russia's nationalist circles—aided and abetted by many senior government officials—Putin and Ivanov and other Kremlin intimates begin hatching plans to make the best of a bad situation. Putin knows his KGB past will dog him through this. He knows his countrymen and the entire world expect an elaborate Soviet-style cover-up about what really happened to their navy's most formidable weapon and its 118 men. He plans to reveal everything, but in due time.

For now, the popular collision claims are politically convenient, and Putin will indulge investigations into their validity; preventing them would only feed the rumors that he's playing into a pro-American cover-up. His general prosecutor, Vladimir Ustinov, has opened a criminal probe to explore whether an as-yet-unnamed party has interfered with a Russian military exercise. And as part of that effort, Ustinov's investigators will try to learn what really caused the tragedy. Putin has also appointed Deputy Prime Minister Ilya Klebanov to conduct a parallel probe aimed at finding out whether the exercises were properly arranged and carried out.

In the end, Putin hopes that an unfettered investigation into this high-profile tragedy will become a bulwark against his critics; the former KGB colonel's government will tell even the most inconvenient truths regarding the Kursk, come what may.

On September 19, Putin announces an initial effort to recover some of the submariners' bodies. A week later, a Russian research vessel, the Akademik Keldysh, brings the two Mir submersibles to the wreck site to study the Kursk's ruins—both to map out the recovery plan and conduct a preliminary search for clues to the tragedy's cause. Russia's two best mini-subs scour the Barents bottom exhaustively until October 2, hunting for traces of foreign submarine parts. They are especially hoping for a glimpse of a foreign sub's railing allegedly sighted on the seabed by one of the rescue submersibles, but all they can find are scattered parts of the Kursk, along with a very unsuspicious hunk of lead.

The findings are quietly acknowledged, but spark little attention anywhere. The alleged American aggression theory still holds sway among the Russian nationalists and the besieged Russian admirals, many of whom increasingly convince themselves of its veracity. As the early probe unfolds with no traces of foreign materials on the scene, the more zealous theorists craft ever more acrobatic scenarios for how the foreign sub could have struck the *Kursk* without leaving any marks. One of their most difficult challenges is how to account for the fact that the foreign sub in question is only one-third of the *Kursk's* size. How could a much smaller Western sub cause such a wreck and get away undamaged?

In any case, to prevent foreigners from getting any ideas about molesting the potential crime scene, Northern Fleet vessels keep watch over the site, occasionally showering it with explosive devices to discourage any approach by unseen foreign submersibles.

29

UNDOING THE BIG LIE:
KOLESNIKOV'S CRY FROM THE DEEP
SOUTHERN BARENTS SEA
OCTOBER 25, 2000

An oil exploration platform hovers over the *Kursk* wreck site as recovery divers probe the ship for some clue to the cause of the blast. They also hope to retrieve any bodies that can safely be reached through the manhole-sized openings they have cut through the stubborn double hull.

Some eighty men from several nations toil aboard the elaborate *Regalia* platform, a floating micro-city whose powerful side thrusters struggle to maintain a fixed satellite-guided position against a steady thirty-five-knot easterly packed with forty-five-knot gusts. Throughout the day, the platform workers try to stay inside the *Regalia*'s many enclosures to avoid the wind-whipped sting of tiny raindrops that strike their exposed skin like needles. Even without the wind, the ambient temperature is a cruel thirty-eight degrees. For the newly trained Russian deep-sea divers down below, the surface weather threatens the operation's safety: as the *Regalia* rises and falls in the heavy swells, it strains the divers' lifelines. The recurring storms have repeatedly tempted authorities to scrap the operation.

The recovery workers expect few big surprises. Over the past two months, Klebanov's fact-finding panel has done a good job of convincing them, and much of the world, that little could have been done to save the *Kursk*'s crew. There were none to save: the tapping noises are now thought to have been nothing more than the expiring sounds of onboard mechanical devices.

During the recovery operation, only Russian divers are allowed outside the diving bell brought in for the effort. The first to enter the *Kursk* are Sergey Shmygin and Andrey Sviagintsev, who are among a handful that trained for this mission on one of the *Kursk*'s sister subs, the *Oryol*. To simulate the wrecked *Kursk*'s interior conditions, the divers repeatedly practiced navigating through the *Oryol* with blindfolds until they knew the layout from memory. To prepare themselves emotionally for the extraction of the dead, some divers spent time at a morgue in St. Petersburg.

Shmygin, the smaller of the two divers, is chosen to enter the hole they've made into the eighth compartment while Sviagintsev assists from atop the *Kursk*'s outer hull. Because the blast wreckage apparently stopped forward of the reactors, experts believe the eighth compartment likely holds some of the most well-preserved bodies. As the divers prepare for Shmygin's entry, stray cod swim through their light beams—along with a large jellyfish slowly throbbing past.

Within the restrictive limits of his air and communications lines, Shmygin explores a small area of the eighth's top deck and finds it empty, then later approaches the watertight door leading into the ninth compartment. The diving director aboard the *Regalia* instructs him to steer clear of a large fish that appears to guard the door, declaring the fish dangerous. The fish slowly moves away, and Shmygin tries to manipulate the door's latching ring with his diving knife. The door briefly resists, until Shmygin gives it a gentle kick with his boot. As the door swings open, Shmygin's helmet camera captures the slow-motion drift of a mattress suspended in the compartment's murky water. He uses a metal rod to move it aside and, slowly, the body of a man floats into the lamp's beam, his facial features obscured by the cloud of churning debris. Carefully maneuvering the body with the rod, Shmygin attaches a cable to the man's legs, and he and Sviagintsev slowly extract the body feetfirst through the outer hull. While Shmygin works further into the ninth, Sviagintsev gently places the submariner's body into a closet-sized yellow steel-mesh box perched on the *Kursk*'s outer deck.

Minutes later, Shmygin is maneuvering the body of a particularly large man whose upper torso has been badly burned. Some diving instructors had urged the divers to look away from the men's faces at such moments, but Shmygin has little choice. The man's head appears oddly flimsy, a ragged black outline with no discernable facial characteristics at all. Then, with some difficulty, they extract a third body before Shmygin becomes concerned that his cables might rupture against the compartment's jagged obstacles.

With the mesh box now holding the bodies of three men, Shmygin and Sviagintsev rest for some hours within their diving bell while they plan a way to probe deeper into the compartment, whose entry quickly drops to a lower deck after a tight gangway. Finally, after midnight, Shmygin retrieves a fourth body, and the divers signal the *Regalia*'s crane operator to lift the box to the surface.

The crane operator skillfully steers the mesh box close to the white shipping container aboard the *Regalia* that will serve as a makeshift examination chamber. Once the bodies are arrayed in the chilled room, the confined atmosphere fills with the smells of salt water and burned flesh. The handful of Russian examiners put on white hygienic coveralls, masks, and latex gloves.

With the initial exams well under way before 0300, Russian Navy pathologist Colonel-Lieutenant Sergey Chernisov studies the body of the man whose torso and head suffered the heavy burns. Because the would-be rescue divers in August had reported seeing carbon-blackened bubbles when they sprang the crippled submarine's hatch, the examiners have been expecting the burns. But these first exams already appear to show something new and shocking: these submariners had time to change clothes in response to the catastrophe; this sailor's beefy lower half is still clothed in the waterproof shell of an emergency escape suit. Top officials had sworn the sailors had all died in a few minutes—*how had this man found time to put on the extra suit?*

Backup Russian diver Renat Gizatullin operates a video camera to keep a record, while pathologist Shamil Shamshudtinov conducts the hands-on exam under Chernisov's direction. Shamshudtinov first concentrates on the dead sailor's torso, carefully peeling away oily black layers of material until a conspicuously congealed clump emerges in the area of the right breast pocket. Shamshudtinov tugs at it, pulling it away from the body. He gingerly tugs again at the clump's top layer, exposing a trace of handwriting on paper. "It appears to be some writing, some letter," Shamshudtinov narrates for both Chernisov and the video record. *What's this?* Chernisov wonders as the note emerges. *He also had time to write a note?*

Diver-cameraman Gizatullin zooms in on a neatly written list of names.

With Chernisov's encouragement, Shamshudtinov further unfolds several pages from a notebook, exposing the stark clarity of a name at the bottom of the top page that he reads aloud: "Kolesnikov." He uses a magnifying glass to briefly study the papers' singed edges. He notes the names "Aryapov" and "Kuznetsov," and then reads portions of the remarkable series of texts.

On one page, this man has written a brief personal message: "Olga! I love you! Do not suffer too much! Regards to G.V.," he has written, using the initials for Olga Kolesnikova's mother. "Regards to mine," he adds, referring to his parents and brother. "No need for despair. Mitya."

In quick succession, officially inconvenient truths present themselves to the handful of Russian recovery workers. Parts of an emergency suit. A note. Then the story the note has to tell. Twenty-three men waited in the ninth compartment, hoping against hope that a new, more humane Russia valued their lives above national pride, the protection of state secrets, and other bad habits left over from the Soviet era.

The facts are excruciatingly simple: *We didn't die in minutes. We desperately tapped out an SOS. We might have had a chance if only our country had called in help from somewhere, anywhere, sometime within those first hours, instead of foolishly banking on grossly outmoded rescue equipment with ill-trained crews.*

Though stunned by the revelations, the tiny exam team maintains their professionalism. They place the note and its explosive contents into a clear plastic bag, as Chernisov orders it forwarded to Rear Admiral Gennady Verich, on board the *Regalia* for the recovery operation. The sub-rescue chief finds Kolesnikov's words disturbing, but there is no suppressing them from his seniors.

An imminent dilemma races up the chain of command from the Barents Sea to the Kremlin. Verich tells Popov. Popov tells Kuroyedov. Kuroyedov tells Klebanov in Moscow. Klebanov tells Putin. Putin makes a decision that will set the tone for the investigation to come.

Meanwhile, in the fourteenth-floor-apartment bedroom of Irina and Roman Kolesnikov, it's still well before dawn on the cool and cloudy October 26. Irina is having a dream about Dima. She sees her "Mitya" sitting on a park bench along one of St. Petersburg's picturesque canals on an uncommonly warm day. As she approaches him, he notices her and beams. She takes him in like a mother does, delighting in his broad smile and the way the sleeves of his T-shirt flutter in the light wind. Mitya was always unabashedly his mother's boy. Whenever he came home on leave, Mitya could easily persuade her to allow him to lounge on the apartment couch with his head in her lap, and coax her to stroke his scalp the way she always did to soothe him as a restless young boy.

From his spot on the bench, Mitya looks up at her suddenly, vulnerable and imploring. "Mama, will you come to see me off?"

"Mitya, of *course* I will," she says, surprised that he thought it necessary to ask at all. The two of them hold each other's smiles while reality begins leaking into the dream and Irina tries to hold on to the image just a little longer because she senses there's a horrifying truth lurking just outside this fragile deep sleep and, oh dear God, it's still there, isn't it, this inescapably monstrous truth. . . .

Irina begins thrashing in the bed. "Roman," she mumbles to her sleeping husband. "Wake up. I think something's happened."

Hours later, Vice Admiral Mikhail Motsak arrives at Northern Fleet headquarters in Severomorsk just after daylight. At 0830 he uses his secure line to check in with his comrade aboard the *Regalia*, Admiral Verich. Verich tells him of the note and its incendiary contents. From Motsak's perspective, the note's existence should not surprise anyone.

He is one of the senior-most fleet authorities who still believes that he and his men clearly heard human tapping from trapped submariners. He has publicly stated that it was last heard on Monday, August 14, at 1100. It's even reasonable to assume they were conscious well past that time.

The widespread reports of tapping until the fourteenth—plus official assertions that discontinued tapping might mean only the men were weak but alive for at least another day—has left many Russians wondering aloud if submariners could still have been saved three days after the blasts.

Roused by the note's implications, Motsak stops by Kuroyedov's office within the headquarters by 0930. Motsak finds it instantly clear that Kuroyedov has already been talking to Moscow about the Kolesnikov note. Motsak is taken aback by the naval chief's statement, but is very glad to hear it: "It is agreed that this note must be made public," says Kuroyedov, "to make clear to all that nobody is concealing anything."

Though Kuroyedov cites Deputy Prime Minister Klebanov as the authority behind this decision, Motsak is convinced it has also been cleared by the Russian president himself. Motsak is impressed at Putin's apparent gambit against tradition; he believes Putin has done the right thing.

At the appropriate time, Kuroyedov instructs, Motsak will broadcast the note's contents to the Russian people. The navy chief tells Motsak to respect the Kolesnikov family's privacy by not publicly disclosing the dying captain-lieutenant's sentiments to his loved ones. "Read only the service part of the note," Kuroyedov says, but withhold the listed names of Kolesnikov's twenty-two trapped comrades. The announcement is slated for the afternoon, 1400, so intermediaries can notify the sailor's loved ones before the broadcast.

In St. Petersburg, the head of a retired submariners' club is asked to alert the Kolesnikov family. For retired Captain First Rank Igor Kurdin, the assignment is more delicate than it would first appear. Kolesnikov's parents and his widow have had a falling out. Despite the brevity of her married life with Dima, Olga Kolesnikova has received the entire $25,000 government payout promised to the dead submariners' families by Putin in August. Olga declined to mention the money to Dima's parents, who learned of it only after they noticed an abrupt coolness from their daughter-in-law before they all departed Vidyayevo. Dima's parents and brother, Alexander, are not included in the compensation plans. The arrangement is standard for all victim families, a reality that has quietly strained relations among the relatives of many dead *Kursk* submariners. The issue has become a thorny obstacle for Kurdin's club, which has tried to keep the peace among bereaved *Kursk* families while also serving as a clearinghouse for outside charity efforts.

With the clock ticking on the public announcement, Captain Kurdin first tries unsuccessfully to reach Kolesnikov's father, Roman, and his brother, Alexander. Then he calls the school where both Irina and Olga work. He gets Irina on the phone and tells her it's "urgent." She asks him what it's about, but he says the news is better conveyed in person. "Be here by one-thirty," says Kurdin. "I really need to talk to you. Bring Olga." "I'll come alone," says Irina, a signal to Kurdin that the rift is still a big issue.

But Olga is duly notified as well, and she arrives at the Submariner's Club five minutes before Irina. The two women refuse to acknowledge each other as Kurdin guides them into his office, where three health care workers await—a general physician, a cardiologist, and a military psychologist. Kurdin shares with the estranged mother and daughter-in-law that navy chief Kuroyedov has just announced that the first submariner's body has been identified as Captain-Lieutenant Dmitry Romanovich Kolesnikov. Irina gasps. Olga remains poker-faced. Kurdin then tells them Dima also left a note, and that a more detailed announcement is planned for several minutes from now on the television, and that they can all watch it together in Kurdin's office.

By the time Vice Admiral Motsak's face appears on the screen, ten people are crowded into Kurdin's small office. Motsak is seen standing outside the Northern Fleet headquarters in Severomorsk, against the backdrop of a dockside memorial to the famed Russian submarine *K-21*, storied for its bold harassment of the German battleship *Tirpiz* in World War II.

Motsak confirms that four bodies have been removed from *Kursk* so far, that the first body identified is that of Kolesnikov, and that Kolesnikov left a note. "The note is of a very private nature and will be passed on to his relatives," says Motsak, "but it also gave us a lot of operational information."

Motsak declines to read the Kolesnikov text verbatim, but broadly describes how it indicates that all men in the *Kursk's* four aft compartments gathered into the last of them to await rescue.

In Kurdin's office, Irina becomes hysterical, prompting the medical team to gather around her. Olga remains quiet.

For Motsak in Severomorsk, this is also an emotional moment. He is acutely aware of the Kolesnikov note's dramatic repudiation of official claims of a quick death for the entire crew. He is acutely aware that this note will ignite a new firestorm of public condemnation, the conclusion to which is anybody's guess. He is also acutely aware that such an announcement could never have happened in Soviet times. He feels the moment's humanity, and nearly chokes up on his admonition to journalists regarding the victim's families. "Don't pry clumsily into our souls," he says. "We're in pain." He then salutes and steps away from the camera.

When Irina Kolesnikova regains her composure, Captain Kurdin warns her and Olga that reporters with cameras are waiting in the hallway outside the club offices, but that the two women should take as much time as they'd like to process their feelings before stepping outside; neither should feel compelled to make any public statement unless they want to.

Roman Kolesnikov soon enters the office and rushes to comfort his wife. He, too, has heard the news. "Mother," he says gently to Irina, "you should be glad that our son has been found."

Roman also declines to acknowledge the presence of his estranged daughter-in-law. Distressed, Olga stands up and asks Captain Kurdin: "May I leave for a cigarette?" Kurdin nods and ushers her into a separate room.

When Kurdin returns moments later, Roman is seated on a bench, suffering chest pain. The cardiologist monitors him with a blood pressure cuff, then administers an injection.

Dima's brother Alexander, or "Sasha," arrives, prompting a new wave of tears as he embraces his mother. Olga, who had returned to the room, abruptly departs again for a cigarette. Sasha senses that his parents' stand-off with Olga is heightening the emotions all around, and quietly urges his parents to attempt making amends. "Why be like this to Olga?" he asks. But his parents are in no mood to initiate a change of terms with their daughter-in-law.

Roman and Irina decline the invitation to grant interviews, but Olga feels differently after her return to the room. "Okay," she says. "I'll give one."

Olga steps into the hallway to a blaze of klieg lights. Few in the media have given her much attention up until now, but her soft beauty and poise instantly captivate. "I heard the official announcement on the television at two p.m.," she stammers through tears. "It's painful, enormously painful. I had had a feeling that my husband did not die immediately, and that was painful for me. Well, this pain turned out to be justified. He is a lovely man. I want to see him one more time. I want to read his letter."

Olga soon retreats from the club, with several cameramen trailing her into the tattered, rainy streets of St. Petersburg.

Shortly after her departure, twenty-two-year-old Sasha makes his own brief statement: "I can't really explain how I feel on hearing this news," he says. "But I am sure I wouldn't wish you or anybody to be in my place now and feel the way I feel."

With the media horde clamoring for the note's text, Russia's ITAR-TASS wire service provides glimpses, courtesy of Admiral Kuroyedov. After Motsak's TV statement, Kuroyedov held back tears while reading some of the text to a number of *Kursk* widows in the North.

"I am writing blindly," the Russian wire service quotes. "It's 13:15. All personnel from sections six, seven and eight have moved to section nine. There are 23 people here. We have made the decision because none of us can escape."

•   •   •

Unremittingly rocky weather over the wreck site prevents a helicopter from transporting the bodies of Kolesnikov and the others to the Russian mainland for four days. The delay allows Kolesnikov's loved ones to arrange flights to Severomorsk, where the submariners' corpses will be held and more formally identified. Kolesnikov's parents and widow will be allowed to view Dima's body if they wish. Surviving former *Kursk*-mates Evgeny Zubkov and Ivan Nessen are also summoned to help identify the remains of their former comrades.

When Dima's parents enter the military morgue, they are shocked by his body's condition. Though warned of the fire's effects on their son's appearance, the brutal scorching of his entire upper body especially devastates his mother. Through sobs, Irina can confirm her son's identification only through an ankle scar suffered in a childhood injury.

When Olga enters the morgue, she rushes to the side of her husband's body and embraces him, kissing the charred remains of his face. A shocked morgue attendant tries unsuccessfully to dissuade her from such intimate contact with a body that has been dead for months.

To the four hundred people who gather in St. Petersburg for Dmitry Kolesnikov's funeral one week later, the man and his note mean many different things. To parents, Roman and Irina, and brother, Sasha, he is obviously a beloved son and brother, but also a great example of Russian character, able to perform his duty with true professionalism under the most horrifying circumstances.

To Olga, he is the soul mate who swept her off her feet and stayed faithful to the last with his pledge to express his love for her in his dying moments.

To many of Kolesnikov's gathered classmates, he is the most perfectly everyday Russian man, "typical" of his generation, a man whose sense of honor and duty compelled him to behave exactly as they would expect him to behave. They all share a deep patriotism that transcends their nation's political turmoil, and it is they who have crafted the simple sign with a selected phrase from his note that gives them comfort in the religious ceremony at St. Petersburg's "sailor's church": "No need for despair."

To friends like drinking mate Maksim Guskov, Mitya requires no special hero worship: such adulation is exactly the sort of thing they might have had a laugh over. Maksim has simply lost the dearest friend he ever had, and he tries to drink the pain away, in a decidedly self-destructive surrender to Russia's greatest national scourge.

To former long-time love Inna, this event marks the tragic wasting of the man she still believes she could have spared from this fate by persuading him into a civilian profession.

To the many gathered senior officials—including Northern Fleet Admiral Vyacheslav Popov—this dead young sailor and his words from beyond the grave represent an entirely new level of nightmare. It is the loss of a good man, of course, but his note's simple words serve as a personal indictment. "None of us can get to the surface. . . . It looks like there are no chances. 10 to 20 percent."

To hopeful observers in the larger world community watching from afar, this man and his note—and the open public outcry they've generated—could herald a possible turning point in the Russian mind-set every bit as sweeping as the Berlin Wall's collapse.

Following the service, an honor guard leads Kolesnikov's casket into the Seraphimovskaya Cemetery, where the Saturday-morning rain abates but the sky remains stubbornly gray. The casket is suspended on boards above a burial hole that occupies the center of one of the cemetery's main paths. In recognition of the *Kursk* submariners' place in Russia's national memory, the path will be filled with the gravesites of other submariners as the recoveries proceed, forcing the creation of new paths in the process.

Mournful music gives way to a round of speeches. A fusillade of gunshots is fired ceremonially into the air. The crowd of nearly one thousand maintains a deep silence as grave diggers lower Kolesnikov's casket into the ground, with their spades soon plying the mounds of soft dark earth, making a smooth *shussing* sound with each shovelful.

The burial site is dubbed "Heroes' Way," and will soon become crowded with the gravesites of many of Kolesnikov's comrades. It closely abuts one of the mass graves of an earlier generation of Kolesnikov's countrymen, whose lives were offered up by the thousands to the Nazis' brutal nine-hundred-day blockade of St. Petersburg. Among the other grave sites jammed into the ever more crowded cemetery are the tombs of the Soviet Union's Afghan soldiers, along with those of modern Russia's victims of the ongoing carnage in Chechnya. All of them have offered blood for the motherland, each in his own way.

And then there are the occasional conspicuous grave sites of the so-called "New Russians," beneficiaries of the best and worst that capitalism has to offer. Their sites are elaborately ornate, often occupying space carved into paths previously considered inviolable to the everyday Russians.

30
THE SEEDS OF ACTIVISM
VIDYAYEVO
FALL 2000

Some of Vidyayevo's most injured families are slow to depart for government-funded free apartments, most of which are clustered around St. Petersburg. They find comfort in the communal grieving, forming even closer bonds among traditionally close neighbors.

Olga Kolesnikova occasionally steps in to share child-care duties with Natalya Tylik, widow of *Kursk* navigator Sergey, who has left her with a one-year-old daughter. Other family members gather for the simple analgesic of conversation, many sharing vivid descriptions of portentous dreams in which their husbands visited to assure them that everything was okay. For months, Irina Lyachina is among the few widows denied such comfort, but she takes a certain satisfaction in another widow's dream: "I saw Genna," Galina Belogun tells Irina excitedly, referring to Irina's husband. "He told me to bring you some grapes." Belogun admits she found the request mystifying, but Irina Lyachina feels she knows exactly what it's about: Genna had always brought her chocolate when he returned from the sea, and Irina finally got up the nerve to tell him chocolate had become a boring cliché; she would prefer something like . . . grapes. Still, Irina remains jealous. She wishes Genna would come to her directly.

Some of the widows gather in their chilled apartments over tea to devise effective methods for organizing their newfound political clout. Even amid their grief, they can see from the few media signals beamed into their settlement how powerful they can be when they speak with one voice.

Though most are still too emotionally fragile to expand their efforts just yet, their network still helps keep the tragedy in the global spotlight. This system aids a Norwegian documentary crew in tracking down Nadezhda Tylik, *Kursk* navigator Sergey's mother, the one who was infamously injected with sedatives after lashing out at the government minister.

As the Oslo-based documentary crew spirits Tylik away from the "closed" settlement of Vidyayevo in a taxi for filming, the sailor's mother regales them with a bitter tale of how Northern Fleet officials had still hoped to keep her muzzled. She says she learned that officials had been telling journalists who sought her out that she was ill and had been taken to an undisclosed psychiatric hospital.

As a centerpiece to the Norwegian film team's story, they bring Nadezhda to a room where she meets with diver Paul Dinesson, one of the two foreign rescuers to reach the *Kursk*. They embrace before Dinesson shares his account of the attempted rescue, and soon the scene switches to a larger gathering of the extended Tylik family—including Sergey's father, widow, and daughter—showing the Norwegian diver their family photo album, depicting their lost Sergey in his prime.

The documentary becomes one of the most powerful of dozens more that will highlight the tragedy's Soviet-era mode of behavior.

The criminal probe into the *Kursk* wreck unfolds through the fall, and Russian Navy insiders become well aware of the dearth of evidence of a foreign submarine's involvement. But chief Kuroyedov finds political value in fomenting the allegations just the same.

The low point comes at a closed gathering in Moscow on the late afternoon of December 4. At his annual "State of the Navy" briefing for Moscow's foreign naval attachés, Kuroyedov takes the podium to address about eighty gathered military diplomats. After a few welcoming words, Kuroyedov launches into a speech calling on all nations to become more open about their submarine operations, and to observe a higher standard of safety in patrol areas. The navy chief then chides "some nations" for their blatant disregard for such basic precautions. He further says he recognizes that "some nations" are still fighting the Cold War, a bad habit for which no sailor should ever have to pay with his life. With U.S. attaché Captain Brannon growing increasingly uncomfortable in the gathered crowd, Kuroyedov finally zeroes in. He proclaims that America's continued refusal to grant a thorough inspection of its suspect submarine's hull is strong evidence of U.S. complicity in the *Kursk* tragedy.

As he says these words, Kuroyedov glowers at Brannon and shakes his fist in the air. He points angrily at the American attaché and calls for an open discussion about submarine safety to prevent such tragedies in the future.

Standing at Brannon's side during the excoriation, his assistant, Commander Warren Wheeler, nudges Brannon at the elbow. "Do you want to leave, boss?"

"No," says Brannon, standing his ground. "That would give him exactly what he wants."

In the reception line after Kuroyedov's speech, Brannon simply glares at the Russian navy chief, refusing to extend his hand.

The next day, U.K. attaché Captain Simon Lister suggests to Brannon that Kuroyedov didn't believe his own allegations; he was simply posturing for the benefit of his fellow nationalists.

The coming of the Arctic winter inexorably deepens the chill over Vidyayevo, turning its small population inward. To leaven the darkening spirits, Northern Fleet officials announce a posthumous awards ceremony to be held at the garrison town's headquarters building for the thirty-one *Kursk* submariners' families who still live there.

On the day of the ceremony, December 12—the wreck's four-month anniversary—officials unveil the awards of valor. Putin will later award a Hero of Russia gold medal to *Kursk* commander Gennady Lyachin, planning to bestow it personally upon the widow, Irina Lyachina, in a Kremlin ceremony.

But the commander's widow attends this ceremony as well, and she is pleased to see that the modest observance displays a certain pomp.

A banner is unfurled. The Russian national anthem is played. The presidential decree is read aloud. Even Northern Fleet commander Popov is in attendance. After the ceremony, all are invited into a separate room for refreshments, where journalists, including a camera crew from independent TV station NTV, await interviews.

Suddenly amid the murmuring, Nadezhda Tylik mounts a rostrum, looking vastly more self-possessed than during her August outburst. "I want the children of the dead men to know when they grow up," she says into the crowd, as startled heads turn to hear, "that their fathers died because of the negligence, bungling, and, quite simply, indifference of the powers that be."

The gathered group watches as if spellbound. Tylik continues: "It so happens that the presentation of the awards at our Vidyayevo garrison coincides with Constitution Day, the day we celebrate the document that protects our rights." She calls the awards and decrees shams that distract from ongoing abuses by nervous officials. She even cites the widely held belief that all of the garrison telephones are bugged. "These are all breaches of our human rights as enshrined in the Constitution," thunders Tylik. "If they try to tell journalists who try to meet me or members of the bereaved families that we are being treated at a psychiatric clinic, don't believe them. This means we are being marched off to prison. . . .

"No," she continues, "I am sincerely sorry for those who are to blame for this tragedy and those who have been forced to lie to the relatives and friends of the dead. They will have to carry in their hearts the heavy burden of a grievous sin. Be brave and repent before it is too late."

As she says these words, Tylik glares directly at Admiral Popov, who departs the hall in disgust.

31
RAISE THE *KURSK*
RUSSIA
SPRING 2001

*One of the problems which arose in recent years in the country is this
distrust of government officials. This confidence can only be restored
if what we promise is fulfilled. In the economy. In the finances. In the
political sphere. Everywhere.*

— Vladimir Putin, explaining to reporters why the
high cost of raising the *Kursk* is justified,
Gazeta.Ru, June 18, 2001

Nothing as enormous as the *Kursk* has ever been lifted from the seabed,
yet this is what President Putin has promised his countrymen will happen. Early cost estimates range from a low of $60 million to a high of
$130 million, but honest accounting could easily propel the tally much
higher. Russia blanches at such a price—most of which will go to foreign
salvage companies—with many perfectly patriotic Russian voices arguing it's completely unnecessary. The *Kursk* can stay where it is. The reactors can be covered over with cement. Channel markers can guide
merchant traffic to keep a safe distance.

Kremlin-friendly journalists try to argue that Putin should honorably
back away from the pledge in the interest of simple fiscal responsibility.
Victims' families even add their voices in support of abandoning the
seemingly foolhardy venture. Time-honored naval tradition dictates that

sea wrecks and their victims may be left where they fall; there is no over-whelming need to change that now. Twelve bodies were recovered along with the Kolesnikov note. Forty tons of wreckage have been hauled up for study. It is enough for the investigators. Why push it?

Throughout the winter, Putin's mission to raise the *Kursk* has become a multinational operation. Dutch contractor Mammoet wins a long-shot proposal, and teams up with Smit Tak International. St. Petersburg's Rubin Design Bureau, which designed the *Kursk*, steps in as the project's primary coordinator on behalf of the Russian government. All involved worry over getting the ambitious plan formed, approved, and under way in time before the fall storms begin sweeping across the Barents. Elaborate new seabed surveys are conducted. New machinery is designed and custom-manufactured at a breakneck pace. Huge pontoons are built in an Arctic Russian shipyard.

And then the perfect news item for conspiracy buffs: Project engineers conclude that the *Kursk*'s shattered bow section—which contains the mysterious remains of the blown torpedo room—poses a destabilizing safety hazard to the lifting process. The multinational team opts to sever the bow from the rest of the submarine, either to be left on the seabed or lifted separately at a later date.

Interested parties howl from all quarters: Pro-collision advocates see a ploy to hide foreign sub damage to protect the alleged Putin-Clinton agreement. Anti-collision advocates suspect a ploy to hide the proof of *no* collision, so as to preserve the Russian nationalists' unifying claim that the West is still a hostile outsider. Torpedo-accident advocates also detect a move to bury the evidence, sparing the Russian Navy any risk of self-blame by leaving the case unsolved. This group includes many Western theorists long convinced that the *Kursk* was secretly testing the superfast Shkval torpedo system when it suffered its catastrophic explosion, and that the Russians don't want to acknowledge its flaws.

Officials launch a special Web site dedicated to covering every aspect of the raising effort—in both Russian and English—offering a remarkable inside view of the daily process. Most journalists hail its information as smart, candid, and largely balanced—if tilted toward collision. But the site also updates the ongoing probes of both Klebanov and Ustinov, with the deputy prime minister favoring collision and the national prosecutor showing skepticism; he hasn't seen any evidence of a foreign sub's involvement.

The raising project's doomsayers become more shrill with the arrival of summer, with only a few workers toiling above the wreck site by late June. Then divers arrive in July to cut holes into carefully chosen points on the hull, where twenty-six giant cables will find anchor. The heavy pillars of a customized hull-cutting chain-saw system are augered into the seabed, straddling the *Kursk* just forward of its sail. The critics grow increasingly quiet as Mammoet-Smit's goliath *Giant 4* salvage vessel sets out from Amsterdam, bound for the Barents.

The hole cutting goes slowly. The sawing cable breaks and needs repair. The Barents skies repeatedly threaten, encouraging the critics but steeling the resolve of the international project managers. Finally, all of the heavy cables are anchored throughout the *Kursk*'s topside and the nose is completely severed. On October 8, cable operators aboard the *Giant 4* carefully winch the lines taut and gauge the ability of each cable to flex vertically with the wave action without creating damage. Then comes the signal to increase the cables' pulling pressures gradually, hoping against hope that the silted seabed offers too little vacuum seal to put up a fight. It doesn't. Almost imperceptibly, the engineers aboard the *Giant 4* can tell from their control panels that the seabed is losing its claim on the *Kursk*. More than a year after it fell, Russia's dead supersub is rising to the surface.

The project's engineers are elated, of course, but keep their emotions in check. It will still take hours for the wreck to rise up into the custom-fitted underbelly of the *Giant*, which must tuck and secure the *Kursk* before its voyage to a dry dock near Murmansk.

The final fitting into the pontoon is almost invisible to nearby surface observers, both in surrounding naval vessels and on the *Giant 4* itself—no aspect of the *Kursk* breaches the surface—but word of the lifting's completion brings great displays of relief to all involved. Amid the excited handshakes and backslapping, Rubin Design Bureau chief Igor Spassky embraces Vice Admiral Motsak and plants a kiss on his cheek. The *Giant 4* then pulls up her lines and sets a course for the Kola Bay.

When the *Giant 4* and her portentous cargo approach the bay on October 10, Northern Fleet vice admiral Motsak is among the officials in the flotilla. He scans the seas and notices a small escort of dolphins leaping alongside the grim but victorious procession. He feels a chill when vessels in the flotilla all sound their foghorns at once, hailing the success of an undertaking that so many had doubted so stridently.

Russian journalists clamor for access to the wreck once it's secured in dry dock, but Northern Fleet admiral Vyacheslav Popov expresses offense at the mere notion of a public display. You must understand, says Popov firmly, to navy men a wrecked vessel is like the body of a dead loved one. It is morbid to expose it in such a fashion for public consumption.

Three layers of security surround the dry dock. The bayside exposure of the sub is shrouded in camouflage. As the flayed leviathan is tethered and prepared for the first wave of forensic investigators hoping to recover bodies quickly before they're exposed to the air, only the tiniest bits of independent reporting emerge.

From his headquarters in Moscow, General Prosecutor Vladimir Ustinov has a difference of opinion with Popov regarding opening the battered *Kursk* for public scrutiny. Popov obviously misunderstands President Putin's mandate. There will be no secrets here. This will be a show of Russian glasnost like the world has never seen.

On November 8, a portly Ustinov arrives at the dry dock in Roslyakovo, dramatically pulling back the *Kursk*'s shroud on national television so that the Russian people may see it. Even with the bow cut cleanly off, the *Kursk*'s exposed front end presents a disturbingly tangled chaos. "What happened inside these compartments was hell," Ustinov narrates in the seven-minute film clip. "The explosion," he gestures, "wiped out everything here. . . . The strong alloys from which these compartments are built were simply ripped apart."

Ustinov then declares, despite only the most preliminary evidence, that investigators believe all compartments were flooded within a "maximum eight hours. . . . Those who think there was a possibility to save our sailors should know that there was no such possibility."

32

NAMING NAMES
MOSCOW
DECEMBER 3, 2001

Several days after holding a Kremlin ceremony congratulating all parties involved in the *Kursk*'s lift, Vladimir Putin holds two back-to-back Saturday meetings. He first meets with General Prosecutor Ustinov for a preliminary report. The prosecutor describes how Northern Fleet leaders committed a disturbing range of safety violations regarding the ill-fated exercise, along with attendant breaches of rescue protocols. He confirms for Putin the grievous offense quietly revealed to Sandy Berger more than a year earlier: that many senior military officials had, indeed, knowingly deceived the Kremlin. Senior officers unduly delayed reports of trouble; the rescue assets proved woefully inadequate for the mission.

Ustinov also discloses that, contrary to countless official proclamations, no evidence at all has been uncovered to support the popular collision claims.

Now armed with the proper ammunition, Putin immediately calls a meeting with Defense Minister Ivanov, navy commander in chief Kuroyedov, and Chief of General Staff Anatoly Kvashnin. The Russian president asks them to draw up a list of the navy's primary offenders, in accord with the investigators' early report. And he wants them now.

Before the evening is out, navy chief Kuroyedov tersely announces the three most prominent sackings on national television: Northern Fleet head Popov; his chief of staff, Mikhail Motsak; and the fleet's submarine flotilla commander, Vice Admiral Oleg Burtsev. Russian wire services indicate a total of fourteen Northern Fleet officers have been singled out for punishment, and soon a detailed listing of all the punished officers is also published. It includes fleet combat training chief Boyarkin, Russian Navy rescue chief Verich, and his Northern Fleet counterpart, Teslenko. In keeping with Russian tradition, most of the officers demoted or dismissed will soon be offered attractive posts in other areas of the Russian government.

Putin adds a modest postscript to the day's events, specifically directed at collision supporters. "It should be admitted that, despite the large amount of work done," he tells journalists, "no objective evidence proving this theory has been received up to now."

These first reckonings cause split reactions in the coming weeks. Aggrieved *Kursk* families remain mystified over repeated official statements that the demotions and dismissals are not directly related to the tragedy, only to poor management of the exercise in which it happened. Some Russian newspaper pundits find fault with the list of officers who were singled out, many insisting they are just scapegoats. The staunchly independent *Novaya Gazeta* leads a charge against what it sees as the mysterious preservation of the man who approved of the entire exercise plan and then presided over its political shakeout—naval chief Kuroyedov. Some observers of Russia's military-political culture attribute Kuroyedov's job security to his close ties with Putin, who in July 2000 found time to attend personally the admiral's oral defense of his dissertation, which outlined a brighter future for the Russian Navy.

Throughout the early winter of 2002, Russians bear witness to a steady parade of headlines updating the list of sailors whose remains have been confirmed amid the heavy metal layers of wreckage. With each new name, senior forensic spokesmen try to lower expectations of how many remains might still be found, yet workers sifting the frozen submarine's compartments keep the identifications coming.

The families' vigils are, each in their own way, long and painful. But the *Kursk* commander's widow is especially pelted with inquiries. *Have they found Gennady Lyachin yet? Will they ever find him, since he was so close to the explosions?*

Irina Lyachina becomes obsessively proprietary about the wait as the winter weeks drag on with no news, and she desperately commands the investigators: "If you find my Genna," she says, "don't touch my boy." Of course the request makes no practical sense, but the investigators' polite assent gives her the illusion of control.

At one point the investigators summon Irina north to Severomorsk, saying they may have found her husband. As she makes her lonely pilgrimage, Irina finds herself talking to Genna, hoping she can somehow will his body to return to her. When she arrives, she is dismayed to learn the investigators have made a mistake; these are not the remains of her husband. Irina feels as if she has "lost him one more time."

Weeks later the investigators get it right, a fact confirmed by Irina. "This is mine," she thinks while examining the modest identifiable traces of her husband and parts of his distinctive uniform.

In one last grand ceremony on Saturday, March 23, Commander Lyachin is interred along "Heroes' Way" in St. Petersburg, along with those of seven other *Kursk* crew, joining Kolesnikov and other submariners buried there earlier. These last crewmen also include division weapons officer Murat Baigarin, torpedo control officer Alexey Ivanov-Pavlov, and navigator Sergey Tylik. Their grave sites bring the total in the St. Petersburg site to thirty-two. The families of the rest have chosen sites throughout western Russia. The only *Kursk* sailors forever missing are Seaman Dmitry Kotkov, torpedist Ivan Nefedkov, and Dagdizel engineer Mamed Gadzhiev.

After the public attention wanes, Irina Lyachina feels more empty than ever, as if there is nothing more to wait for.

Except in her dreams, where Genna comes to her at last. She sees him in his most formal dress uniform against a black backdrop. She wants to run to him and touch him, but some unseen gulf keeps them apart. He simply looks at her sadly and says, "I'm sorry."

33

TELL THE PEOPLE THE TRUTH
MOSCOW
JULY 22, 2002

When the Ustinov report finally emerges in July, the findings are announced by the prosecutor general himself in an impressive recitation of conclusions at a formal press conference.

A leaky Fat Girl torpedo—without a warhead—doomed the *Kursk*, Ustinov proclaims. An assistant investigator displays the twisted weapon's actual remains and guides the gathered journalists through a schematic of how the weapon is supposed to work and why it failed.

The ill-fated Fat Girl was in the *Kursk's* fourth tube, lower port bank. Its technical description is that of an SS-N-16 torpedo, product number 398. Investigators believe its HTP oxidizer leaked through microcracks in the oxidizer tank's casing. When it contacted certain metal elements inside the torpedo-firing device, it instantly decomposed. The oxidizer tank and the firing tube exploded with a force of "50,000 atmospheres"—about twenty-five thousand times the force of an average passenger car's tire blowout—igniting a fire in the torpedo room and blowing a hole through both the inner and outer hulls immediately forward of the firing tube. Metal fragments shot throughout the torpedo room, puncturing fuel tanks and igniting hardened warhead materials. As the fire reached as high as 5,400 degrees Fahrenheit over the next two minutes and fifteen seconds, at least four nearby combat torpedoes reached their maximum heat threshold and detonated.

The profoundly destructive second blast sent damage as far back as the bulkhead dividing two sections of the fifth compartment, just forward of the sixth compartment that contained the twin nuclear reactors. Ustinov declares that his investigators have recovered fifty fragments of the exploded Fat Girl, and ten pieces of its fourth firing tube. He says careful studies of all the fragments testify that the Fat Girl's HTP caused the initial explosion.

He says all of the sailors forward of the reactors died within a few minutes, and that most of the twenty-three men found in the ninth compartment expired within eight hours, as flooding proceeded into their last refuge and a fire ignited.

Ustinov says that no rescue efforts from anywhere could have changed the tragedy's outcome.

He further reports that, while the exercise was poorly planned and executed, no individuals have been found to have acted in a manner that could constitute criminal behavior. There are no guilty parties.

Finally, Ustinov highlights the work performed to arrive at these conclusions. He says that 1,500 experts conducted "2,000 investigatory actions." He cites a tally of 1,200 witness interviews and 8,000 objects examined—with 200 of them considered material evidence. He says 211 "forensic examinations" were performed, and that 1,000 customized experiments contributed to the conclusions.

Ustinov says the final report contains too many state secrets and cannot be fully disclosed to the public.

Some of the report's key volumes are stamped "confidential," and reportedly cannot be opened for twenty-five years. Still, the Ustinov disclosures constitute a level of glasnost previously unseen by the Russian people.

But the Kursk mysteries still burn. The people are not completely satisfied. Hardcore collision adherents won't let go. Many constituencies continue to whisper of a cover-up. Few express comfort with the idea that no one will be held responsible.

Most families of the ninth compartment's twenty-three blast survivors protest the conclusion that all of their men died within eight hours. If that were so, they ask, then what do top officials make of the persistent reports that human tapping was still heard rising up from the deep as late as 1100 on Monday, August 14?

Wishful hearing, the officials proclaim. There was nothing but mechanical noise.

The haunting questions continue to plague the Russian people through August 2002. Many still feel unsettled as they prepare to mark the tragedy's second anniversary on the twelfth. Just northwest of St. Petersburg, the city of Kronstadt plans a special memorial to the lost sailors in their Orthodox Christian cathedral, and the church's leaders hurry to place a heavy new gilded cross atop their dome for the occasion. On August 8, a heavy crane hoists the enormous cross to its post, but the crane's tethers slip. The cross slowly leans off center, then topples away, crashing and tumbling off the roof and pounding into the asphalt street below.

The entire sequence is captured on video, and it plays out on Russian national television that evening, echoing a national tragedy that refuses to release its grip.

Of all the media to pry open the *Kursk*'s remaining secrets, few would have expected it to come from the one Russian newspaper many perceive as the Kremlin's own mouthpiece, *Rossiiskaya Gazeta*. Yet the broadsheet splashes a lengthy and remarkably candid account of the tragedy in its August 29, 2002, edition, bitterly reproaching the shortcomings of the Ustinov report. Entitled "Anti-State Secret," the broadside names the names that Ustinov withheld, sarcastically citing many of the most damning passages from the thirty-three bound volumes compiled by the tragedy's investigators. "Alas," its author remarks at one point, reacting to a citation that Vice Admiral Boyarkin and Captain First Rank Teslenko failed to schedule a key submarine rescue exercise, "They didn't prepare an exercise and had to nail up coffins." The newspaper goes on to mock the continued spirit of secrecy that shields the Northern Fleet's deepest areas of incompetency. Even everyday Russians are shocked at the article's seemingly unrestrained criticisms, which are widely echoed in other national media.

In the coming months, Boris Kuznetsov, a lawyer representing the families of the ninth compartment's twenty-three blast survivors, will win his quest for full access to the investigation's thirty-three volumes. He files a legal complaint to reopen the case, to revisit the conclusions about survival times and the fleet's rescue response. His complaint is rejected by a military court in April 2004, prompting an immediate appeal. As of this writing, the appeal has yet to be heard.

POSTSCRIPT

WHOSE LEGACY?

More than most people, it seems, Russians trade freely in dreams and omens. And so it is with the families left behind by the *Kursk* tragedy, who like to think their lives and losses are governed by some higher design.

Olga Kolesnikova describes a recurring dream in which she learns that her celebrated husband mysteriously survived the catastrophe but suffered heavy burns to his face and upper body. In the dream, Dima has quietly retreated back to Vidyayevo and has persuaded his neighbors to keep his return a secret. He would prefer that Olga believe he died heroically, anything to keep her from seeing his grotesque disfigurement.

Olga now lives in a new apartment on the outskirts of St. Petersburg, where she clings to at least two talismans she believes indicate Dima's awareness of his coming fate: on a hook near their apartment door in Vidyayevo, on a neck chain that her husband never failed to wear when he left for the docks, hang his crucifix and dog tags.

Olga Lubushkina, Sergey's widow, has also seen her share of dreams and omens, but she keeps them to herself. She has moved to an apartment in Severodvinsk, which she shares with a younger sister. In one of Lubushkina's first attempts to resume a normal life, she took herself to see the popular movie *Titanic*. She stayed for the "love story" part of the film, but left before the wreck.

For Khalima Aryapova, the most chilling dream came before the tragedy. Shortly after she married Rashid in Uzbekistan on May 3, 2000, she dreamed a number of elderly women from her village came to her home. They wanted to express their alarm over why she had "married a dead man."

Then came the omen. When Khalima and Rashid took their long train ride to Murmansk weeks after their wedding, they stopped for twenty-four hours in St. Petersburg. As part of their whirlwind sightseeing tour, Rashid took Khalima to a lushly shaded fountain just off Palace Square. He told her that according to the fountain's legend, couples who throw coins into its waters are destined to return to it someday. Khalima liked that idea, and she threw coins that Rashid had given her into the water. Then it dawned on her: he had given her all his coins; there were none left for him to throw. Khalima fretted that they had violated the fountain's rules. Rashid dismissed her worries with a laugh.

Khalima gave birth to their son, Ilgiz, on February 12, 2001, precisely six months after the wreck of the *Kursk*. She hopes Ilgiz will help her complete the circle that she and Rashid could not. "I think that when Ilgiz is big," she says, "I will take him to this fountain."

Khalima rents a new apartment in Tolyatti, an industrial city in central western Russia that straddles the Volga River. Her mother has moved in to help her raise Ilgiz. Rashid's parents have left Uzbekistan and live in a rural apartment an hour from Khalima and close to Rashid's grave site.

The event that affected the *Kursk* families so catastrophically has become pivotal to their nation's new course. The government's handling of the tragedy provoked one of Russia's most democratic moments. But in the years since, that moment has emerged as an anomaly: the predicted authoritarianism of Putin's Russia has risen with a vengeance, just as some critics said it would when he first appeared on the world stage.

With his nomination in January 2000, cynical observers brayed that Putin's KGB past heralded a shift toward a more Soviet-styled government. One of Putin's first acts appeared to confirm their worries. In answer to the rise of maverick governors in Russia's eighty-nine regions, Putin, with the Duma's blessing, dismissed regional governors who displeased him and was granted the power to dissolve regional legislatures whose governance strayed too far from the Kremlin line. He also carved the eighty-nine regions into seven federal districts and appointed each district an administrator—each of them a loyalist, five of them military leaders—to control the regions on his behalf.

These were only his most visible moves toward centralizing all power in Moscow, a campaign that was just finding traction when the *Kursk* tragedy intruded. For a few moments, Putin had to make adjustments: one of the immediate upshots of the disaster was that Putin's plans for a return to global military power were temporarily stalled; he canceled his navy's ambitious deployment to the Mediterranean in the fall of 2000.

With so many of his country's shortcomings exposed by the tragedy, Putin, on this one occasion at least, bowed to the will of his people. They were demanding an end to government deceit, and Putin acquiesced, ordering his admirals to broadcast publicly the incendiary contents of Dmitry Kolesnikov's note within hours of their discovery. Putin did this knowing full well that Kolesnikov's message nakedly refuted his own proclamations that the submariners all died a mercifully quick death. He also had to know that the gesture would send a powerful signal to Russian investigators that the truth would be told, at least in matters regarding the *Kursk*, regardless of who the truth would favor. Furthermore, Putin kept his promise to raise the dead sub and recover the submariners' bodies, rebuilding a reservoir of trust among the Russian people that propelled his approval ratings to a remarkably steady 70 percent and higher.

But in the event's long aftermath, Putin has returned to the authoritarian course. With shockingly little protest from the masses—and with impotent opposition groups further nullified by the electorate's deepening confidence in Putin's honesty—the president has set about retooling his nation's character.

He has presided over an alarming series of media crackdowns, allowing his agents to seize control of all major television stations, to shut down some newspapers, and to force ownership changes in others to guarantee more Kremlin-friendly coverage. Russia's remaining independent media have been broadly cowed by the crackdowns.

Many former owners of these media operations, the oligarchs, have been further targeted by Putin's prosecutors. The most prominent has been Mikhail Khodorkovsky, Russia's wealthiest man, who was suddenly jailed in 2003 for alleged crimes committed in his acquisition of former Soviet oil interests. Many other Russian businessmen committed similar "crimes" during the chaotic 1990s, but critics believe Putin targeted Khodorkovsky because he funded political opposition efforts.

Prosecutors have also resumed a zealous pursuit of citizens who aid foreign parties in certain areas of research—especially in the environmental and nuclear energy sectors—bringing a series of dubious jailings and a seeming disregard of anything that might resemble due process for those detained.

Such prosecutions have created new concerns for Russians whose work routinely brings them into contact with foreigners. And rightly so. Russian FSB agents—latter-day operatives of the dreaded KGB—have celebrated their rising clout by announcing an annual tally of foreigners caught seeking information that is often arbitrarily deemed a "state secret." Russia's worried social critics have dubbed the trend "spy mania."

Sometimes Western actions have aided the FSB's efforts. In March 2001—in response to the U.S. expulsion of several Russian diplomats after the FBI's Robert Hanssen spy scandal—the FSB reciprocated with expulsions of American diplomats. By the time the tit for tat was over, fifty diplomats from each side had been ousted, including American naval attaché Robert Brannon.

In addition, Putin has brought back the national anthem of the Soviet Union, but modified some of its more objectionable lyrics. He has restored his army's Soviet-era emblem, the red star. And he has soft-pedaled the legacy of Joseph Stalin, tacitly endorsing older Russians' enduring veneration of one of history's bloodiest dictators.

Even the gains in public accountability displayed in the *Kursk* probe have quickly reverted to their pre-2000 level. One prominent example of this came in October 2002, when Chechen rebels seized a Moscow theater filled with nine hundred people. Police ended the standoff by pumping a narcotic knockout gas into the building. Police then stormed in, killing the dozens of hostage takers and allowing emergency workers to remove the unconscious hostages. When the victims arrived in area hospitals, doctors demanded to know the knockout agent so they could administer antidotes. Authorities refused, and 129 of the hostages died. The mystery agent has still not been publicly identified, and Putin's government has refused to order a probe. His government has argued persuasively that the risks posed by the knockout gas were a better alternative than surrendering all nine hundred lives to the terrorists' likely mass suicide bombing.

The intense television coverage of that incident prompted a new round of media regulations, severely curtailing broadcast journalists' coverage of hostage takers' demands.

The new media restrictions didn't stop there. Months in advance of the nation's parliamentary elections in December 2003, all media were prohibited from covering any candidates or issues in ways that displayed any form of bias. Media outlets could now be shuttered just for quoting people who favored one candidate or position over another. Though media operators decried the restrictions as too vague and arbitrary, they soon learned that enforcement would apply only to coverage of reformist candidates not allied with Kremlin positions and parties. Putin himself endorsed his candidates via the media, and widely proclaimed the political factions he favored. Media that uncritically accommodated Putin's endorsements suffered no ill consequences, bringing about a landslide sweep of pro-Putin nationalists into Parliament and leaving only a handful of the liberals who had been the vanguard of Russia's tortured first bid for democracy.

Similar methods guaranteed Putin's victory in March 2004 for a second presidential term. With the Duma now thick with nationalists and other members of the right wing, and with key government posts increasingly filled with former members of the security services, the new Russia looks ever more poised to become a police state.

Yet a steady parade of public opinion polls by respected independent Russian organizations shows Putin is doing exactly what the majority of Russian citizens want him to do. Many see the dismissed reformers as architects of their country's unacceptable chaos. Many more see the oligarchs as criminals. They distrust the oligarch-funded media's harsh criticisms of Putin's Kremlin and don't necessarily see the crackdowns as censorship.

Russians like Putin's sobriety. They like his calm. They like his stability, and the fact that wages are increasingly paid on time. They like his consistent bridge building between Soviet stalwarts and Russia's new generation. They are reassured by several of his government's gestures toward reversing widespread corruption in Russia's public institutions.

A surprisingly high number of Russians believe that early changes in the name of "democracy" have only harmed their lives. This is especially true of older Russians, who have lost the social safety nets of the Soviet era. For these disenfranchised citizens, the fact that Western thumbprints are so indelibly linked with these changes only increases the East-West gulf of distrust. "If this is democracy," goes a common refrain for many Russians over forty, "then we don't need democracy."

The younger generation is more optimistic, but seemingly unconcerned with losing their forebears' hard-won, if modest, gains. In large numbers, the twenty-somethings are becoming politically inactive.

Meanwhile, Putin's Russia has laid a new foundation for its place in the world community, forging a complex relationship with the European Union, even winning a seat at the elite gathering of the world's richest nations, traditionally known as the G-7. When Russia is at the table, the G-7 becomes the G-8. Russia is far from a rich nation, but it is heavily endowed with enormous real estate, vast oil and gas reserves, and the world's second-largest arsenal of nuclear weapons. Still, Putin observers have declared that he "plays a weak hand well."

One of his grandest displays of such statesmanship came in the immediate wake of the September 11 terrorist attacks on the United States, when Putin hurriedly called U.S. president George W. Bush to offer support in the "War on Terror." Though the gesture was at first deemed acceptable by most of his countrymen, Putin's hard-core cadre of nationalists bristled. Chief among their concerns was Putin's agreement to let American military facilities operate on former Soviet territory, particularly in Uzbekistan and Kyrgyzstan, each of which now host small U.S. air bases. The establishment of the U.S. base in Kyrgyzstan prompted a remarkable response from Putin's Ministry of Defense: his military men persuaded the Kyrgyz government also to allow a Russian air base, and with Putin's blessing they quickly flew a handful of Russian military jets to an existing airfield just nineteen miles away from the American site.

Such lingering Cold War behavior also haunts Russia's western border with Europe, as the West's economic juggernaut moves into former Eastern Bloc nations, bringing with it an expanding round of new NATO memberships. To Russia's ascendant nationalists, the expansions feel like military encirclement by their Cold War foe. For their part, senior NATO officials have also embarked on an awkward courtship with Russia, most recently through a parallel structure to the G-8 model: When NATO's twenty-six members occasionally meet with their Russian partners to share strategies and explore common objectives, the gathering is called the "NATO-Russia Council."

This combined NATO-Russia group has found some common ground, and has presided over a number of joint military exercises. (They have also finally forged plans to work together in future submarine rescue efforts.) Perhaps the most intriguing talk among these partners in 2004 is that, as NATO has lost its mission to protect Western Europe from Soviet/Russian aggressions, the new battlefront is shifting southward: an enlarged NATO might join forces against the common threat of fundamental Islamic terrorism.

But Putin's opposition to the U.S.-U.K. war in Iraq has slowed the momentum of this partnership and its ideas, and added to the lingering East-West rift. At the war's outset, 80 percent of the twenty-eight thousand Russians in a phone poll conducted by the former liberal-leaning TVS said they hoped Saddam Hussein would win. A number of retired Russian military officials even flew to Baghdad independent of their government to advise the Iraqi dictator on how to defeat the Americans.

Some Russian weapons suppliers continued to arm Saddam's military with night-vision technology and satellite-jamming equipment.

In February 2004, to further enhance Russia's image as a viable opponent to the United States in future global disagreements—especially in the wake of America's abdication of Cold War treaties guaranteeing nuclear parity—Putin presided over a series of new military displays. In actions reminiscent of the buildup before the *Kursk* exercise, Putin boarded a Northern Fleet sub, intending to witness the launching of two nuclear missiles from a neighboring Russian sub. State-controlled media were invited to the event, with all parties hoping to capture the now-seasoned president overseeing the dramatic new demonstrations. With the cameras rolling, Putin waited for twenty-five minutes for the launches, which failed.

Confident that the absence of independent media on site guaranteed state control over the message, navy commander in chief Admiral Kuroyedov declared that the launches were intended all along to be simulations. But not all official sources cooperated with the ruse, and the remaining vestiges of independent media quickly exposed the truth. Then the problem repeated itself, in a way that left no room for doubt. The day after the first missile failures, the navy attempted a second demonstration. That missile strayed dangerously off course, forcing its self-destruction in midair.

Putin is both the leader who forced sweeping candor in the wake of Russia's greatest naval disaster, and an efficient authoritarian hedging his bets toward new opposition in the West. Nothing if not pragmatic, Putin is leading Russia on its so-called "third path," which many have come to call "managed democracy," and which might settle into something like a kinder and gentler dictatorship. Given Russia's unpleasant first encounters with so-called "democracy," Putin's authoritarian course looks like a more palatable alternative, at least for the time being.

But regardless of how Russia's course unfolds in the coming years, the *Kursk* and the Kolesnikov note will cast a long shadow. In the near term, Putin's administration came clean and told the truth, but it also happened with a relatively unrestrained media, and in a freer society with an empowered collective voice that could demand an accountable government. Those qualities have been seriously diminished in Putin's new Russia, setting the stage for Soviet-style deceits to emerge once again.

At a modest café sandwiched between small shops in a suburban St. Petersburg shopping mall, a group of Dima Kolesnikov's classmates have regularly gathered since their 1990 graduation. They come together to drink coffee or alcohol, grab a few smokes, and chat about their lives. Whenever he was home on leave, Dima would join them.

In the weeks immediately after their friend's death, his classmates planned a number of memorial efforts, including the installation of a plaque at the high school they'd all attended. But they also wanted to find a way to help repair their intimate circle, and so they proposed a solution. If a majority of them agreed, they would nominate Dima's younger brother, Sasha, to take his spot in the group. After a quick show of hands, Sasha was in.

At the subsequent swearing-in ceremony, classmate Denis Popov raised a toast "to the newest member of our class." Sasha, tall, dark-haired, and angular, quietly expressed his thanks, declaring that he was "proud to be part of such a circle."

They downed drinks and shared stories, and Sasha described his last meeting with Dima at the dock just a couple of days before the *Kursk* set out. Sasha had summoned Dima topside to wish him a happy twenty-seventh birthday when Commander Lyachin suddenly appeared, wondering why Captain-Lieutenant Kolesnikov was not at his post. When Lyachin learned that the dark-haired stranger was Kolesnikov's younger brother, the commander's face softened into a big smile. "Ah, your brother!" With an avuncular enthusiasm, Lyachin proposed that he fill out some paperwork to bring Sasha along for the exercise. The paperwork didn't come through in time, and Sasha was left with complex feelings about having escaped his brother's fate.

As classmate Irina Goreva listened, her eyes closed, Sasha's voice sounded exactly like that of his wild red-haired brother, and she couldn't help feeling that Sasha perfectly embodied Dima's spirit. When Sasha had finished telling his story, Irina and the other classmates unanimously urged him to consider transferring out of the submarine service.

Then they raised a toast to the memory of Dima, whose stark note about the *Kursk*'s fate forced a grand, if temporary, reckoning in how their government would weigh the balance between national pride and human life.

ACKNOWLEDGMENTS

Though the U.S. Navy studiously avoids talking about submarine operations and declined to participate closely in this effort, they did grant me some key exceptions. Most notably, they arranged for my personal dockside orientation in Norfolk aboard the USS *Scranton*, which, like American subs operating in the Barents Sea when the *Kursk* exploded, is a Los Angeles–class vessel. Her commander, Captain Clarence Earl Carter, candidly explained the *Scranton*'s details, along with life aboard a sub, during his guided tour.

Prominent U.S. author Norman Polmar, the leading U.S. expert in nonfiction submarine literature, provided some pivotal early guidance until another commitment posed a conflict.

My most tireless instructor in the ways of submarining was Lars Hanson, whose remarkably well organized tutorials filled my inbox for months. Lars is also a skilled graphics designer, and would often spontaneously craft top-quality illustrations of key aspects of sub design and torpedoes and their launching mechanisms, and so forth. I'm convinced he's amassed enough material now to publish his own submariner's handbook.

This book's technical reviewer, retired Rear Admiral Thomas Evans, also guided me through a hands-on orientation of Cold War–era submarines at the Smithsonian Institution's exhibit at the National Museum of American History.

For the more specific orientation to the USS *Memphis*, her former combat systems officer, Lieutenant Charles Gales, skillfully advised me on the unclassified particulars of this cutting-edge platform for U.S. submarine surveillance work.

Other key contributors on the U.S. side included Sherry Sontag, coauthor of the celebrated *Blind Man's Bluff*, Peter Huchthausen, author of the fine book *K-19: The Widowmaker*, and naval affairs journalist Robert Hamilton, who works at the *Day* newspaper in New London, Connecticut.

Thanks also to former submarine commander Peter Vogelberger, the father of a childhood friend, for becoming my very first U.S. submarine guide and for showing perfect patience during my earliest efforts.

On the Russian side, my most skilled advisor was retired Soviet submarine commander Captain First Rank Ryurik Ketov, aided by his right-hand man and translator Rouslan Kotov. Ketov also made a special sojourn to Vidyayevo to gather some details on this book's behalf, and his skill at communicating with the other Russian submariners in their own lingo advanced the book's authenticity.

Prominent Russian author Nikolay Cherkashin kindly provided my first handful of phone numbers. One of his longtime associates, retired Captain First Rank Igor Kurdin, also provided some initial guidance, and filled in key details on the tragedy's human fallout. Another helpful close associate of Cherkashin's was Mikhail Volzhiensky, who energetically laid out the *Kursk's* circumstances during its final maneuvers.

Though he was one of the central subjects held partially accountable for the *Kursk's* demise, Vice Admiral Mikhail Motsak proved steadily candid throughout a series of probing interviews. He gave many answers that authoritatively shed light on the disaster's mysteries, and continues to strike me as a standout member of Russia's older generation who most emphatically embraced the fruits of post-Soviet glasnost.

For my introductions to the special universe that is Russia—and how its history brought a special bearing on the *Kursk* disaster—I am indebted to former *Baltimore Sun* Moscow correspondents Will Englund and Kathy Lally, who graciously allowed me to use their bureau offices as a launching pad, and made time amid their heavy schedule to offer insights.

They linked me with translator-fixer Andrey Mironov, a tireless walking encyclopedia of Russian history and contemporary affairs who provided a crash course in both the darkest and brightest aspects of his fellow countrymen.

Perhaps the most sage guide on the big picture that surrounded the *Kursk* tragedy was prominent journalist Masha Lipman, who, at the time we met in Moscow, was still the deputy editor of the once-powerful independent newsmagazine *Itogi*.

The other key Russian journalists who took special time with me were Pavel Felgenhauer and Alexander Golts, both independent Russian analysts who specialize in military affairs.

The American expat journalist in St. Petersburg whom I described in the preface as retrieving me from that lovely city's rainy streets was Charles Digges, who, at the time we met, was an editor at the *St. Petersburg Times*. Digges introduced me to the eccentric café The Idiot— where he briefed me at length and provided still more story leads and connections.

Digges pointed me to one of his key sources on the demise of the *Kursk*, Alexander Nikitin. Nikitin was a former Russian navy officer who had assisted the Oslo-based environmental group, the Bellona Foundation, in identifying major sites of nuclear contamination. When I visited, two of the foundation's key officers, Nils Bohmer and Igor Kudrik, authoritatively indulged my wide-ranging questions.

The translator whom Digges's wife had found for me was Anna Korovina, who added an entirely new perspective to the big Russian picture: unlike many members of the older generation who still pined for Soviet times, Korovina took a decided joy in the nascent freedoms and opportunities of the postreform era.

One of my first breakthroughs with Korovina's assistance was the introduction to Russian TV journalist Dmitry Skrilov, who had contributed to some of NTV's most incisive reports on the *Kursk*. When I solicited Skrilov's insights, he responded by providing some twenty or so key sources and their phone numbers.

Some of the primary subjects of the *Kursk* story went well out of their way to provide insights to the lives of their departed submariners. This was especially true of the Kolesnikov parents, Roman and Irina, who graciously submitted to my repeated inquisitions. Among Kolesnikov's classmates, Irina Goreva became my advocate and guide in helping me make a number of key connections.

The widows portrayed herein also demonstrated a powerful willingness to aid my efforts to candidly memorialize their husbands. These especially include Khalima Aryapova, Olga Lubushkina, and Irina Lyachina. Svetlana Baigarina, widow of division torpedo officer Murat, bravely provided a remarkable breakthrough in untangling the *Kursk*'s intrigues. Svetlana puzzled together some of the unusual activities surrounding her husband's sudden last-minute assignment to the *Kursk*'s last voyage, and, during our telephone interviews, she provided cornerstone information about the torpedo crew's advance worries regarding one particular torpedo, and further illuminated the special pressure that *Kursk* commander Lyachin was under to manage the problem.

For special insights into Commander Lyachin's professional character aboard the *Kursk*, I am indebted to his former first mate, Captain Second Rank Mikhail Kotsegub. Kotsegub had to travel some distance to meet with me in Murmansk, yet thought it was the least he could do to help honor the man who had been an uncle figure to him from his earliest memories. Kotsegub's entire life was spent in Vidyayevo, and his father was a submariner who had also once served with Lyachin.

The key *Kursk* crew survivors who gave so generously of their time were Captain Third Rank Evgeny Zubkov (who had left the *Kursk* crew sometime earlier but remained close with her men), and Warrant Officer Ivan Nessen. Both Zubkov and Nessen stand as powerful testimony to the ability of everyday Russian sailors to endure unfathomable loss while continuing to shoulder their country's security burdens.

When it came time to assemble some of the more far-flung story elements, aid came from surprising places. I'd heard of the searing early documentary produced in Norway in the fall of 2000, and was welcomed at the Oslo offices of TV-2 by the award-winning film's producer, Odd Isungset. After sharing key sources and insights, Isungset quickly assembled a customized video of his material.

Understanding the vast complexities of deep-sea saturation diving also became central to this effort, and I was enthusiastically aided in this area by commercial diving expert Garry Ball.

Getting a handle on the little-known properties of high-test hydrogen peroxide, the volatile chemical at the core of the *Kursk* disaster, was made easier for me under the tutelage of Dr. William L. Hufferd. The doctor and two of his associates at the Chemical Propulsion Information Agency sat down with me at their research headquarters in Columbia, Maryland, and Dr. Hufferd later followed up with a series of smartly composed e-mail guides laying out the most likely *Kursk* torpedo blast scenario based on the found details as I reported them to him. Dr. Hufferd's scenario spelled out almost exactly the chain of events that were articulated months later in the formal presentation of a team of Russian *Kursk* investigators' conclusions.

Top-quality research was crucial at every turn in assembling *Cry from the Deep*, and Russian language specialist Robert "Rip" Burns, as detailed in the preface, quickly made himself indispensable. Aficionados of Russian naval affairs should visit his regularly updated Web site, which can be found at http://www.ctirip.com.

One of the best sites for tracking Russian military affairs, at least as they relate to nuclear issues, is through a Web site provided by the Monterey

Institute for International Studies, which posts very cogent summaries of targeted Russian news coverage via its Center for Nonproliferation Studies. Their Web site can be found at this address: http://cns.miis.edu. One of their most skillful researchers in tracking the *Kursk* catastrophe was Cristina Chuen, who generously offered guidance when I sought obscure details from her efforts.

By far the most helpful Russian news aggregation service is provided by David Johnson, who crafts a twice-daily online newsletter known to committed Russophiles as Johnson's Russia List.

From the outset, I felt this book had to distinguish itself as the definitive account of how the West responded to the unfolding crisis in the Barents Sea, particularly regarding the actions of the former Soviet Union's erstwhile superpower rival, the United States. The breakthrough source here was NSC Russian specialist Mark Medish. Medish displayed both candor and authority from the very beginning, and never dodged even my most difficult questions. He remained responsive and available throughout my research, and never had to modify his story as new information developed. This was true of the other primary subjects in the United States who also recounted their actions regarding the *Kursk* affair, including Strobe Talbott, Frank Miller, Debra Cagan, Walter Slocombe, Captain Robert Brannon, and Pentagon background guide Jeffrey Starr. None of these officials made excuses or ducked responsibility.

For his exclusive recounting of his first reactions to news of the *Kursk* tragedy, I am grateful that now-retired admiral Harold W. Gehman Jr. found a way to carve time from a very demanding post-naval career undertaking.

For the British angle on the story, I am especially grateful for the contributions of a handful of sources. These include Commander Alan Hoskins, a key figure in the early organization of the British rescue bid. Commodore David Russell, who appears throughout the book's central chapters, always found the time to indulge even my most needling queries. One of his associates, Commander Jonathan "Jonty" Powis, was willing to take me behind the scenes in the British Royal Navy's rescue coordination center in the course of several telephone interviews. Naval attaché Captain Geoffrey McCready took time out for my visit to his location in Portsmouth and later remained available by phone as I continued to puzzle through time-line issues.

The most pivotal source in Norway was Admiral Einar Skorgen, who endured many telephone rounds with me over the course of months and then years.

For the most detailed inside account of response events at NATO headquarters in Brussels, I was lucky to find retired Dutch vice admiral Egmond van Rijn, who served as American admiral Gehman's representative to the alliance. Admiral van Rijn crafted for me an authoritative narrative of events as they unfolded in Brussels, a time line that helped immeasurably.

The art section of *Cry from the Deep* is anchored by what I consider to be the most definitive illustration of the *Kursk* at the moment of its first blast. The dramatic cutaway was produced by Doug Stern, who graciously suffered a seemingly endless parade of technical revisions and new detail requests from Lars Hanson and me. I can't imagine an illustrator who could better handle such perfectionist revisions, but the result speaks for itself. The publisher has printed the image in black and white for this hardcover edition, but I'm hoping we can portray it in its proper colors on the book's companion Web site, http://www.cryfromthedeep.com.

The other heavy-lifting art contribution worthy of special mention is the montage of nautical and seabed charts that depict the disaster sequence in its geographic context. The materials were masterfully pulled together and smartly manipulated by Chris Robinson, who performed his special magic on a very tight deadline. The satellite-seabed image was custom-produced for this project by NOAA mapping scientist

Dr. Peter Sloss, employing a little-used imaging technology that penetrates the sea surface to reveal the landforms below.

The plotting of the primary vessel positions and activities at the time of the *Kursk*'s blasts was skillfully crafted by Lars Hanson, using a number of previously unreleased details based on my original reporting.

Pulling all of this effort together into a book became possible through the endless patience and understanding of a hardworking nucleus of editors at HarperCollins Publishers: Mark Bryant, David Hirshey, Jeff Kellogg, and Emily McDonald.

But before it became a book, of course, *Cry from the Deep* was a magazine story in *Men's Journal*. The editor who tirelessly guided and sharpened it from its infancy was Mark Cohen, a former colleague from our mutual early days at *Baltimore* magazine. Cohen's masterful magazine editing helped form the "voice" of the book that still dominates that of the book.

I would express eternal gratitude to my literary agent, but *Cry from the Deep* came into being without one. My attorney in Baltimore, James Astrachan, reviewed the contract as offered and gave his proper blessing.

None of this would have been possible without the constant support of my parents, Mary Jane and Bill Flynn, who found endless ways to help relieve the pressures posed by my ever-deepening absences to travel, research, and write. Those same obligations also brought about an entirely new level of dedication from my wife, Betty, who made every sacrifice necessary to see this effort through to its completion. The juggling naturally put special demands on caring for our amazing young boys, William and Hunter, whose grandmother, Betty Boniecki, stepped in to fill the void on critical needs—after-school pickups and child care.

•   •   •

To all of the above contributors to *Cry from the Deep*—and to the many more I have failed to mention—here's hoping that you've helped create a piece of work that improves the dialogue in our ever-shrinking community of nations. And my sincerest thanks to each of you.

NOTES

CHAPTER 1: WIVES' DAY

1. *The wives hush:* The sequence described here was videotaped and broadcast in various reports. I obtained a copy of the video from a Norwegian documentary producer for Norway's TV2, Odd Isungset. Unrecorded details were provided through personal interviews with participants Olga Lubushkina and Khalima Aryapova. Weather details come from the meteorological station in nearby Murmansk for the described time of day.

2. *Vidyayevo's cinder-block apartment buildings:* Descriptions of Vidyayevo come from my own visit to the garrison town, along with interviews of many residents.

4. *Dmitry Romanovich Kolesnikov had foundered:* Information about Dmitry Kolesnikov's background comes from my interviews with his family members, friends, high-school teachers, and acquaintants. His battle with alcohol was known among Kolesnikov intimates.

4. *He was especially close:* Details about Kolesnikov's relationship with Maksim Guskov and Inna (her last name was about to change because of a pending divorce), were provided to me by Guskov and Inna.

5. *the three men suddenly made excuses:* The story of how all three friends pooled their modest funds for Sergey Lubushkin's first date with his future wife was first reported in *Izvestia* on December 21, 2000.

6. *The concern was well founded:* The fact of a shape-up-or-ship-out ultimatum from Commander Lyachin comes from Olga Lubushkina.

6. *she'd spotted a pretty young biology teacher:* Kolesnikov's courtship of Olga Borisova were described to me by Kolesnikov's mother, Irina, and was detailed in a well-done 2001 book by Russian author and friend Nikolay Cherkashin entitled *Taken by the Abyss: The Death of the Kursk: Chronicle, Versions, Fates.* Most of the key exchanges of dialogue between Kolesnikov and Olga are adapted from his book. The phrase "I thought I'd married the poorest officer..." was provided by Kolesnikov's mother, Irina.

9. *With the matter settled, Dima persuaded a friend:* The anecdote about Kolesnikov summoning a friend to drive him and his new wife from Vidyayevo to

the train station in Murmansk comes from my interview with that friend, *Kursk* warrant officer Ivan Nessen.

CHAPTER 2: LOADING UP

10. *The leviathan* Kursk *floats quietly:* The description of the *Kursk* at the loading dock in Zapadnaya Litsa Bay comes from multiple sources, including an associate's interviews with a Northern Fleet submarine division commander, Rear Admiral Mikhail Kuznetsov, my own interviews via translator with Admiral Mikhail Motsak—who was both the Northern Fleet's chief of staff as well as the base commander of the facility where the torpedoes were being loaded. Further details were provided by Vice Admiral Yuri Boyarkin, who personally inspected the *Kursk* and its commander days before they set out. Background details were provided by *Kursk* warrant officer Ivan Nessen, along with the observations of two civilian residents of Vidyayevo who asked not to be named. Weather descriptions for these hours come from the reporting station in nearby Murmansk.

10. *a 14,700-ton predator:* Technical descriptions of the *Kursk* come from the Web sites of reputable defense-reporting organizations, most prominently *Jane's Defence Weekly.* Some of the details also come from my personal interview with independent defense analyst Pavel Felgenhauer, who operates from Moscow. The detail about the cat named Vasily comes from my interview with that cat's owner, former *Kursk* assistant to the commander, Captain Second Rank Mikhail Kotsegub. (Neither Kotsegub nor his cat were aboard the *Kursk* when it went down.) Chief technical adviser Lars Hanson helped guide the description's accuracy.

11. *The command structure makes Rashid senior to Dima:* Descriptions of working dynamics between Kolesnikov and Aryapov aboard the *Kursk* come from Kolesnikov's father, Roman, along with formal explanations by technical adviser Lars Hanson. Former *Kursk* officer Evgeny Zubkov provided the anecdote about Sergey Lubushkin's "rite of passage" in one of a series of personal interviews. Khalima Aryapova and Olga Lubushkina offered their best assessments of their husbands' states of mind before setting out.

12. *From President Vladimir Putin on down:* The material on Russia's international frustrations amid military decline are gleaned from hundreds of international reports regarding Russia in mainstream media online, but also from a host of analytical organizations such as the Brookings Institution, the Center for Defense Information, and the Council on Foreign Affairs. I also visited the Bellona Foundation's headquarters in Oslo, which closely monitors Russian nuclear submarines as part of their mission to track nuclear issues throughout the Arctic region. The detail on the status of the Mir submersibles during the Barents exercise came from a report in an October

edition of the *Moscow Times* by Pavel Felgenhauer, supported by Internet research.

13. *Safety has become a casualty of the economic collapse:* Most of the information regarding the decline of Russia's submarine rescue assets prior to the *Kursk* event come from interviews conducted in Moscow with the former head of the Soviet sub rescue fleet, retired admiral Yuri Senatsky.

13. *But they also lack equipment:* Some key details regarding Russia's deep-sea-diver capabilities at the time of the wreck come from a Moscow interview with Colonel Sergey Nikonov, chief surgeon for Russian diving operations. Several other divers who wish to remain anonymous corroborated details in this depiction.

13. *the* Kursk *has its own clever rescue system:* Details regarding the *Kursk*'s built-in escape pod are well known and described on many Web sites dedicated to understanding the disaster, but the fact that its capacity is 115 submariners came from an interview with Admiral Mikhail Motsak.

13. *The summer's war games have been well advertised:* Notification of the Barents exercise plan, including its date, was published on Russia's Military News Agency Web site in May 2000.

14. *"NATO is an agent of war, not peace":* Uttered by Russian general Leonid Ivashov, this was widely quoted by wire services on or near April 3, 1999.

15. *Some of Lyachin's officers fondly recall:* Multiple sources on the *Kursk*'s mission to the Mediterranean, including an interview with Commander Lyachin's widow, Irina. An early report from the (U.K.) *Electronic Telegraph*'s Marcus Warren mentioned Commander Lyachin's boast about the mission's success. A more colorful report came from an *Izvestia* article on December 21, 2001, in which former *Kursk* crewmen described the voyage.

15. *The* Kursk *soon homed in on the primary target:* I first learned of the *Kursk*'s 1999 tracking of the USS *Roosevelt* off the Yugoslavian coast from an early account in *USA Today*, which I later supplemented with verbatim congressional testimony from U.S. admiral Daniel J. Murphy.

16. *The deployment's only serious blemish:* The detail that the *Kursk* suffered an aft compartment fire while on the Mediterranean mission to the best of my knowledge has never been reported before. It came from a source close to the postwreck probe who was intimately familiar with the *Kursk*'s onboard tape recordings.

16. *When Lyachin and his men debarked:* The depiction of *Kursk* commander Gennady Lyachin celebrating his Mediterranean mission's success comes from Russian TV footage of the event.

16. *Buoyed by the* Kursk's *Mediterranean adventure:* The remaining factual aspects of this chapter are gleaned from dozens of consensus media reports regarding Russia's plans for the Barents and beyond.

CHAPTER 3: ENDLESS SPYING GAME

19.   *The entire 542,000-square-mile Barents basin:* Western intelligence-gathering methods and apparatus regarding the Barents Sea are generally well known, and this opening recitation is tailored to the scenario for August 2000.

19.   *The tiny* NR-1 *research sub lingers to the west:* The existence of the U.S. *NR-1* research submarine on the Barents perimeter during the exercise would have been entirely missed by the media were it not for the reporting of journalist Robert Hamilton, who covers affairs at the naval facilities in Groton, Connecticut, for the *Day* in New London. I located and interviewed William R. Merz, the *NR-1's* commander at the time, who acknowledged his vessel's capabilities regarding the exercise but said his primary mission was separate and classified. (The *NR-1* is sometimes used to maintain NATO's secret undersea system of listening cables.) Merz did not deny that his deployment's timing was also linked with the Barents exercise. He also said that after reports circulated about the *Kursk* wreck, he signaled to U.S. authorities that his vessel was ready and able to assist, but that his offer was never accepted.

20.   *The* Memphis *is the American navy's premier testing platform:* Details regarding upgrades on the USS *Memphis* submarine that tracked the *Kursk* were generally provided by active and former members of the *Memphis's* crew. All of them appeared to exercise great caution not to disclose details that would compromise U.S. national security, but active crewmen would talk only on conditions that their names would not be published. One former officer from the *Memphis* who was able to explain some declassified issues on the record was Charles Gales, who served as the *Memphis's* combat systems officer but left the navy in March 2000.

21.   *Vladimir Putin's Kremlin finds itself on the defensive:* The litany of domestic pressures weighing on Russia on the eve of its naval exercise was gathered from multiple reports in the mainstream Russian media. Hard data on issues like the number of homeless children on the streets of the larger cities is difficult to come by and much disputed. Anecdotally, I came upon street children by the score around the metro systems of Moscow and St. Petersburg, and easily believe the figures that claim upward of fifty thousand such children in each of those cities.

22.   Putin must settle a long-running public squabble: The defense priorities debate at the Kremlin on the eve of the exercise was widely reported in mainstream media.

CHAPTER 4: DANGEROUSLY LATE

24.   *Hours past the* Kursk's *intended departure time:* Depictions of the *Kursk's* torpedo-loading problems at the Bolshaya Lopatka dock—and the fact that these problems delayed the *Kursk's* departure time—come from many of the same sources described in Chapter 2. Some of the human sources whose interviews helped round

out these scenes include Warrant Officer Ivan Nessen and the commander's widow, Irina Lyachina. In addition, one of five known *Kursk* crewmen who were spared from her ill-fated last voyage gave a rare interview to the *Obshchaya Gazeta* newspaper. In its issue from August 24, 2001, Senior Warrant Officer Nikolay Mizyak described in great detail the *Kursk*'s last-minute loading frustrations.

24. *This particular torpedo:* The Fat Girl torpedo's troubled history was quite scattered. Some weapons research sites offered essential descriptions, but key details came from far-flung sources. One of the more revealing sources was a report from the Vladivostok bureau of the Russian newspaper *Daily News* dated January 4, 2002. Unearthed by senior research director Robert Burns, the report disclosed the Fat Girl's little-known history as a bone of contention in East-West arms talks, especially when its guidance system was disabled to support a nuclear warhead for striking coastal facilities. Other Russian media also provided details on the Fat Girl's troubled history, including a cogent summary in the formerly independent TV station NTV.

24. *Salty weapons handlers also like to joke:* The comment that some weapons men joked that the Fat Girl was designed by a "very lonely woman" arose in my Moscow interview with Duma deputy Valery Dorogin, a retired Russian vice admiral who was a member of the Klebanov commission that probed the *Kursk*'s sinking.

25. *the Fat Girl employs high-test hydrogen peroxide:* My most authoritative guide on the volatile scientific properties of the Fat Girl's HTP oxidizer was Dr. William L. Hufferd, director of the Chemical Propulsion Information Agency attached to Johns Hopkins University.

25. *at a cost to the Soviet state of 300,000 rubles:* The cost per unit of manufacturing the Fat Girls within the Soviet era came from a detail in the incisive reporting of Elena Milashina, who has done some of the most remarkable reporting on the *Kursk*'s mysteries for the reformist newspaper *Novaya Gazeta*. The cost detail came from Milashina's account in that paper's edition of August 12, 2002.

27. *Though Western navies once tried:* Details on the West's unhappy HTP experiments came from two primary sources. The British case of the ill-fated HMS *Sidon* submarine's wreck came to light in a BBC documentary of August 7, 2001. The U.S. case of an attempt to power the experimental *X-1* mini-sub with HTP was detailed for me in an interview with that sub's chief experimenter, Richard Boyle.

27. *One of the first reports:* The account of the Russian diesel sub *B-37*'s destruction from an unstable gas-steam torpedo was provided to me in a St. Petersburg interview with that sub's commander, Captain First Rank Anatoly Begeba.

29. *a flood of paperwork irregularities:* The most authoritative report on the *Kursk* Fat Girl's paperwork and maintenance irregularities came in a searing broadside in the Kremlin-linked *Rossiiskaya Gazeta* of August 29, 2002. The report, by Russian journalist Yuri Yemelyanenkov, is cited with his permission.

29. *the long-neglected crane's heavy slings and rusty chains:* I first learned of the Russian Navy's loading cranes crisis from a German TV documentary produced by ZDF-TV Moscow correspondent Dietmar Schumann. Schumann kindly sent me his verbatim script. Schumann's account was based partly on a report in *Komsomolskaya Pravda* by military affairs reporter Viktor Baranets. I learned of further crane system details through a Russian media summary posted online by Cristina Chuen, a research associate with the Newly Independent States Nonproliferation Program at the Monterey Institute of International Studies. More details came from an April 6, 2000, report in the now-defunct *Segodnya* (well in advance of the August maneuvers), a September 22, 2000, report in *Vesti.Ru*, and from a November 15, 2001, report in *Moskovsky Komsomolets*. In the course of interviews with Northern Fleet admirals Motsak, Burtsev, and Boyarkin, all variously minimized the cranes as an issue for the *Kursk*. They also dismissed the practicality of removing all combat torpedoes from vessels before participation in an exercise.

29. *forcing the crane's operator to lower it roughly back to the pier:* In a February 2002 series headed up by *Komsomolskaya Pravda*'s Baranets, he reiterated an earlier claim that a Fat Girl torpedo "crashed to the pier" during loading. I met with Baranets at his office in Moscow to gauge the veracity of his claim and came away doubting it; he could claim only that he had an anonymous source. Through subsequent reporting efforts, I was unable to verify the Baranets "crashing" account, but I accepted a later modified version in which the Fat Girl simply suffered rough handling from the demonstrably decrepit cranes.

29. *As an added precaution:* The detail that a torpedo base systems commander personally inspected the *Kursk* Fat Girl's HTP monitoring system came in a series of interviews with Mikhail Motsak conducted in my absence by Anna Korovina.

31. *other fleet sub commanders will share the* Kursk's *additional weapons risks:* The fact that other vessels in the exercise were also firing Fat Girl torpedoes first came to my attention through an interview with Admiral Burtsev via Anna Korovina. It was further confirmed in a recent book by Igor Spassky, the head of the submarine bureau that designed the *Kursk*, the Rubin Maritime Technology Central Design Bureau.

32. *Lyachin intends to retire after this exercise:* Most of Commander Lyachin's biographical details were provided in interviews with his widow, Irina Lyachina.

32. *Lyachin had hunted for Baigarin:* The story of Commander Lyachin's anxious pursuit of Fat Girl torpedo expert Captain Third Rank Murat Baigarin was jointly provided through interviews with *Kursk* warrant officer Ivan Nessen and by Baigarin's widow, Svetlana Baigarina. To my knowledge, Baigarin's last-minute substitution for this duty is well known, but the concerted campaign to sway Baigarin to go on one last *Kursk* voyage has not been previously reported.

32. *the lead torpedo man designated and trained to handle the weapon was suddenly hospitalized:* The report that *Kursk's* originally designated lead torpedo man was injured in a fight cannot be proved. Several of my sources in Vidyayevo said this missing crewman, Chief Petty Officer Oleg Sucharev, broke his nose, which I did not believe would likely cause his absence. Others said he got injured in a fight and couldn't get out of the hospital in time for the *Kursk's* final departure from Zapadnaya Litsa. In any case, I can confirm that Sucharev did not take his post on the *Kursk* for that exercise, and he declined the repeated requests for interviews that I relayed through Vidyayevo intermediaries. Neither my research associates nor I have ever found credible media accounts of Sucharev's testimony, and my Russian correspondent Anna Korovina later heard he'd been reassigned to a new submarine crew in Russia's Pacific Fleet.

33. *a quiet ripple of rumors around Vidyayeo:* The detail of rumors regarding a torpedo problem aboard the *Kursk* were well substantiated in my interviews with Ivan Nessen and Svetlana Baigarina. Nadezhda Tylik revealed to several media outlets — and repeated to correspondent Korovina — that her son declared "We have death onboard" before his departure, but she acknowledges she can't prove her son was talking about the Fat Girl torpedo.

34. *As the long day approaches 2200, sunset:* All sunrise and sunset times come from tables for the relevant coordinates.

34. *"Davai poyekhali":* Commander Lyachin's parting comment was not witnessed by any of our sources, though they consider it a reasonably modest conjecture.

34. *twenty tons of TNT:* The *Kursk's* total weapons TNT equivalent is based on a combination of her standard combat load, plus a detailed multiweek weapons-loading schedule provided to me by Admiral Mikhail Motsak.

CHAPTER 5: GETTING UNDER WAY

35. *topside crewmen clear away gear:* Much of the description of the *Kursk* setting out from its dock is extrapolated from known procedures and described by my chief technical adviser, Lars Hanson. Some of the initial descriptions came from an early Russian associate who'd set out from this site many times, retired Russian Navy captain first rank Ryurik Ketov. (One of Ketov's greatest distinctions as a Soviet submariner is that he reportedly commanded the only submarine to slip through the American naval blockade during 1962's Cuban Missile Crisis.) The weather conditions for the fjord at the moment of setting out come from the Russian weather station in nearby Murmansk.

37. *"This is a drill! General quarters!":* The *Kursk's* onboard dialogue, beginning with Commander Lyachin's announcement of a fire drill, come from verbatim tape recordings whose highlights were transcribed for me from a source close to the

Kursk's postwreck investigations. Nearly all succeeding dialogues aboard *Kursk* prior to its sinking come from this same source. Neither these dialogues, nor the ironic detail that Commander Lyachin put his crew through a fire drill that substantially simulated much of the scenario the crew was to experience for real the following day, have, to my knowledge, been published elsewhere.

38. *Olga Kolesnikova helps her mother gather the fruit crop:* The account of Olga Kolesnikova's actions and state of mind on August 11 are based on her interviews with a number of mainstream media operations, and also on more detailed description in the *Kursk* book written by author Nikolay Cherkashin.

38. *taking a bus from their home in St. Petersburg:* The similar account of Dmitry Kolesnikov's parents that day come from my own series of interviews with both parents.

39. *Khalima found the garrison town's surroundings:* All three of the remaining people's accounts in this chapter come from my interviews with the subjects themselves.

CHAPTER 6: USS *MEMPHIS* PROWLS

42. *Commander Mark Breor slowly rotates the periscope:* A number of crew from the USS *Memphis* carefully aided in the portrayal of their own sub. Though I also contacted *Memphis* commander Mark Breor on several occasions to solicit his input, he was unable to obtain permission from higher authorities to do so. Descriptions of Breor's manner and style come from some of his former officers and crew.

43. *submarine commanders find it hard to resist "peeking":* My chief technical adviser Lars Hanson, who has operated as a submariner in the Barents Sea, added standard operational details and guided the portrayal for accuracy.

43. *Great submariners have been rewarded for closely shadowing:* General principles of how American and Russian subs have shadowed each other during the Cold War and beyond were broadly extracted from *Blind Man's Bluff: The Untold Story of American Submarine Espionage,* one of the best nonfiction books ever written about modern submarining, coauthored by Sherry Sontag and Christopher Drew (Thorndike, Me.: Thorndike Press, 1992).

43. *The* Memphis's *new listening equipment:* The *Memphis*'s recent commercial upgrades—at least those that could be declassified—were patiently explained to me by former *Memphis* weapons systems officer Charles Gales.

44. *One of the group's tunes, "There Beyond the Mists":* *Kursk* wreck investigators found many of the crew's recreational musical tapes in the debris, and one of the most common tapes was from the popular Russian folk-rock group Lubeh. Commander Lyachin's widow, Irina, reported the name of his favorite Lubeh song, the lyrics to which were gleaned from the Internet by my chief researcher, Robert Burns.

44. "*Peter the Great,*" *Captain Lyachin says into his radio microphone:* The *Kursk* dialogues used here come from the same source described in Chapter 5, along with some confirmation and explanation from Admiral Burtsev.

45. *the* Kursk *settles to a keel depth of 165 feet:* The *Kursk's* movements during this exercise are gleaned from consensus reconstructions in the Russian media. One of the earliest reliable accounts of these details came from Russian author Vladimir Shigin's excellent book *Empty Moorage.* More authoritative material was later published in Yuri Yemelyanenkov's *Rossiiskaya Gazeta* account in August 2002.

45–46. *giving sailors from bow to stern a sensation:* The description of what it feels like when a submarine fires a missile comes from a comment by former submariner Bill Whalen, quoted on a Web site hosted by public television's WGBH in Boston. The site is a companion to a NOVA documentary entitled *Submarines, Secrets, and Spies.*

46. *the second missile failed to properly eject:* The *Kursk's* successful firing of her first cruise missile on August 11 is well documented and widely reported. I could not find any reports on the failure of her second attempted missile launch, and learned of it from the same source who supplied me with the underway dialogues.

46. *"I received your message!":* Kursk *dialogues from ibid.*

47. *Lyachin still can't hide some disappointment:* References to Commander Lyachin's underway reactions and state of mind cannot be verified, but are generally linked with the content of his dialogue comments. Advisers Ryurik Ketov and Lars Hanson have aided in interpreting a sub commander's state of mind in the sequences described.

47. *he offered to eat all the ice cream himself:* The story of Commander Lyachin treating some of his men to a round of ice creams appeared in the book *Empty Moorage* by Russian journalist Vladimir Shigin, who quoted former *Kursk* crew reserve commander Oleg Yakubin.

48. *In his afternoon meeting with Yasser Arafat:* Accounts of Putin's Kremlin schedule, his actions, and general assessments are extrapolated from consensus media reports, and also from subsequent public statements made by a number of the principals.

48. *preside over his squabbling military men:* Former Russian defense minister Sergeyev's assertion that his Defense Ministry rival was "criminally insane" was reported in a number of mainstream media accounts.

49. *"If sailors almost never put to sea":* President Putin's quotes about the state of Russia's military come from a partial transcript of his statements at the opening of the Kremlin meeting.

49. *"We have noted a pressure increase":* The detail of the log notation made by *Kursk* torpedo control officer Ivanov-Pavlov came from the August 2002 account in *Rossiiskaya Gazeta.*

CHAPTER 7: SHOOTING PRACTICE

50. *dawn bursts rapidly over the sharp horizon at 0316:* Sunrise time and weather conditions from same sources cited for Chapter 1, page 1.

51. *Admiral Boyarkin is vaguely apprehensive:* Boyarkin's thoughts and actions come from interviews with Boyarkin, the provided radio dialogues, and also from some Russian media reconstructions of the events depicted.

51. *complained on the record, frequently and pointedly:* Boyarkin's record of public complaints about naval funding shortfalls was especially well detailed in an obscure Boyarkin interview found by my researcher Robert Burns in a February 1999, edition of *Morskoy Sbornik*.

52. *saw himself standing in an open tomb:* Ivan Nessen's dream was recounted to me by Nessen.

CHAPTER 8: FAILING TO TAME THE FAT GIRL

53. *The original plan called for shooting two smaller USET-80 torpedoes:* It is well established that the two USET-80s were scheduled to be first. I am basing my assertion that "all agree" that the Fat Girl should be moved to first in the shooting lineup on the demonstrable truth that the *Kursk* torpedo crew was deeply worried about the Fat Girl, and the actual fact that it was prepared for firing and inserted in its tube with the breech door shut.

53. *Abdulkadir Ildarov, a swarthy even-tempered forty-year-old:* The biographical details of the torpedo men aboard *Kursk* derive from interviews with their families conducted by Anna Korovina.

55. *Though he is impressed with Ivanov-Pavlov's general weapons smarts, Baigarin wishes:* Relationship dynamics described between Murat Baigarin and Alexey Ivanov-Pavlov are based on the known circumstances of their working together on the dubiously procured Fat Girl, and also on character sketches of both men that were provided by their survivors.

55. *At 1005, the Kursk's sonar room detects two echoes:* The *Kursk's* maneuvers and times are derived from time lines by Shigin, Milashina, and Yemelyanenkov.

55. *each keeping two nautical miles apart from the other:* The detail that the *Peter the Great* and her two partner vessels were sailing two nautical miles apart was provided by Admiral Burtsev in his Moscow interview via Anna Korovina.

56. *Admiral Popov hovers closely over the planning table:* Details of circumstances on the bridge of the *Peter the Great* before the torpedo firing were provided in interviews with Admirals Boyarkin and Burtsev. In his interview, Burtsev stated that the Russian *Akula*-class sub *Leopard* also fired a practice torpedo, a detail not mentioned in any of the other *Kursk* accounts I've studied. My technical reviewer retired Rear Admiral Thomas Evans, believes this may be because *Leopard's* participation in the

exercise was classified, as the practice of smaller Russian attack subs escorting missile carriers is a little-known routine developed by the Russian Navy's forerunners in the latter years of the Soviet Union.

56. *This is really magnificent, thinks Admiral Boyarkin:* Boyarkin's sentiment here was expressed in an interview via Korovina.

56. *"one more prize":* Quote supplied by Burtsev.

56. *Aboard the* Kursk *at 1112, now over thirty miles away:* The *Kursk's* maneuvers and time line from similar sources cited for page 55 above.

56–57. *sailors not involved in the torpedo exercise trickle into the fourth compart-ment's upper deck:* The detail of the timing of *Kursk's* lunch shift and her crew's relaxed state of "Battle Readiness Two" come from interviews with Mikhail Motsak.

57. *What if the HTP leaks now? How will they know?:* Details of the torpedo team's heightening worries regarding the Fat Girl after it was enclosed in its tube are derived from the known fact that the torpedo's oxidizer-monitoring system must be detached for this phase. The notion that the torpedo was "warming" at this point is extrapolated from the subsequent investigation that demonstrated the likelihood of an HTP leak leading up to the torpedo's explosion. It is known that this process ini-tially develops gradually.

57. *Ildarov is called back to the control compartment:* Assertion that the torpedo room chief was summoned to the CCP before the blast is based on the demonstra-ble likelihood that the torpedo team knew that it had an unfolding concern. That is coupled with the fact that forensic investigators who later combed through the *Kursk's* wreckage found Ildarov's remains associated with those of other men known to be in the CCP at the time of the blast. Conversely, the remains of Gadzhiev and Nefedkov were never recovered, supporting the belief that they were still in the tor-pedo room during the explosions. (The *Kursk's* shredded torpedo room was severed from the rest of the sub prior to its lifting from the seabed. After Russian investigators sifted its contents, it was later blown up.)

57. *the sound of a muffled hiss from within the tube:* The description of sounds and sensations leading up to the first blast are adapted from X-1 experimenter Richard Boyle's description of the HTP blast that destroyed his sub.

58. *Much of tube four's after end is shattered, adding to the shrapnel spray:* The initial blast dynamics as described come from a combination of details provided by Russian general prosecutor Vladimir Ustinov in his final report on the causes of the disaster, along with other postulations offered by my HTP and propulsion expert, Dr. William Hufferd.

58. *explosive force equal to 220 pounds of TNT:* The TNT equivalent of the first blast was a widely reported estimate derived from seismic sites.

58. *kills or stuns most of the men in the second compartment's CCP through the open door:* The first published assertion I ever saw that the *Kursk's* torpedo room door was left open into the CCP came from the series by Victor Baranets et al in *Komsomolskaya Pravda* in February 2002. This possibility had been debated since shortly after the tragedy, as purists asserted that strict rules dictated that all watertight doors should be closed and locked prior to weapons firings. An open watertight door could mean Commander Lyachin had broken rules that may have exacerbated the catastrophe. Lyachin defenders said the commander routinely allowed the variance as a humanitarian gesture, as it relieved the shock of the blasts when the torpedo crew fired their weapons. In any case, Mikhail Motsak and Valery Dorogin, both members of the Klebanov commission that helped study the disaster, say that examiners declared the watertight door to the torpedo room was open.

58. *the* Kursk *begins to slowly nose into a dive:* The *Kursk's* initial postblast movements are based on what tech adviser Lars Hanson and I deemed to be the most plausible aspects in the most credible published accounts. Hanson also applied his formidable engineering skills to reconstruct the *Kursk's* progressive response to the first blast.

58–59. *They jam the passageways and ladders between decks:* The description of crewmen jamming the *Kursk's* forward passageways comes from the forensic examiners' discovery of the clustered remains of men in those locations.

59. *Erasov snakes through the tangle of frightened sailors to retrieve the coding equipment:* The detail about *Kursk* warrant officer Igor Erasov retrieving the submarine's secret codes box came from a report by Victor Baranets in *Komsomolskaya Pravda* that summarized some of the early forensic findings. A slightly enhanced version of this detail was published in the Russian online publication *Grani.Ru* on March 26, 2002.

59. *the tube four blast has also damaged the smaller torpedo tube above it, opening a path to the sea:* That the *Kursk's* torpedo room was subjected to flooding after the first blast was hotly disputed by many experts. Prosecutor Ustinov's team concluded that it indeed flooded, but did not explain how the water failed to douse the torpedo room's fire. In one of his interviews via Korovina, Admiral Motsak attributed this phenomenon to the relatively small size of the *Kursk's* initial exposure to the open sea through a hole in the forward pressure hull, and to the low water pressure at periscope depth. Weapons expert Hufferd also helped piece together how many of the flammable components in the *Kursk's* torpedo room would continue to burn even when doused with seawater.

60. *designed to withstand a fuel-fired temperature of 1,600 degrees Fahrenheit:* The fire-resistance level of Russian torpedoes and other combat weapons comes

from multiple sources, but was fleshed in with greater detail by propulsion expert Hufferd.

60. *the USS* Memphis, *now tracking the* Kursk *from twenty-five miles northwest:* My assertion here that the *Memphis* was actually twenty-five miles from the *Kursk* at the moment of its first blast might raise eyebrows. Because of American submariners' checkered history regarding collisions with Russian subs in the Barents, the U.S. Navy has adopted a recommendation that U.S. subs should conduct surveillance from no closer than seventy miles. In most previous accounts of the *Kursk* tragedy, journalists have posited a distance between the two subs of sixty to seventy miles. In my correspondence with seasoned submarine reporter Robert Hamilton of the *Day* newspaper in New London, he inferred that sources in Groton intimated that the *Memphis* was closer than five miles from the *Kursk,* using a well-established but risky surveillance technique called "wake shadowing." After shuttling back and forth with several other informed sources, I settled on a distance of "less than twenty miles away." This provoked a reaction by the Pentagon's Frank Miller, who sternly asserted that the *Memphis* was "tens of miles" away from the *Kursk.* I followed up with an interview with former undersecretary of defense Walter Slocombe, where I'd posited that the vessels were within twenty-five miles of each other. Slocombe did not argue. Miller also stopped arguing. I knew both men had carefully reviewed the vessels' relative positions at a briefing at the Pentagon presented by naval officers equipped with charts and graphs. At a later point, I'd interviewed Admiral Harold Gehman, who'd been particularly vexed over the proximity issue from his perch as the head of NATO's submarine operations in the Atlantic. When I briefed the admiral on my understanding of events so far, I mentioned the twenty-five-mile distance. His response was, "That sounds about right."

60. *"What the hell is this?":* Exclamations by an unnamed sonar man aboard the USS *Memphis* are suppositional, but were endorsed by at least two members of the *Memphis's* crew.

60. *Even the NATO's secret hydrophones west of the Barents detect the blast:* The general description of the way that intelligence data proceeds from the Barents environment to analysts in the United States comes from basic Internet research along with an assist from John Pike, a security and intelligence expert from GlobalSecurity.org.

61. *It shows what looks like a temblor, 2.2 on the Richter scale:* The first blast's Richter scale equivalent comes from widely reported data provided by seismographic measurement sites.

61. *she excitedly opens a letter from her beloved husband of four months:* Olga Kolesnikova's depiction as receiving her husband's letter on the day of the wreck

comes from an interview she gave to *People* magazine that was published on November 13, 2000.

61. *In Estonia, Dima's parents relax at a health spa:* The midday activities on August 12, 2000, described by the Kolesnikov parents, Khalima Aryapova, Olga Lubushkina, Irina Lyachina, and Ivan Nessen come from my interviews with these people.

62. *Putin himself is still stuck in the Kremlin:* Putin's Kremlin activities at that hour were widely reported in mainstream Russian media.

CHAPTER 9: KILLER BLOW

63. *Shocked survivors toward the aft take small comfort in the sub's return to a level angle, hoping the worst is over:* A number of careful studies contributed to the blast description sequence, but not all of them agree about the exact position of the crippled *Kursk* at the moment of the second blast. Some early seismic analyses concluded the second blast occurred just above the seabed. Tech adviser Lars Hanson says that, because the *Kursk* is five stories high and its explosives-laden torpedo room was on the top deck, the difference could have affected the early analytical interpretations. The most recent report to affect the portrayal in this book was written by *Kursk* design bureau chief Igor Spassky in his book entitled *Kursk: After August 12, 2000.*

64. *Some will also revise its Richter scale reading to 4.2:* The timing of the *Kursk's* second blast is universally agreed upon. Some of the farthest seismographic sites to register the blast included those in the Ukraine, Germany, Alaska, and Africa. Seismographic analysts Terry C. Wallace and Keith D. Koper of the University of Arizona revised the blast's Richter scale equivalent after intensive study.

64. *Even men without headphones hear the extraordinary blast:* Blast reactions aboard USS *Memphis* are from the same *Memphis* sources cited earlier.

64. *Thirty-two miles to the northwest, the Russian missile sub* Karelia *is also rocked:* I'd first heard about blast reactions aboard Russian missile sub the *Karelia* as rumors but did not see a credible published report until stumbling upon an item from *Komsomolskaya Pravda's* edition of October 19, 2000. At least one Russian Web chat room frequented by submariners provided other small details about the reactions aboard the *Karelia.* Robert Moore's account of the *Karelia* commander's blast reaction in his book *A Time to Die: The Untold Story of the* Kursk *Tragedy* (New York: Random House, 2003) added further detail, as did another account in *Krasnaya Zvezda* in March 2003.

64. *the super-quiet Akula-class* Leopard—*is even closer to the* Kursk: The first report that the Russian vessel closest to the blast was the Akula-class attack sub the *Leopard* came in one of our interviews with Vice Admiral Mikhail Motsak. He also explained how the *Leopard's* angle relative to the *Kursk* likely prevented its crew from feeling any significant shock wave.

64. *The* Leopard *is acting as an escort to the* Karelia: The postulation about the *Leopard*'s purpose in relation to the *Karelia* comes from my senior reviewer, retired rear admiral Thomas Evans, who learned of the described secret escort practice during the latter days of the Soviet Navy's submarine operations.

64. *On the surface, the* Peter the Great *registers the shudder:* Details regarding blast reactions aboard the *Peter the Great* are most authoritatively spelled out in Yemelyanenkov's *Rossiiskaya Gazeta*'s broadside from August 2002. Even more recently, an attorney representing parents of the *Kursk*'s short-term survivors in a civil filing describes one officer on the nuclear cruiser's bridge as having to steady himself on a railing to keep from falling down. Despite some modest corroboration from Vice Admiral Boyarkin on these phenomena, his partner, Vice Admiral Burtsev, asserted in his interview with us that there was no such data provided at all. Burtsev's assertion stands starkly at odds with all knowledgeable other sources. But in his defense, it also appears possible from his own testimony that Burtsev was not on the bridge at this moment, but in a separate enclosure elsewhere on the vessel.

65. *Boyarkin considers it just another small bit of data amid a stream of other coordination challenges:* Boyarkin's internal deliberations about the blast reports came in his interviews with us.

65. *Aboard the* Kursk, *the strained first bulkhead has broken loose:* Much of the initial description of the physical progression of the second blast through the *Kursk*'s hull came from an early newspaper account that quoted Klebanov commission member Valery Dorogin, who is also a retired submarine commander and was a member of the Russian Duma at the time I interviewed him further in Moscow. A more formal explication called the "Stralevern Report" arrived in May 2001. It was drafted by Norwegian members of the Joint Norwegian-Russian Expert Group for Investigation of Radioactive Contamination in the Northern Areas, and helped establish a reliable template for further research. This report was paralleled by researchers at the Bellona Foundation based in Oslo, a nuclear watchdog group whose officers I visited. Other details came from a series of published interviews in various Russian media with senior-level investigators Arthur Egiev and Viktor Shein. One of the earliest and best of these arrived in the December 8, 2001, issue of the Russian newsmagazine *Itogi*. Other Russian publications that provided excellent factual descriptions of the blast were *Strana.Ru*'s issue of December 20, 2001; *Komsomolskaya Pravda*'s October 31, 2001; *Rossiiskaya Gazeta*'s January 30, 2002; along with select reports on forensic findings from *Nezavisimaya Gazeta* and its partner paper *Nezavisimoye Voyennoye Obozreniye*. Additionally, Russian journalist Igor Zhevelyuk contributed an authoritative account of forensic results for a Web site dedicated to Russian submariners. My account is based on very discriminating sifting from these publications and many others, along with a six-hour interview in Moscow with

prominent Russian *Kursk* expert Mikhail Volzhiensky. Senior tech adviser Lars Hanson researched the blast dynamics independently, and carefully guided much of the depiction.

66. *Captain Breor and others on the* Memphis *keep listening:* Continuing reactions aboard USS *Memphis* from the same group of sources cited for page 42 of Chapter 6.

66. *none dare to initiate contact with the Northern Fleet to ask if it needs assistance:* The external silence from NATO observers regarding the prospect of informing the Russians about the blasts on-site and in the moment are confirmed by my interviews with the Northern Fleet's senior officers. Several Pentagon officials I quizzed about this scoff at the notion that Western observers should ever communicate with the targets of their surveillance without top-level clearance, though one source did suggest that a quiet "colonel-to-colonel-level" contact would have certainly been possible. In his interviews with us, Vice Admiral Motsak expressed frustration that no such contact was initiated by Western forces, and even points out that the Norwegian surface surveillance vessel *Marjatta* has a standing protocol for being able to call the Northern Fleet's headquarters duty officer at any time. Motsak suggested that such a bold action might have made for a better outcome. In an interview with Russian journalist Alexander Sabov in *Rossiiskaya Gazeta*'s issue of November 28, 2001, Admiral Popov also expressed chagrin: "Unfortunately," Popov said, "the lack of such a treaty . . . results in regular collisions. We cannot even talk mutual assistance under such circumstances. Nobody will even announce that somebody else's submarine is in trouble due to a collision. This may result in a serious conflict someday."

67. *Some on the bridge scan the seas with binoculars:* Description of inactivity aboard the bridge of the *Peter the Great* from multiple Russian media reports, and confirmed in interviews with Boyarkin and Burtsev.

67. *Four thousand miles across the Atlantic:* Western naval intelligence protocol from John Pike of GlobalSecurity.org.

67. *No NATO rescue assets are contacted:* This assertion is based on my interviews with former U.S. submarine rescue chief Captain William Orr; U.K. submarine rescue chief Commodore David Russell, and Norwegian admiral Einar Skorgen. Of the three, I found Russell and some of his subordinates to be most disturbed by this. In the United Kingdom, sub-rescue efforts were coordinated at the time by Commander Jonathan "Jonty" Powis. When I interviewed him by phone, Powis described nearly spilling his coffee into his computer keyboard early on the morning of Monday, August 14, after the overnight watch stander informed him that U.K. intelligence officers had been observing the Russian submarine crisis throughout the weekend.

CHAPTER 10: STRUGGLING FOR SURVIVAL

68. Kursk *sailors in the aft compartments try to move about*: The *Kursk* crew's re-actions in the aft are based on many of the forensic reports cited above for Chapter 9. *Kursk* author Vladimir Shigin also blazed a trail here, acquiring the first exclusive medical results that demonstrated through their bodies' metabolic changes that the aft survivors put their initial panic aside so they could function methodically. His material was first published on a special Web site produced by *Strana.Ru* and dedi-cated to candid *Kursk* findings. Other reports demonstrated that the survivors per-formed damage control efforts, and their compartments' emergency phones were all unwrapped from their packages and left out. The extrapolation required for this sec-tion, and for others to come, qualifies as what I have come to call "informed sce-nario." Much of it was also guided by the engineering and nautical wisdom of my chief tech adviser, Lars Hanson.

69. *The trapped men can try sealing themselves, one at a time, into the trunk with emergency escape suits*: Material on stricken-submarine escape protocols is drawn from a number of sources, including some reports supplied to me by survival in-structors at the U.S. Submarine School in Groton, Connecticut, and by former Pen-tagon sub-rescue chief Captain William Orr. But submarine escape protocols are not altogether universal, so I relied on the advice of former Soviet sub-rescue chief Admiral Yuri Senatsky, along with any credible details that I could find among dozens of relevant Russian media reports. Commercial diving supervisor Garry Ball, who works for the company that aided in the initial rescue effort, Stolt Offshore, sup-plied me with voluminous testimony about what he'd learned about Russian tech-niques after working so closely with the Russians themselves.

69. *"Zolotoy!" says Rashid*: Dialogue between Kolesnikov and Aryapov here is in-formed scenario. It is known that their close friend Sergey Lubushkin was trapped on the other side of the *Kursk* reactors amidships and that the watertight door into Lubushkin's compartment was jammed shut by the blast. In fact, it is quite likely that Lubushkin and his comrades in compartments five and five-b lived for a significant amount of time after the blasts, as it was later found that flooding into these com-partments proceeded more slowly than in all the others. In any case, it is hard to imagine that Kolesnikov and Aryapov would not have shared their concerns very early on about the fate of their dear friend. Regarding the detail about "securing the reactors," forensic examiners found that the relevant manuals lay open in front of the station where this process had to occur, and also that the reactors had, indeed, been manually secured. This is a remarkably selfless act that has received little public at-tention anywhere and none other than Rashid Aryapov was in charge of the *Kursk's* reactor systems.

70. *Dima tests the aft emergency buoy's internal release lever:* The detail that there is a manual lever in the *Kursk's* eighth compartment to activate the aft emergency buoy comes from the testimony of Russian chief prosecutor Ustinov, who described it in an interview with the newsmagazine *Itogi* in their issue of December 17, 2001. The fact that no one aboard the stricken *Kursk* could have activated this crucial device is not in dispute. In its remarkable *Kursk* broadside from August 2002, *Rossiiskaya Gazeta* disclosed a series of disturbing findings. When the buoy was first shipped from its factory for installation aboard the *Kursk,* its mechanisms were secured with immobilizing straps, and accompanied with instructions to remove the straps before installation. When investigators studied the buoy, they found the factory straps still affixed. This also meant that the series of *Kursk* submariners whose job it was to test and update the buoy system had never done so. I consider Kolesnikov's likely discovery and concern over this undeployable buoy to be reasonable supposition.

71. *"13:15. All personnel from compartments six, seven and eight . . .":* The text of Kolesnikov's note comes from widely publicized copies of the note's contents. I should say here that specific translations vary remarkably—though not so much in their essence. (The same is true of nearly all of the Russian-language communications that I saw translated by different news agencies.)

71. It could have been a dud, *thinks Admiral Popov:* Popov's first thoughts about the *Kursk's* unfolding mystery are based on several rare interviews in which he was pressed to explain his inaction. Other sources, including Admirals Motsak and Boyarkin and even some Western submariners, assert that some of Popov's reasons for denying the worst-case scenario are quite plausible.

72. *The yawning silence from the* Kursk *has become acute:* Boyarkin and Burtsev reactions from interviews with Boyarkin and Burtsev.

72. *As a wave of thunderstorms moves in from the Northwest:* In one of his interviews, Popov attributed his failure to return to the *Peter the Great* to stormy weather. I obtained records from a Russian full-service weather station at Teriberka, on the Kola Peninsula's northern coast very near the *Kursk's* wreck site, which confirmed Popov's assertion. The conditions from those weather records also inform the scene's portrayal.

73. *"At 1350 we start to operate on the worst variant":* This detail from the *Peter the Great's* logbook comes from a remarkable narrative reconstruction by *Novaya Gazeta's* Elena Milashina in that newspaper's issue of July 16, 2001.

73. *Should the Northern Fleet leadership suddenly choose to act on its worries:* This "what-if" litany comes from my own inquiries among a wide range of experts. Several NATO figures informed me of the recent years of rebuffed overtures toward Russia to partner with NATO on sub-rescue exercises.

73. *the traditional East-West spy game might consider a time-out:* Sources similar to those cited for page 67 in chapter 9. As applied here, the dilemma poses a question that only Popov is in a good position to answer, and he declined my repeated requests for an interview.

74. *could also rouse the commercial sector:* Regarding the option of soliciting rescue assets from nearby commercial oil-drilling operations, this idea was emphatically endorsed during my interview with the Halliburton company's Dennis Wright, a retired U.S. naval captain who believes commercial diving equipment is far more "robust" than any military equivalent. (Halliburton won the contract to recover some of the first *Kursk* submariner's bodies in October 2000.) Wright asserted that if anyone had called Halliburton's commercial oil division right away, "there might have been a very different outcome." He described how a commercial mini-sub could perform a "hot tap" operation into the stricken *Kursk*'s hull to provide air and communication instantly. In my interviews with dozens of other experts in sub rescue, few had heard of such a procedure—until I came upon Stolt Offshore's Garry Ball, who could actually name the tool used to perform the operation, the little-known "Cox's bolt gun."

74. *If the fleet carried properly equipped divers to submarine exercises as a routine safety precaution:* The idea of routinely bringing sub-rescue vessels along on fleet-wide weapons exercises reflects my own incredulity. Don't ambulances and their crews wait nearby for major league sports events? Despite being mocked for the mere suggestion, I've chosen to keep it in the book.

74. *attach air hoses with communications lines through exterior valves:* The valves referred to here were first mentioned to me by former Soviet sub-rescue chief Senatsky, who called them "bugle-horn valves." I came to find that few experts, even sub-rescue specialists, had ever heard of them. That was until I was introduced to Ramsey Martin, a U.K. submarine-rescue and salvage expert who studied the *Kursk*'s sister sub at its dock in Severomorsk. Martin kept an attentive eye out for these valves but spotted none. I subsequently learned from a Russian source close to the forensic studies that the *Kursk* and its fellow Oscar II–class subs had done away with these valves. Chief tech adviser Lars Hanson offered an explanation: Such valves constitute "hull penetrations" that would seldom, if ever, be used. Engineers committed to designing an airtight sub will go to great efforts to reduce the number of hull penetrations to the bare minimum.

74. *if the fleet immediately summoned the storied rescue submarine* Lenok: The tragic story of the scrapping of the *Lenok* and its associated mini-subs came from my Moscow interview with former Soviet rescue chief Senatsky.

74. *Popov contemplates finally sounding the alarm:* Popov's further ruminations from previously cited Popov interviews in the Russian media. Additionally, the fleet chief shared some of his thoughts with *Nezavisimaya Gazeta*'s late Valery Alexin in

that paper's edition of November 21, 2000. (Before his death to cancer, Alexin, a re-tired Russian admiral highly skilled in sub wreck analysis, compiled some of the most authoritative material on the *Kursk*'s mysteries.)

74. *Popov knows there are no rewards for delivering bad news to superiors:* The idea of the Russian military culture's long-standing reluctance to readily communicate bad news to higher authorities was first posited to me by Russian independent de-fense analyst Pavel Felgenhauer during an interview in Moscow.

75. *hatchmarks and checkmarks in the left margin, plus signs to the right:* Kolesnikov's notations from previously cited found notes. The details about the "sta-tus marks" in the margins of each surviving submariner's name comes from a video photo still supplied to me by one of the forensic examiners present for Kolesnikov's autopsy aboard *Regalia*.

75. *elected to bang on the escape trunk in hopes of attracting searchers:* The pur-ported "fact" of the trapped submariners banging on the hull in the hopes of sum-moning rescuers is hotly disputed. Many dozens of Northern Fleet officers and sailors swear they heard tapping of a human origin, and they specifically cite the interna-tional SOS code, along with the Russian code for "water rising in compartment." I personally find it unfathomable to imagine trapped sailors sitting quietly and making no such effort at all. Still, there are no contemporaneous witnesses to such signals be-ing generated, because there were no Russian vessels close enough to the *Kursk* to hear it during the eight hours the submariners purportedly remained alive. But there were two physical details to support the claims that tapping occurred. First, there is an embossed metal code table affixed to the ninth compartment's watertight door that spells out the code that water is rising in the compartment. Second, according to a summary of *Kursk* forensic developments on the Russian *Dris.ru* site dated April 17, 2002, investigators found a series of scratches on the bottom hatch of the ninth com-partment's escape trunk. From the beginning, the "pro-knocking" experts have said this is the surface that a code-tapping sailor would most likely seek out, as it offers the perfect direct contact of metal surface to sea, which would maximize the distance that such knocking sounds would travel underwater.

75. *The sound of water slowly leaking in from below:* Regeneration plates and early leaking in the compartment from multiple forensic accounts, but especially well de-tailed by Shigin is Strana.ru.

76. *The pressurized nitrogen will then enter a submariner's bloodstream at ten times its normal rate:* Pressure and narcosis effects from Shigin, Larson, and Stolt Off-shore's Ball.

76. *For the* Kursk, *the ninth compartment is inherently vulnerable:* Ninth compart-ment flooding paths and rates were elaborately calculated by chief technical adviser Hanson.

77. *the trunk's ladder lies stowed away, detached from its base:* Escape trunk ladder found in this position by investigators.

77. *assess the gathered emergency escape suits, and soon learn that their country's poverty has even found its way here:* Missing metal parts vital to the function of the escape suits comes from little-noticed details in the note written by Sadilenko. As brass is one of the valuable metals treasured by Russia's zealous metals thieves, the assumption that they were pilfered is highly likely.

78. *"It is dark to write here, but I'll try by feel":* Kolesnikov notations from the many translations of his actual note's contents.

78. *The meeting started at 1400, and Putin tries to hurry it along:* Putin meeting actions from published accounts of his activities found in the Russian media.

78. *Byrd places an urgent call from the Pentagon to Robert Tyrer at 0830 Eastern Time:* Call disclosed by both subjects in telephone interviews.

79. *Cohen thanks Byrd, but issues no orders:* Timing and content of Byrd call to Cohen disclosed by Byrd.

CHAPTER 11: AMERICAN DILEMMA

80. *"We're following reports of a large underwater explosion in the Barents . . .":* Scene of Medish's notice from the White House Situation Room mostly from Medish interviews. Some details corroborated by tennis partner Steve Roberts. Weather details from nearby stations reporting at that hour.

81. *Of course, Putin is still an enigma to the Clinton White House:* Summary of the NSC's collective view of Russia, Yeltsin, and Putin comes from interviews with Medish, former ambassadors Strobe Talbott and Stephen Sestanovich, NSC aide Andrew Weiss, and a professional intimate of former security advisor Sandy Berger, who declined to be named.

81. *Yeltsin lurched about Blair House in his undershorts:* Account of Yeltsin's "pizza" stunt, etc., comes from Strobe Talbott's excellent book *The Russia Hand: A Memoir of Presidential Diplomacy* (New York: Random House, 2002) in which he recounts his time as the Clinton administration's adviser to Russia.

81–82. *Berger wants to know how quickly he can reach his counterpart:* Recounting of Berger's actions come from a source close to Berger. For this item and all Berger-related items to follow, the source should be understood to be a person with whom Berger has shared his detailed thinking regarding the *Kursk* affair.

82. *Conspicuously absent from the early Saturday intelligence loop:* Verification that U.S. and British embassies in Moscow were not notified through internal channels comes from naval attachés at both embassies, including Captains Geoffrey McCready and Simon Lister at the British embassy, and Captain Robert Brannon at the U.S. embassy.

CHAPTER 12: A WORRIED FLEET

83.   *Russian fleet rules dictate:* Rules regarding reaction times were widely disseminated in Russian media.

83.   *"Report on your location and status!":* The *Peter the Great*'s first attempts to summon the *Kursk* via voice command were relayed to me in an interview with former Russian "space communications" specialist Igor Archipchenko, later roughly confirmed by Admiral Boyarkin and a time line reconstruction by journalist Vladimir Shigin.

83.   *Boyarkin quickly relays news of the failed contacts:* Acceleration of actions by Popov, Motsak, and Boyarkin from ibid. Some elements enhanced with time-line details from Shigin and *Novaya Gazeta* reporter Elena Milashina. Some of Popov's ruminations drawn from reporter Alexin's interview with Popov in *Nezavisimaya Gazeta*, Cherkashin's in *Rossiiskaya Gazeta*, Baranets's in *Komsomolskaya Pravda*, and an unbylined interview in the Russian military paper *Krasnaya Zvezda*.

84.   *Word then reaches the fleet's rescue chief:* Alert scenario regarding Teslenko and the *Mikhail Rudnitsky* crew comes from a combination of key sources. The first came from an authoritative account in a Web site run by the St. Petersburg Central Naval Museum's Leonid Kharitonov. Kharitonov's account was enhanced by the testimony of fleet rescue chief Teslenko himself, who gave an interview to *Na Strazhe Zapolyar'ya*, a small-circulation Northern Fleet paper in Severomorsk, in which he detailed key parts of his time line. That account was translated by the Bellona Foundation's Igor Kudrik, who graciously furnished me with the original during my Oslo visit. Further details came from *Novaya Gazeta*'s Elena Milashina, Shigin, and in the *Rossiiskaya Gazeta* broadside.

84.   *fleet commanders hand binoculars to a number of sharp-eyed sailors:* This detail from aboard the *Peter the Great* was found in the general archives of a Russian paper called *Zhizn*.

84.   *Despite the low clouds, visibility remains high:* Site weather details from nearby weather records for that time and location.

84.   *The Il-38s depart for the* Kursk's *designated sector by 1852:* Timing of search planes dispatch from Milashina's *Novaya Gazeta* report of July 16, 2001. Other air reconnaissance details from Shigin and *Rossiiskaya Gazeta*'s Yemelyanenkov.

84.   *lingering near Kildin Island twenty miles west:* Altay tug detail from *Rossiiskaya Gazeta*.

84.   *detected a weak and unstable signal:* "Vintik" detail from *Novaya Gazeta* of July 16, 2001 and also from my interviews with Motsak.

85.   *debating with himself whether it's time to tell Moscow:* Popov's "late afternoon" deliberations from previously cited interviews with Popov in Russian media.

85. *Boyarkin has been transmitting to Popov in ten-minute intervals:* Popov and Boyarkin actions from combined accounts by Shigin, and from my interviews with Boyarkin and Burtsev.

CHAPTER 13: WHITE HOUSE SITUATION ROOM

86. *Medish thinks the key concern remains whether the Russian leadership understands the crisis yet:* Actions, statements, and thoughts of Medish, Miller and Cagan come from interviews with subjects. Depiction of Berger from note relating p. 112.

88. *But Ivanov does not know. Putin does not know:* My assertions that Putin and Ivanov do "not know" are based on the subsequently published statements of both men, which are consistent with their behaviors and have held up over time.

88. *Medish turns to a naval officer attached to the NSC staff:* NSC naval liaison Captain Cullom's assignment was confirmed in my telephone interview with Cullom.

89. *No one in the U.S. embassy in Moscow is alerted of anything:* Non-notification of U.S. and U.K. embassies for second day confirmed by previously mentioned naval attachés.

89. *no one from the British MOD's intelligence operations notifies anyone outside their cloistered circle:* My assertion that neither U.S. nor U.K. submarine-rescue systems were alerted of the crisis for a second day was confirmed by the principals.

CHAPTER 14: FLEET BREAKING POINT

91. *At 1928 Moscow time:* Putin's aircraft departure time from Moscow reported in *Rossiiskaya Gazeta*.

91. *"Did you observe K-141's work?":* Depiction of Popov ordering reports from the Leopard and from the closest torpedo-catcher vessel comes from reporting by Shigin.

91. *it does not occur to rescue coordinators to quiz the Karelia's captain:* Rationale for Popov's not soliciting a report from the *Karelia* missile sub at this point is my own "informed scenario," which was accepted by chief technical adviser Larson and technical reviewer Evans.

92. *The first salvo explodes at 2027, the second at 2042:* Detail of the *Peter the Great* employing grenades to summon the *Kursk* based on the large report from *Rossiiskaya Gazeta*'s Yemelyanenkov.

92. *They create a tangled scarlet veil:* Vidyayevo weather details from a combination of nearby station records for that moment and the recollection of Lyachina.

92. *now that she's alone:* Based on personal interview with Lyachina.

93. *at a bearing of zero-nine-six:* Detail of the *Peter the Great's* Boyarkin receiving the report of the day's earlier blast report coordinates is based on accounts from *Novaya*

Gazeta's Milashina, author Shigin, the *Rossiiskaya Gazeta* account, and from author Robert Moore's detail regarding the *Karelia's* report.

94. *He's risking his career:* Popov Saturday-night worries based on Felgenhauer interview cited for Chapter 10, page 107.

94. *dismayed to learn that it still hasn't left its dock:* Status of stalled rescue efforts based on time lines provided by Shigin, Milashina, and Yemelyanenkov.

94. *Popov turns to the landline phone in his Severomorsk office:* Details of Popov's call to Kuroyedov captured in multiple published interviews from both subjects. The most detailed (and contentious) interview regarding Kuroyedov in this moment was reported by *Novaya Gazeta's* Milashina on August 13, 2001.

94. *not to disturb the president on vacation in Sochi until officials get more information:* Sergeyev notification and rationale for delaying his call to the Russian president was revealed in an interview on Russian television station ORT on August 21, 2000.

94. *Shortly after midnight, one of the Voronezh's senior officers:* Call to Zubkov reported by Zubkov in series of personal and telephone interviews.

94. *his submarine had been designated to participate:* Details on switch of the *Voronezh* submarine with the *Kursk* revealed in Zubkov interviews.

CHAPTER 15: EMERGENCY SEARCH

96. *proceed at maximum speed to a rendezvous point near Kildin Island:* Rudnitsky and *Altay* movements detailed in Yemelyanenkov's *Rossiiskaya Gazeta* report.

96–97. *As Golodenko listens intently, he notes that the faint pulses:* First reports of sounds arising from the Barents were widely reconstructed by many Russian journalists, including Milashina and Shigin. The most authoritative report from *Rossiiskaya Gazeta* is used here.

97. *daylight slowly brightens the low cloud cover:* Scene weather details from nearby weather station records for this hour.

98. *The Peter the Great's echo sounder detects an "anomaly" on the seabed:* Timing of this development was initially derived from Kharitonov's museum Web site.

99. *Sergeyev orders the flight grounded:* Detail asserted by Kuroyedov to *Novaya Gazeta's* Milashina.

99. *By 0715, Defense Minister Sergeyev reluctantly:* Sergeyev's call to Putin derived from report in the United Kingdom's the *Guardian* of August 30, 2000. Further details by Putin when he recounted his time line with the families in Vidyayevo on August 22, an event recorded by Russian journalist Andrey Kolesnikov for *Kommersant* and later transcribed into English for the *Moscow Times.*

99. *misses the scheduled rendezvous entirely:* Rudnitsky navigational error based on account in *Rossiiskaya Gazeta.*

CHAPTER 16: RUMORS COME ASHORE

101. *Though he applies his best skills:* Zubkov's activities on the *Voronezh* from interviews with Zubkov.

102. *A slight ray of hope arrives:* Activities regarding the *Peter the Great* and the *Mikhail Rudnitsky* based on Yemelyanenkov's *Rossiiskaya Gazeta* report.

102. *The* AS-15 *is a thirty-six-man Kashalot design:* The existence of a secret submarine deployed to inspect the *Kursk* is little reported. It was referred to in passing by Kharitonov's Web site very early, and then expanded upon in later reporting by Shigin. I was able to flesh in the *AS-15 's* specifications from a Web site database posted by *World Navies Today* and compiled by Andrew Toppan. The Russian state's level of sensitivity regarding this top-secret intelligence vessel was illustrated vividly on January 29, 2004, when FSB agents raided the offices of the newspaper *Versiya*. The previous September, *Versiya's* military reporter wrote in some detail about the vessel, which was illustrated with a video still of the submarine on the *Kursk* site that was inadvertently captured by the state's RTR TV.

102. *A "terrifying hole"—as one official would later describe it—gaping:* The "terrifying hole" comment was uttered by Deputy Prime Minister Ilya Klebanov when he addressed journalists on Thursday, August 17, 2000.

103. *another flurry of excitement arises:* The reported sightings of purportedly foreign buoys near the *Kursk* site was widely disseminated in mainstream media, and those reports' veracity is still hotly disputed. Some of the key details rendered here are based on Yemelyanenkov's *Rossiiskaya Gazeta* report.

103. *When Captain Evgeny:* Zubkov actions from Zubkov interviews.

103. *One of them joins a line of residents:* The anecdote about a *Kursk* searcher in the Vidyayevo breadline comes from a report by Amelia Gentleman in the United Kingdom's the *Guardian* of August 9, 2001. As the dialogue and actions are repeated nearly verbatim, this item is used with permission.

103. *Olga Lubushkina soon hears:* Reports of actions by Lyachina and Lubushkina from interviews with both women.

105. *Admiral Skorgen greets the pair:* Skorgen's activities are based on a series of telephone interviews with Skorgen.

107. *the phone rings in Admiral Harold W. Gehman Jr.'s home:* Actions of U.S. admirals Gehman and Grossenbacher based on series of telephone interviews with Gehman.

107. *Gehman is a patrician fifty-eight-year-old:* Brief biographical sketch of Gehman based on comments by two Pentagon officials, a profile in the *Virginian-Pilot* of February 25, 2003, by Dale Eisman, and a telephone interview with Gehman's former spokesman, Captain John Carman.

108. *Concerned that U.S. leaders might too hastily dismiss*: Account of Gehman's call to Shelton based on Gehman interviews.

CHAPTER 17: DISHEARTENING SIGNS

109. *At 1327 hours, while finding a place to anchor*: Continuing rescue account from Yemelyanenkov's *Rossiiskaya Gazeta* report.

109. *Shortly after 1400, Admiral Popov's*: Popov's return to the *Peter the Great* roughly agreed by the multiple time-line reports.

110. *After 1800, the AS-34's Maisak reports*: Continuing rescue account from Yemelyanenkov.

CHAPTER 18: WESTERN PARALYSIS

112. *the group focuses on Cagan's lingering question*: Recounting of Sunday meeting in United States derived from interviews with the four mentioned principals.

113. *The dramatic display unfolded just the previous summer*: Russian Pristina incident portrayal based on widely disseminated accounts in mainstream media.

113. *Yeltsin later claimed in his memoirs*: Based on account in his memoir, *Midnight Diaries* (New York: Public Affairs, 2000).

114. *Talbott had distinguished himself as an advocate*: Brief biographical sketches of Sunday meeting principals based on my own reporting, plus background research via Internet of various media reports.

115. *For their own reasons, each of four key countries*: Multicountry silence assertion through remainder of Sunday, August 13, is self-evident.

115. *Meanwhile, the entire U.S. embassy in Moscow*: U.S. embassy still out of loop confirmed by attaché Brannon.

115. *A distraught Olga Lubushkina calls her parents*: Reported by Lubushkina.

CHAPTER 19: LYING TO THE PEOPLE

116. *On state-controlled radio*: Russian media announcement widely disseminated. In my two personal interviews with spokesman Dygalo in which I proposed that he could explain the origin of the apparently deceitful series of announcements, he proposed successive interview times in which he would explain himself. He repeatedly failed to follow through. Of the many Russian officials I quizzed about the issue of Dygalo's apparent deceits, they often pointed out that Dygalo acts on the orders of his boss, Russian Navy commander in chief Vladimir Kuroyedov.

116. *In the United Kingdom, British Navy commodore David Russell*: Initial reactions in U.S. embassy and U.K. submarine rescue circles recounted by the principals.

117. *Khalima thinks Olga is joking*: Aryapova reaction recounted in her personal interviews.

117. *Watching the news from his brother Dima's:* Sasha Kolesnikov reaction recounted in interviews.

118. *In the United States and around the world:* Timing of first CNN broadcast to the United States found in that network's news archives.

118. *On his small farm in Devon:* McCready account based on personal interview in Portsmouth and follow-up telephone interviews with McCready.

119. *Lister calls the Royal Navy HQ:* Lister account based on personal interview at British embassy in Moscow.

119. *In Norway, the scientific director of the NORSAR:* Seismologist Ringdal account based on multiple mainstream media reports and NORSAR Web site postings, plus my brief e-mail exchanges with Ringdal.

119. *Alarmed, Norway's Defense Ministry urges:* Norwegian Defense Ministry actions described to me in Oslo interviews with General Kjells Grandhagen, spokesman for the Supreme Commander of Norwegian Defense; Steinar Gil, head of Norwegian Ministry of Foreign Affairs for Russia and the CIS; plus a series of telephone interviews with Skorgen. Other Norwegian reaction details came in my personal interviews in Moscow with Ole Terje Horpestad, the Norwegian embassy's deputy head of mission, and with his defense attaché, Brigadier General Jorn Buo.

119. *John Spellar faxes a formal rescue offer:* I obtained a copy of the U.K. minister of defence's fax to Russia from the offices of duty minister John Spellar; this is a verbatim rendering of that fax.

120. *NATO similarly offers its services as a bloc:* NATO reactions are based on internal NATO memoranda, which officials based in Brussels shared with me. Other documents were also provided by former Gehman spokesman Carman.

120. *Out on the Barents Sea, the Northern Fleet's AS-34:* Barents rescue details from Yemelyanenkov's account in *Rossiiskaya Gazeta*.

120. *Within hours of the U.K. and NATO offers:* Details of the Berger-Ivanov telephone exchange based on recounting by Medish, and also from a key source close to Berger.

121. *"There are reasons to believe there has been a big and serious collision":* I have learned that some authorities dispute that Kuroyedov made the collision allegations as early as Monday, August 14, but this fact was reported widely by independent media. A UPI account quotes Admiral Kuroyedov's statement on the fourteenth, citing Russia's official Itar-Tass news agency: "There are signs of a major and serious collision." The UPI account goes on to cite a Northern Fleet spokesman as saying that "somewhere out there a foreign submarine is also damaged, and it may not be far from the *Kursk*." Similar quotes and time frames are attributed more specifically to Kuroyedov by CNN, the *Washington Times*, the *London Telegraph*, and other mainstream media.

121. *On learning of Kuroyedov's unsubtle allegation:* U.S. reactions to the collision allegations are recounted by multiple sources, though it should be said that Talbott's "ripshit" quote was mentioned to me casually in an interview with an NSC aide.

121. *Submarines avoid sending signals:* Berger's "panic attack" was mentioned to me by an indignant senior Pentagon official. I explored the propriety of Berger's order with some interest until Admiral Gehman described his own parallel actions taken on an even earlier time line.

CHAPTER 20: THE GLOBAL WHIPSAW

123. *Out on the Barents, the would-be rescuers:* Continuing rescue efforts from previously cited time-line reports.

123. *The reporters are also barred:* Media dynamics are extrapolated from my analysis of hundreds of Russian and international reports from these first days, along with anecdotal statements contributed by Russian subjects.

124. *To Khalima Aryapova:* Details regarding Lyachina, Aryapova, and Lubushkina from my interviews with all three women.

124. *These domestic critics go beyond:* Some of the critics cited here include people I encountered. In particular, my first Moscow translator, Andrey Mironov, is a former political prisoner, torture victim, and human rights activist whose views were hardened by years in the Soviet gulag. Much of our copious time together was filled with Andrey's conflicted feelings about his country, and his thoughts left an impression on me. Mironov also served as translator for an extensive personal interview with Duma member Sergey Kovalyov, another former political prisoner and human rights activist who held forth eloquently regarding modern Russia's struggle to free itself from Soviet-era values.

126. *Cloistered in his vacation dacha:* Putin's activities in Sochi were well covered in the Russian media during this period.

126. *aging senior members of Russia's Ministry of Defense:* Though Russian and foreign journalists reported heavily on the apparent clash of priorities within the Ministry of Defense, I have never seen an authoritative account that actually named individuals who held particular points of view.

126. *NATO instantly agrees:* The initial NATO coordination with the Russians is based on NATO memoranda, along with interviews of several NATO officials, including spokesman Jamie Shea, military committee head General Klaus Naumann, and Vice Admiral Egmond van Rijn, who represented Gehman's interests in Brussels. Other elements are based on telephone interviews with Russell and with a Russian officer to NATO who asked not to be named.

127. *Naval attaché Captain Brannon presides over a draft:* Brannon's actions regarding the Cohen fax come from Brannon interviews.

127. *"Dear Marshal Sergeyev . . .":* The text of the Cohen letter is a verbatim rendering of the fax itself, a copy of which I obtained through a Pentagon spokesman.

127. *Brannon tucks the folded sheet:* Brannon actions from Brannon interviews.

128. *But during the course of Brannon's charm campaign:* The detail that Brannon's mission was complicated by a quid pro quo demand from an authority figure in the Department of Defense was first mentioned to me by Brannon. Other Pentagon officials, including Frank Miller, have denied knowledge of the arrangement. The State Department's Debra Cagan confirmed the arrangement, and voiced the impression that it was a consensus decision among key decision makers in the administration, but NSC sources say they were unaware of it. Brannon recalls only that the order came in a telephone request from a naval captain based at the Pentagon. Logic would certainly infer that such a condition could not have been relayed to the Russian Ministry of Defense without the authority of Defense Secretary Cohen, who declined my repeated requests for an interview.

129. *While maintaining the aloof posture with the United States:* Depictions of continuing actions of Russian officials based on voluminous consensus accounts in Russian and foreign media.

130. *One world leader successfully reaches out:* Detail of Barak call to Putin in Sochi based on Russian TV report.

CHAPTER 21: OPENING THE GATES

131. *Dygalo renews his defense of the rebuffs:* Dygalo's announcements widely reported; his deceptions were widely dissected in Russian and foreign media.

131. *Even the United Kingdom's Commodore Russell calculates his early strategy:* Russell calculations on faulty data from Russell interviews.

132. *The visibility is fine, says Pobozhy:* Russell exchanges with Pobozhy based on Russell interviews.

132. *In the southern Barents, one of the struggling:* Continuing rescue efforts from previously cited time-line account.

133. *"To repair AS-34," the telegram begins ominously:* The listing of missing parts needed by the *Mikhail Rudnitsky* was spelled out in Yemelyanenkov's *Rossiiskaya Gazeta* report.

133. *The United Kingdom's LR5 lifts off:* U.K. and Norway activities portrayed by NATO sources listed above, along with Russell and associates and Skorgen.

133. *On the Black Sea past midday:* Putin's Sochi activities portrayed by various Russian media; earlier jet-ski sequence broadcast by ORT TV.

134. *Clinton hopes to apply some persuasion:* Clinton-Putin phone call recounted by Medish, who served as the call's translator.

135. *Within an hour, Putin dramatically reverses course:* Putin's Sochi reversal reported widely in mainstream media.

135. *Admiral Popov is among those who feel betrayed:* My assertion that Popov felt chagrin over Putin's decision to admit foreigners to the rescue effort is based on a little-noticed quote from Popov reported by Shigin well after the fact: "I didn't need foreigners. The decision on their help was taken without me."

135. *"Einar," says Popov:* Content and timing of Popov call to Skorgen recounted by Skorgen.

135. *Other Russian officials simultaneously open up:* Russian back-and-forth regarding the U.K. rescue bid recounted by Russell.

136. *In an emotional evening news conference in Moscow:* Dygalo acknowledgment of ceased tapping reports widely disseminated by Russian and mainstream media.

136. *Losing his composure, Dygalo holds up:* Detail regarding Dygalo's holding up an icon gleaned from report in German newsmagazine *Der Spiegel*, August 21, 2000.

136. *He details how the well-equipped* Avalon *and* Mystic: U.S. proclamations by Navy spokesman Quigley derived from Department of Defense transcript of that press conference.

CHAPTER 22: GOING INTERNATIONAL

137. *They are telling us they have no information:* Milyutina's comment about officials advising her to "ask journalists" for updates was reported in a *Washington Post* account. Coincidentally, Milyutin repeated the same line to me in a personal interview in St. Petersburg.

137. *Angling to end the mystery:* Komsomolskaya Pravda's account of its acquisition of the *Kursk's* crew list based on that paper's own report.

137. *In Brussels, Belgium, Russian Vice Admiral Pobozhy:* NATO teleconference described by Russell, Gehman, and van Rijn.

138. *In the annals of Russia-NATO:* Pobozhy context portrayal from ibid, along with NATO memoranda and some background information from Brannon.

139. *"From our experience with Soviet submarine forces . . .":* Pobozhy's Brussels comments were widely disseminated in mainstream media.

139. *one of the Northern Fleet's submersibles:* Russian mini-sub suffering battery drain from Kharitonov's Web site and other Russian media reports.

139. *Despite the Northern Fleet's official request:* Skorgen frustrations with Northern Fleet recounted by Skorgen.

140. *Popov's response is all business:* Skorgen-Popov exchanges regarding Norwegian airspace incident based on Skorgen interviews.

140. *But then the picture becomes even clearer to Skorgen:* Russian media portrayal of the USS *Memphis* "limping" along the Norwegian coast was widely disseminated in Russia, and then echoed in foreign media.

141. *They must prepare and extract all of the acoustic data: Memphis* actions in Haakonsvern and beyond are based on my interviews with *Memphis* sources, and on portrayals of the same events by *New York Times* reporters Steven Lee Myers and Christopher Drew on August 29, 2000, which was quickly followed by another in-depth report by the *Washington Post*'s Roberto Suro the next day, and then two days after that by Robert Hamilton in the *Day*, based in New London, Connecticut.

141. *Along Norway's northwestern coast:* Progress of the *Seaway Eagle* based on contemporaneous media reports.

142. *Skorgen lays down strict orders:* Skorgen's handling of sensitive issues surrounding military divers and Russian security concerns recounted by Skorgen.

142. *With the* Normand Pioneer *well under way:* Vessel's progress based on contemporaneous media reports and on interviews with Russell and some of his associates in the United Kingdom.

142. *a high-speed flight through Norway's coastal fiords:* Russell and Lister helicopter flight based on interview with Lister.

143. *The relentless assaults finally score a direct hit:* Evolving Putin perspective in Sochi based on his subsequent published comments regarding his decision to linger on the Black Sea. Sergeyev's public comments corroborated some of Putin's view.

143. *But within minutes of boarding a vessel:* The detail about Putin pacing on the ferry from Sochi to Yalta comes from a report by a Russian journalist named "Medvedev" in the September 1, 2000, issue of *Rossiiskaya Gazeta.*

145. *A trim and fit black belt in judo:* Putin's biographical details are based on multiple accounts. One of the most prominent was a lengthy profile by Maureen Orth in the October 2000 issue of *Vanity Fair.* Another is a surprisingly candid book, *First Person,* in which Putin describes at some length the Dresden moment referred to above, which I have also explicated in this chapter. *First Person* is an authorized biography that was aimed at rapidly introducing Putin to the Russian people for his shotgun presidential election in March 2000.

145. The detail that Putin's KGB office building was a "gray villa" on "number 4 Angelikastrasse" comes from a portrayal of Putin's KGB time in the *Washington Post* by former Moscow correspondent David Hoffman.

146. *When Putin described this rite of passage:* The perspective of Putin's personal

friends regarding his life as a spy was based partly on comments in the book *First Person*, and also on my personal interview in St. Petersburg with one of Putin's closest lifelong friends, Sergey Roldugin.

147. *Out on the Barents Sea, Northern Fleet rescuers:* Continuing rescue efforts from previously cited time-line accounts.

CHAPTER 23: DEMOCRACY, UP CLOSE AND PERSONAL

148. *Taking his position at the podium:* Klebanov visit to families in Vidyayevo widely reported in mainstream Russian and international media. My assertion that this is a people he "barely recognizes" is based on comments Klebanov later made to the United Kingdom's Russell during their meeting aboard the *Peter the Great*.

149. *Some of the young wives are in the auditorium:* Details on Aryapova, Lubushkina, and Dima Kolesnikov's parents provided by the subjects. Kolesnikova details provided in interviews with Aryapova and Lubushkina.

149. *Nadezhda Tylik shoots to her feet:* Tylik incident captured by Russian media TV camera and later broadcast worldwide. Translations of the quotes attributed to her range widely. Tylik herself has given differing accounts regarding the context of this incident. She even told the *London Times* in an August 29, 2000, report that the incident was misunderstood by the foreign media; she said her husband had requested the medical intervention to protect her heart from the exertion. But Tylik reversed her position months later, claiming in a revised report that her husband had confessed that he'd deceived her about this rationale to calm her down in the incident's aftermath. During a 2001 telephone interview conducted with Tylik via special correspondent Korovina, Tylik affirmed her belief that she had been forcibly sedated to suppress her outburst.

149. *A shaken Klebanov tries to regain his composure:* The actions of Ms. Sadilenko regarding Klebanov were recounted in my personal interviews in Murmansk and St. Petersburg with Tylik's daughter, Natalya, who said she'd witnessed both nearly simultaneous incidents.

150. *Olga Kolesnikova's arrival:* Kolesnikova's actions regarding her two friends were recounted in interviews with those two friends.

150. *Mitya, she thinks, you have to breathe:* Kolesnikova's thoughts about her husband at this moment based on her published recounting.

151. *Many of the Western rescuers are unaware:* Western rescuers' expectations based on interviews with British diver Tony Scott, Norwegian diver Dinesson, dive supervisor Ball.

151. *The Eagle's dive supervisors:* Nankivell's appointment of Scott based on telephone interviews with Scott.

151. *He will fly to Moscow at the earliest opportunity:* Putin's Yalta shift based on multiple Russian media reports.

151. *In Moscow, word circulates:* CIA's Tenet visit widely reported in Russian media, along with the rising conspiracy theories.

151. *U.S. attaché Brannon even shared dinner:* Tenet-Brannon dinner recounted in Brannon interviews.

152. *Over a dinner conversation:* Ushakov-Medish dinner recounted in Medish interviews.

CHAPTER 24: KEEPING THE WEST AT BAY

153. *David Russell takes a helicopter to Norway's* Seaway Eagle: Russell–Lister departure for the *Seaway Eagle* recounted in interviews with both men.

153. *"I understand your security concerns":* Russell's exchanges with Verich detailed in interviews with Russell and Ball.

154. *Minutes later, men aboard the* Pioneer: Burtsev visit to the *Normand Pioneer* based on interviews with Russell and Burtsev.

155. *Officials on the* Peter the Great *order the* Pioneer: Russian barring of *Normand Pioneer* based on Russell interviews.

156. *"Our worst expectations have come true . . .":* Motsak declaration based on consensus media accounts, along with my interviews with Motsak.

156. *But then the* Seaway Eagle, *too, is ordered:* Seaway Eagle's holdup based on interviews with Ball and Skorgen.

156. *Soon after learning of the Motsak statements:* Russell vow to "fight on" based on U.K. media accounts, and Russell's confirmation.

157. *In moments, several of the* Eagle's *experts:* Verich team's orientation of the *Seaway Eagle* recounted by Ball.

157. *The five-year-old* Seaway Eagle *carries eighty crew:* the *Seaway Eagle's* specifications based on Ball interviews.

157. *none of the foreigners plan on billing the Russians:* Based on interviews with Russell and Skorgen.

158. *Anticipating that Verich will finally approve:* Nankivell actions with Dive Team One based on interviews with diver Scott.

158. *Then Graham Mann meets with Admiral Verich:* Depiction of impasse between Mann and Verich based on Robert Moore's reporting in *A Time to Die.*

CHAPTER 25: DOWN TO BUSINESS

159. *In one of the* Eagle's *video monitoring rooms:* Verich reactions to ROV exploration based on interviews with Ball.

159. *Tony Scott leaves the bell minutes later:* First rescue dive depiction based on interviews with Ball, Scott, and Dinesson, and on multiple clips of video footage of the dive taken from television documentaries.

161. *aboard the* Eagle, *the crew wonders:* Concerns over possibility of a trapped submariner in the escape trunk—and its implications and eventual solution—were first conveyed to me in Dinesson interviews and confirmed by Ball.

161. *Diver Tony Scott uses the moment to pose:* The clockwise-counterclockwise issue was listed in a series of initial complaints by Skorgen.

162. *Just as this new impasse appears:* Popov visit to *Eagle* and dispatch of Ball and Nankivell to a sister sub in Severomorsk based on interviews with Ball.

162. *As he debarks from the helicopter onto the* Peter the Great's *deck:* Ball's observations aboard the *Peter the Great* from interviews with Ball.

162. *Moments later, Northern Fleet chief Popov places a radio call:* Shift on *LR5* question based on Russell interviews.

162. *No one is watching when the outer hatch:* Mechanism and timing of the *Kursk's* upper hatch releasing during the night from the use of a "buoyant bag" based on Moscow interview with Lister.

162. *The development constitutes progress:* Deliberations regarding opening the *Kursk's* lower hatch based on interviews with Ball.

163. *When the ROV punches open the lower hatch:* Description of reactions aboard the *Seaway Eagle* to lower hatch opening based on interviews with Ball, along with documentary footage of the event aired in subsequent television reports.

163. *Some of them note that the glistening bubbles:* Report that rising hatch bubbles had darkened interiors based on interviews with diver Dinesson.

163. *Watching the live television footage:* Sentiment expressed by Olga Kolesnikova regarding her sense of the rising bubbles "soaring heavenward" based on Kolesnikova's published statements about her feelings in that moment.

163. *Vladimir Kuroyedov invites the United Kingdom's senior man:* Account of Russell and Lister's lunch aboard the *Peter the Great* based on interviews with both men.

164. *Back on the* Pioneer, *Russell gathers his men:* Normand Pioneer crew's wreath-laying gesture widely reported in mainstream media.

164. *Later in the afternoon, Norway's Admiral Skorgen:* Skorgen's call to Popov recounted by Skorgen.

164. *By evening, Popov has summoned the strength:* Popov's evening statements on Russian TV widely reported in both Russian and international media.

165. *Nearly sixty fathoms down:* This depiction of the twenty-three dead submariners in the ninth compartment comes from a wide-ranging number of sources. As conditions in the ninth compartment were of great interest to Russian investigators, enterprising journalists focused heavily on conditions there in their queries with forensics experts. One of the earliest and best accounts of this scene was published on *Strana.Ru's* official *Kursk* Web site by author Vladimir Shigin. His rendering

authoritatively disclosed for the first time how the sailors in the last compartment died of a flash fire from one of the oxygen-regeneration plates coming into contact with the oily water. Though his report was not conclusive regarding the timing of that flash fire's onset, my chief technical adviser, Lars Hanson, conducted a remarkable analysis that used the compartment's flood rate as a marker of time. Because we'd learned from our reporting efforts the approximate level of the water on the compartment's top deck at the moment the fire broke out—just below a standing submariner's knee—Hanson was able to persuasively argue to within a half hour when the fire broke out. If Hanson's calculations are correct, they appear to corroborate the Russian investigators' conclusion regarding the survival time of the ninth compartment's twenty-three sailors—about eight hours at the most. This time of death would, for practical purposes, render moot any delays in rescue efforts. The only argument against this time limit is the continuing assertion by many authorities—borne out by acoustics logs composed at the search scene—that humanlike tapping was heard up until about 1100 on Monday, August 14. Even Admiral Mikhail Motsak, who, as a member of the Klebanov commission, agrees with the official conclusion, continues to believe that human tapping was rising up from the *Kursk* on Monday, August 14. When pressed about the apparent discrepancy, Motsak posits that such sounds may have come from a handful of sailors trapped in the stricken submarine's five-B compartment, which was found to have flooded last. Forensic examiners had reported that bodies found there were very intact. When I quizzed chief forensic examiner Victor Kolkutin via interviews with my correspondent Anna Korovina regarding five-B's conditions, he answered that the men there were alive for at least three hours. When I asked for specifics, Kolkutin declared that information contained in original forensic records would cost a fee. As I have avoided all requests for fees in exchange for information for this book, I declined Kolkutin's offer. In any case, as Motsak admits, the men in five-B could not have reached an escape hatch, as the watertight door toward the aft was jammed shut. (At least two published accounts of forensic results described finding one sailor's body slumped against this particular door.)

CHAPTER 26: PUTIN MEETS THE FAMILIES

167. *Effective tomorrow, Wednesday, August 23, 2000:* Putin's decree widely reported in Russian media.

167. *A small retinue gathers to escort the president:* Putin's preliminary actions regarding visit to the Kola Peninsula from ibid, plus further details from interviews with Lyachina.

168. *A sheet of paper is tacked to the door:* Detail of paper posted on Vidyayevo chapel door based on reporting by Shigin.

168. *The diminutive Putin steps to the podium:* Putin's lengthy talk with families in Vidyayevo based on verbatim transcript provided by *Kommersant* reporter Kolesnikov, as translated in the *Moscow Times.*

CHAPTER 27: FACING THE NATION

173. *Vladimir Putin sits somberly in a black suit:* Putin's address to the nation based on a transcript of his RTR interview.

174. *Russian defense minister Sergeyev leads the charge:* Sergeyev allegation details widely covered in both Russian and international media. Sergeyev also reported the claim that seabed searchers had found parts of a foreign submarine, including the railing of a conning tower. These allegations eventually proved false.

175. *"It was not any accident with the ship's equipment . . .":* Nationalist manifesto was published in *Zavtra,* August 22, 2000.

175. *"America Wins First Round of World War III":* Headline in *Komsomolets Zapolarya* published on September 1, 2000.

175. *Other explanations for the tragedy's cause:* Range of theories posted on Kharitonov's museum Web site.

175. *Defense Minister Sergeyev forwards a formal request:* Though it is a matter of record that U.S. officials declined to allow Russian inspection of the *Memphis's* hull below the waterline while docked in Norway, Norway's General Grandhagen told me during our interview that his country invited international journalists to view the American spy sub *above* the waterline. To the best of his knowledge, no Russian journalists attended.

176. *Slocombe and Miller easily satisfy themselves:* Depiction of Slocombe and Miller reviewing the *Memphis's* position relative to the *Kursk* at the time of its explosion based on interviews with both men.

176. *While the U.S. embassy in Moscow offers condolences:* The U.S. diplomatic community's "black humor" regarding the Ostankino tower fire was mentioned to me by journalist Will Englund, who was the Moscow bureau chief for the *Baltimore Sun* at that time.

176. *Voronezh officer Evgeny Zubkov repeatedly catches himself:* Emotional state of Vidyayevo in the tragedy's early aftermath based on interviews with the subjects mentioned.

176. *The widowed mother names her child Abdul:* Detail about the September 6 birth of the *Kursk* torpedo compartment chief's son based on Russian media reports.

177. *the actions of a Russian military culture that the Russian president increasingly distrusts:* My assertion here is based on information disclosed by Putin's close associate, Ivanov.

CHAPTER 28: SUMMIT MEETING

178. *"I am genuinely sorry for what you've been through . . ."*: Opening exchange between Clinton and Putin based on contemporaneous notes taken by Deputy Secretary of State Talbott, which he later shared with me.

179. *"Get a load of Ivanov's teeth!"*: Detail based on my Washington interview with Sestanovich.

180. *the United States had initially denied two previous Barents collisions, then later retracted the denials*: Comment by Mamedov to Talbott and Medish based on Medish interviews.

180. *But in a side room, security chief Ivanov*: Rendering of intelligence material handover to Ivanov based on interviews with Medish, and also on a source very close to Berger with whom Berger shared his impressions.

180. *Berger and Medish view Ivanov as favoring transparency*: Berger and Medish hopes based on Medish interviews.

180. *After returning to Moscow*: Putin and Ivanov's reversion to form based on widely disseminated media reports of their post–New York actions and statements, or lack thereof.

181. *As the anti-American allegations rage unabated*: The Russian officials who most prominently kept up the public pro-collision claims were Klebanov, Sergeyev, and Kuroyedov. Sergeyev was soon replaced by Ivanov, and Klebanov was demoted before the conclusion of the *Kursk* investigations. Though Russian pundits suggested that Klebanov's demotion was based in some part on the shrill collision claims that Putin later refuted, the Kremlin offered no credible explanation.

181. *He plans to reveal everything, but in due time*: My assertions regarding Putin's long-term strategy regarding the *Kursk* probe is based on a series of demonstrably true developments: first, Putin's decision to publish the Kolesnikov note; second, Ivanov's admission that he and Putin were aware their navy officials were providing bad information regarding the collision claims; and third, the obvious high quality of the *Kursk* probe and the prevailing integrity of its conclusions.

181. *A week later, a Russian research vessel*: Seabed probe by Mir submersibles based on report by Felgenhauer in the October 19, 2000, *Moscow Times*.

182. *As the early probe unfolds with no traces of foreign*: A prominent proponent of one of the more "acrobatic scenarios" whereby a smaller Western sub could hit the *Kursk* without suffering its own demise was Mikhail Volzhiensky, who laid out his complex case to me in a Moscow interview.

182. *In any case, to prevent foreigners*: Detail about multiple detonations of grenades at the *Kursk* wreck site to discourage would-be snoops is based on reports by seismic stations, including NORSAR.

CHAPTER 29: UNDOING THE BIG LIE

183. *An oil exploration platform hovers over the* Kursk: General scene of the *Regalia's* activities based on consensus media reports, which were fed by daily official updates by *Regalia* operator Halliburton.

183. *a steady thirty-five-knot easterly packed with forty-five-knot gusts:* Site weather details from records of nearby weather station for that date and time.

183. *During the recovery operation, only Russian divers:* Diving operation details based on perfunctory exchanges between correspondent Korovina and divers Shmygin and Sviagintsev. Depiction was further rounded out by my lengthier interviews in St. Petersburg and Moscow with key dive team sources who asked not to be named. One of these sources shared with me the actual video footage of the extraction of the first bodies from the submarine, along with the subsequent preliminary autopsy exam of Kolesnikov and the discovery of his note.

186. *They place the note and its explosive contents:* Chain of custody regarding decision-making dilemma about whether to publicly reveal the Kolesnikov note based on a series of interviews with Motsak.

187. *Meanwhile, in the fourteenth-floor apartment bedroom:* Irina Kolesnikova's dream based on personal St. Petersburg interview with Irina Kolesnikova.

188. *Roused by the note's implications, Motsak stops by Kuroyedov's office:* Motsak-Kuroyedov exchange based on interviews with Motsak.

188. *In St. Petersburg, the head of a retired:* Kolesnikov family notification sequence and individual reactions based on interviews with Kurdin. Family conflict issues confirmed by family members.

190. *Motsak confirms that four bodies have been removed:* Details associated with Motsak's public announcement regarding Kolesnikov note based on Motsak interviews.

191. *Olga steps into the hallway:* Olga and Sasha public statements based on multimedia accounts of their statements.

191. *With the media horde clamoring:* Kuroyedov statement in Vidyayevo from contemporaneous account by ITAR-TASS.

192. *Surviving former* Kursk-*mates:* Zubkov and Nessen identification of bodies in Severomorsk based on interviews with Zubkov and Nessen.

192. *When Dima's parents enter the military morgue:* Kolesnikov parents' identification detail based on recounting by Dmitry's high-school classmates.

192. *When Olga enters the morgue:* Details of Olga Kolesnikova's encounter with her husband's body based on published account of Russian author Cherkashin's interviews with Kolesnikova.

192. *To the four hundred people who gather:* Perspectives of Kolesnikov intimates

regarding their view of Kolesnikov's loss based on my interviews with the principals or, in the case of Olga Kolesnikova, on her other published statements.

192. *To the many gathered senior officials:* Depiction of Popov's view of Kolesnikov based solely on context.

193. *To hopeful observers:* My summary assertion of a larger worldview of Kolesnikov and his note is based on my broad reading of relevant analytical accounts of the tragedy.

193. *The casket is suspended on boards above a burial hole:* Portrayal of Kolesnikov funeral details based on multiple media accounts, plus my own on-site observations of the burial of a *Kursk* submariner whose ceremonies immediately followed those of Kolesnikov.

CHAPTER 30: SEEDS OF ACTIVISM

195. *They find comfort in the communal grieving:* Portrayal of Vidyayevo based on interviews with many of its residents.

196. *This system helps a Norwegian documentary crew to track down Nadezhda Tylik:* Norwegian documentary provided by TV-2's Isungset during Oslo visit.

196. *The low point comes:* Kuroyedov's closed-meeting stunt involving Brannon based on interviews with Brannon.

198. *Suddenly amid the murmuring:* Details regarding Tylik's announcement after an awards ceremony in Vidyayevo based on contemporaneous account by NTV.

CHAPTER 31: RAISE THE *KURSK*

199. *"One of the problems which arose in recent years . . ."*: Putin's quote in *Gazeta.Ru* regarding the value of raising the *Kursk* from Gazeta.ru Web site.

199. *Early cost estimates range:* Reports of the actual cost of lifting the *Kursk* varied widely in media reports, many of which also posited that the chosen contractors might perform such work at a loss because the project's high visibility would establish their value for future business.

200. *Throughout the winter, Putin's mission:* Details on the lifting effort's preparations and execution were very well covered by *Strana.Ru*'s official *Kursk* Web site. The contractors also provided authoritative updates and photos on their separate Web site.

200. *And then the perfect news item:* The Russian government's decision to cut off the *Kursk*'s jagged bow was widely reported on and well debated. Conspiracy theorists on all sides can now cite the "missing bow" detail as a trump card for all eternity: after sifting its remains, officials opted to blow it up on the seabed.

201. *Amid the excited handshakes:* The detail of Rubin's Spassky planting a kiss on the cheek of Motsak was captured in a contemporaneous photograph.

202. *He scans the seas and notices:* Motsak sighting of dolphins on arrival into Kola Bay and his emotional reaction to them was shared in a press conference he gave via video hookup from aboard the *Peter the Great* immediately after the effort's completion.

202. *You must understand, says Popov firmly:* Popov's objection to the wrecked *Kursk's* public display based on account in *Moscow Times* of October 11, 2001.

202. *On November 8, a portly Ustinov arrives:* Ustinov's public display of *Kursk* in dry-dock widely played on Russian national television stations.

CHAPTER 32: NAMING NAMES

203. *He first meets with General Prosecutor Ustinov:* The portrayal of Putin's Saturday Kremlin meetings and subsequent sackings is based primarily on contemporaneous news reports in *Gazeta*, RIA Novosti, the *New York Times*, and the news agency Reuters.

204. *The families' vigils are, each in their own way:* Account of people repeatedly asking Irina Lyachina about developments regarding the search for her husband's body based on interviews with Lyachina.

205. *If you find my Genna:* Lyachina's admonition to body searchers from ibid.

205. *In one last grand ceremony:* Portrayal of Lyachin funeral based mostly on account by Irina Titova in the *St. Petersburg Times*.

205. *Except in her dreams:* Lyachina dream of her husband based on Lyachina interview in St. Petersburg.

CHAPTER 33: TELL THE PEOPLE THE TRUTH

206. *When the Ustinov report finally emerges:* Ustinov report presentation widely reported in mainstream media. This depiction relies primarily on details described in *Strana.Ru*'s account of July 22, 2002.

208. *Many still feel unsettled:* Portrayal of cross tumbling from steeple in Kronstadt captured in RTR TV report, a video file of which was located by chief researcher Burns.

208. *Of all the media:* Authoritative *Rossiiskaya Gazeta* report by Yemelyanenkov.

209. *In the coming months:* Lawyer Kuznetsov's lawsuit on behalf of families of the twenty-three men in the ninth compartment has been steadily chronicled in *Novaya Gazeta*. Kuznetsov sent me a formal copy of the complaint and some supporting documents in March 2004. As of this writing, his case has not been completely adjudicated.

POSTSCRIPT: WHOSE LEGACY?

211. *Olga Kolesnikova describes:* Kolesnikova dream based on her account as published in Cherkashin's book.

211. *Olga now lives in a new apartment:* Kolesnikova details regarding the talismans her husband left behind widely reported in published accounts.

211. *In one of Lubushkina's first attempts:* Lubushkina account of current status based on my interviews with Lubushkina at her apartment in Severodvinsk and with follow-up telephone calls via correspondent Korovina.

211. *For Khalima Aryapova, the most chilling:* Aryapova dream and omen and current status based on personal interviews with Aryapova at her new apartment in Tolyatti.

212. *the predicted authoritarianism of Putin's Russia:* Account of Putin's early efforts to secure central authority in Moscow were widely reported in the mainstream media.

213. *But in the event's long aftermath:* All of the gestures listed as evidence of Putin's accelerating authoritarianism have been widely reported and heavily analyzed by a veritable army of Russia experts.

215. *Yet a steady parade of public opinion polls:* Russian sentiments regarding Putin have been extensively documented in a wide variety of opinion polls. Outside observers generally hold the credibility of Russian opinion polls in high regard, but at least one alarming change has come about: reportedly after becoming disenchanted with the line of questioning in polls crafted by one of Russia's most respected agencies, the All-Russia Center for Public Opinion, Putin's intermediaries arranged for the ousting of that agency's director and replaced him with a Kremlin acolyte. The ousted director, Yuri Levada, soon formed a new agency.

217. *The establishment of the U.S. base in Kyrgyzstan:* Distance between new U.S. and Russian air bases in Kyrgyzstan derived from half a dozen reports, which range from fifteen miles to thirty-five. A report in the United Kingdom's *Independent* dated October 24, 2003, pegs the distance at nineteen miles.

217. *This combined NATO-Russia group:* Summary of Russia–NATO and Russia–European Union issues based on widely disseminated foreign-policy media reports.

217. *But Putin's opposition:* Summary of Russia-Iraq dynamics based on mainstream reports; detail of Russian TV poll results from the same range of polling groups noted above.

218. *In February 2004, to further enhance:* Account of 2004 missile launch failures based on widely disseminated Western media reports of the incident.

219. *At a modest café:* Ending anecdote portraying Kolesnikov classmates inviting Sasha to take his brother's place in the group based on interviews with Sasha and with Dima's classmates.

INDEX